THE SEALED TRAIN

THE
SEALED TRAIN

by *Michael Pearson*

G. P. PUTNAM'S SONS *New York*

To Julian Bach

Foreword

IN MARCH, 1917, Lenin was living in Zurich in poverty, the exiled head of a small extremist revolutionary party that had relatively little following even within Russia. Eight months later, he assumed the rule of 160,000,000 people occupying one-sixth of the inhabited surface of the world.

The Sealed Train is the story of those thirty-four fantastic weeks. The train itself and the bizarre journey across Germany, then at war with Russia, are a vital and dramatic link in the story. For without the train, Lenin could not have reached St. Petersburg when he did, and if Lenin had not returned to Russia, the history of the world would have been very different. For not one of his comrades had the sense of timing, the strength of will, the mental agility, the subtle understanding of the ever-changing mood of the people and the sheer intellectual power of Lenin.

It is one of the great ironies of history that without the help of the German Emperor—the archproponent of the imperialist capitalist system that Lenin was dedicated to destroy—Lenin could never have achieved what he did. His establishment of a socialist state, the first stage in what he hoped would be a world Communist system, was made possible only by German cooperation, a German train and the massive German finance that followed it.

In the unifying of opposing interests that the Sealed Train symbolized, both Lenin and Kaiser Wilhelm took an enormous risk. For Lenin, the tarnish of enemy association, the "unclean hands" with which the train invested him, was highly dangerous politically and nearly destroyed him.

For the Kaiser, the risk, though he discounted it, was that

Lenin's plan for world revolution would spread across the Russian borders to threaten him with the same fate that had already overtaken his cousin, the Tsar.

Strangely, although their interests were opposed, both men achieved a large measure of what they sought. Lenin gained his revolution even if it did not assume the immediate global proportions he expected. The Kaiser gained the separate peace he wanted on the Eastern Front so that he could concentrate his forces in France—as well as a side benefit of vast areas of territory that had once formed part of the Tsarist Empire.

In dealing with the problem of spelling that faces any writer on a Russian subject, I have followed by and large the Library of Congress standard, though I have departed from this in the case of names or words that seemed to me to appear more natural spelled in other ways—such as Zinoviev.

The number of people in Europe, America and Russia who have assisted with the writing of *The Sealed Train* is too large for them each to be named. However, I would like to express my special thanks to Hannah Kaiser, who paved my way in Moscow and Leningrad and was of enormous help in other ways with the research there, and to Shirin Akiner, my tireless Russian translator in London. The help with translation of Alla Figoff and Kate Oldcorn was also much appreciated.

I should like to state my gratitude to Fritz N. Platten in Zurich for his enormous assistance regarding the Sealed Train and the role played by his father and also to the directors of the Verkehrsmuseum of the Deutsche Bundesbahn in Nuremberg who were extremely cooperative in providing details of the train and German railway systems of 1917.

Professor John Lukacs of Chestnut Hill College, Philadelphia, Harry Willetts and Dr. Harold Shukman of St. Antony's College, Oxford, Professor Leonard Schapiro of the London School of Economics and Political Science and Hilda Kukj of the Hoover Institution on War, Revolution, Peace at Stanford, California, and Dr. Z. A. B. Zeman have all been kind enough to provide research leads or to discuss the more controversial source material. I am also most grateful to Dr. Harold Shukman of St. Antony's College, Oxford, for his diligence in reading the proofs of the book and for his most welcome advice.

I have received great cooperation from the Soviet authorities in Russia in the form of excellent facilities and access for discussion with Soviet historians. It should be stated too that my task in Moscow was made much easier by a highly efficient and extremely intelligent translator and the sheer excellence of the Lenin Library. I would like to name the Russians who helped me within Russia, but even though they acted with approval, it would cause them embarrassment. Any book on the subject of Lenin by a non-Communist Western writer is certain to conflict with official views within Russia, for certain episodes in revolutionary history were altered on the orders of Stalin, and although there have been recent amendments, these have not all been corrected. Trotsky, for example, is barely mentioned in the Soviet Union. The roles played by Kamenev and Zinoviev are discounted. Certainly, the connection with Berlin is heresy, despite the publication of the German Foreign Office papers, though I would like to say to any of my Russian helpers who may see this book that, at the time I was in Russia, it was not my intention to give the weight to this important and highly relevant aspect that this volume now contains.

I am grateful to the staff of the Reading Room of the British Museum, of the Public Record Office and, as always, to Joan Bailey of the London Library for their great assistance. I have also appreciated the help of the librarians in the School of Slavonic Studies, London University, in particular that of Hana Komarkova.

Finally, I would like to thank Averil Lewis and Sylvia Voller for typing the manuscript through its various stages and my wife, Susan, for helping with its correction as well as living with its development.

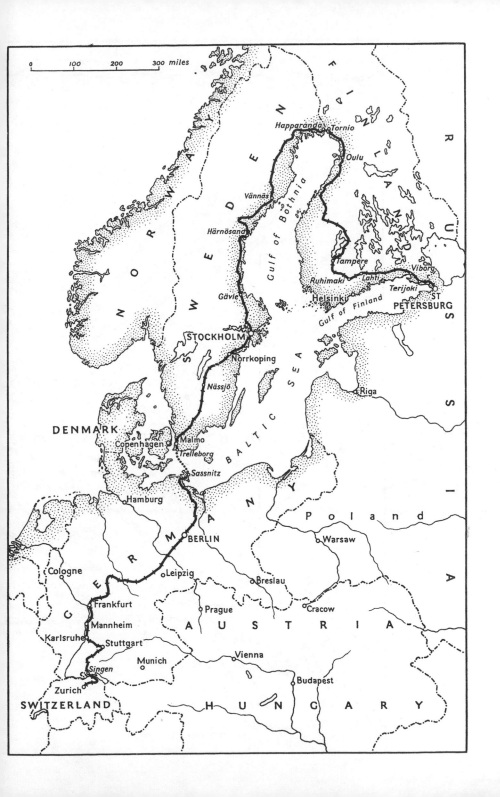

NORWAY

SWEDEN

FINLAND

RUSSIA

Happaranda   Tornio

Oulu

Vännäs

Gulf of Bothnia

Härnösand

Tampere   Viborg

Ruhimaki   Lahti

Gävle   Terijoki

Helsinki   ST PETERSBURG

Gulf of Finland

STOCKHOLM

Norrkoping

Nässjö

Riga

BALTIC SEA

DENMARK

Copenhagen   Malmo

Trelleborg

Sassnitz

Hamburg

Poland

GERMANY

BERLIN   Warsaw

Cologne

Leipzig   Breslau

Frankfurt   Prague   Cracow

Mannheim   AUSTRIA

Karlsruhe   Stuttgart

Munich   Vienna

Singen   Budapest

Zurich

SWITZERLAND   HUNGARY

RUSSIA

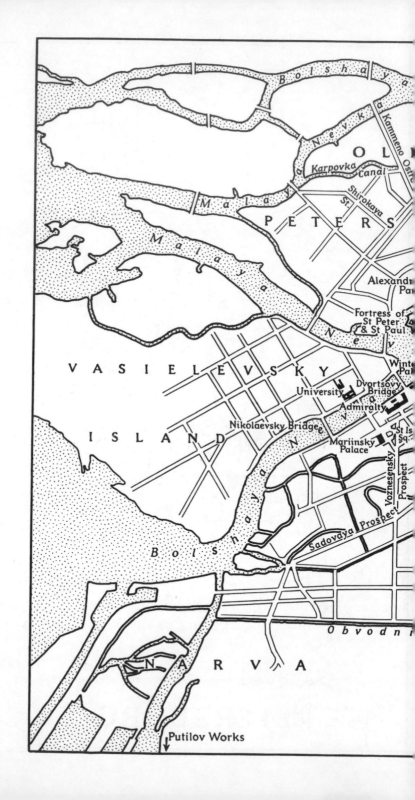

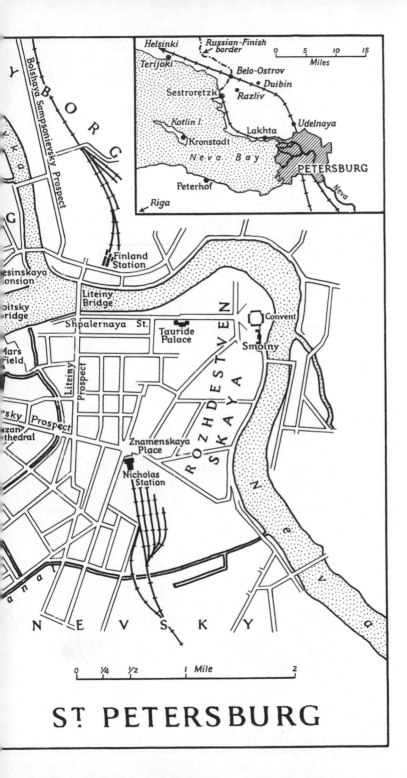

Helsinki
Russian-Finish border
Terijoki
Belo-Ostrov
Sestroretzk
Duibin
Razliv
Kotlin I.
Lakhta
Udelnaya
Kronstadt
Neva Bay
PETERSBURG
Peterhof
Neva
Riga

0   5   10   15
Miles

BORG

Bolshaya Sampsonievsky Prospect

Finland Station

esinskaya ansion

Liteiny Bridge

oitsky ridge

Shpalernaya St.

Tauride Palace

Convent

Smolny

Mars Field

Liteiny Prospect

R O Z H D E S T V E N S K A Y A

sky Prospect

zan thedral

Znamenskaya Place

Nicholas Station

N   E   V   S   K   Y

N e v a

0   ¼   ½   1 Mile   2

ST. PETERSBURG

They transported Lenin in a Sealed Train like
a plague bacillus from Switzerland to Russia.

—WINSTON CHURCHILL, *World Crisis*

Illustrations will be found following page 160.

Chapter 1

THE LIBRARY in the "Old Town" of Zurich was in a strange site. It was housed in the steepled Predigerkirche, a sixteenth century "Preacher's Church," no longer used for worship, in the complex of the Dominican friary that formed one side of the treelined square called the Zahringerplatz.[1]

It was there on March 15, 1917, that Vladimir Ilyich Ulyanov—better known among revolutionaries by his cover name of Lenin—spent the morning working, as indeed he spent every day, except Thursday afternoons when the library was closed.

As usual, soon after midday, he straightened the books on the table in front of him, so that they were neat and aligned, for he had a passion for order, and struggled into an old worn gray overcoat to return home for lunch.

He walked out the library door, which was at the side of the friary buildings, and cut through the Prediger, a narrow passage of oak-beamed shops. Striding fast and noisily in the studded mountain boots he always wore, he was a short, wiry figure, hunched within his coat beneath a black brimmed hat that seemed too large for his head.

He turned into the Neumarkt, passed the Eintracht, a workers' social club where he sometimes spent the evenings, and began to climb the Spiegelgasse, a steep cobbled alley of tall, gloomy ancient houses. As he strode up the lane, Lenin could smell the stench from the sausage factory at the top of the hill.

The single room at No. 14 that he shared with his wife, Nadya, was dark and drably furnished. During the daytime, when the

17]

sausage factory was in operation, they could not open the windows, though in truth in recent months this had been no great problem, for the weather had been bitterly cold. It had been a bad winter. Nadya had been ill for weeks, and she had still not fully recovered. Communications with Russia had been even sparser than usual since 1914, and contact with the members of the small extremist revolutionary party that Lenin directed had been minimal. Locked in Switzerland, surrounded by warring nations, Lenin and Nadya had been overwhelmed by a sense of endless isolation. Worse, they were desperately short of money—poorer by far than they had ever been in the seventeen years since they had been released from exile in Siberia.

Lenin was now forty-seven. He had a round head that was bald except for a ring of red hair, small dark Mongol eyes and a short, pointed beard. Always, his clothes were crumpled, his trousers baggy and a little too long. "To look at," his friend Gleb Krzhizhanovsky once remarked, "he is like a well-heeled peasant . . . a cunning little muzhik."

Most people found him unimpressive on first meeting, and later it was always his eyes, which narrowed sometimes when he smiled into slits, that gripped them. They gave to his face a mobility of expression that could display an exceptional scale of emotion, ranging according to Valentinov, an early comrade, through "thoughtfulness, mockery, biting contempt, impenetrable coldness, extreme fury."

Nadya* was a year older than her husband—plain, her body thickening in middle age, her broad face marked by bulging eyes, owing to a thyroid condition that caused Lenin's sister Anna to comment cruelly that she looked like a herring.

After lunch that day, Lenin prepared to return to the library. While Nadya swilled the plates in the handbasin on the washstand, he eased himself awkwardly into his overcoat. Suddenly, there was a hammering on the door, and Mieczyslav

---

*Nadya is known by most historians as Krupskaya, which was both her main cover name and her maiden name. However, since my characters refer to her either as Nadya or Nadezhda Konstantinovna, I am following their lead.

Bronski, a young Polish revolutionary, burst into the room, his eyes bright with excitement. The scene that confronted him was identical with what he would have witnessed at this time on almost any afternoon—the Ulyanovs in their daily routine—and its sheer subdued normality, by contrast with the facts he had to tell them, must have amazed him.

"Haven't you heard the news?" he exclaimed, according to Nadya. "There's a revolution in Russia!"

Bronski's jubilant announcement was so completely incredible to Lenin that he was shocked into confused silence—"bewildered," as Nadya was to describe it in *Pravda*. It was thirty years, almost to the day, since Lenin, as a seventeen-year-old boy in his hometown of Simbirsk on the Volga River, had had to break the news to his mother that Sasha, her eldest son, had been arrested in St. Petersburg as a terrorist; only two months less since he had been sent for by his schoolteacher to be told that Sasha had been hanged. His elder sister, Anna, arrested at the same time, had been banished to their grandfather's estate at Kokushkino. In December he himself had been expelled as a first-term undergraduate from Kazan University—technically because of his marginal role in student unrest but truly because he was Sasha's brother.

In Simbirsk the family had been shunned. Even their neighbors avoided them. Not one of their liberal friends would accompany Maria Alexandrovna, Lenin's widowed mother, to St. Petersburg to attend the trial of her son—which may have contributed something to the contempt that Lenin had felt for liberals ever since. There was no background of terrorism in the family. They were solid gentry. Lenin's father had been a civil servant, an area inspector of schools, entitled, as were most men of even minor position in Russia, to the title of "Excellency." They talked radical politics of course, but in Russia of the 1880's it was fashionable to speak as a radical.

Almost ever since that traumatic year,[2] Lenin had devoted himself to revolution—at first as a young lawyer within Russia, until he was arrested and sentenced to three years in the Siberian village of Shushenskoye. Then after his release for most of the next seventeen years in foreign exile, moving from city to city in Western Europe with the tiny group of comrades who helped him direct the "Bolsheviks," a breakaway section of the Russian Social Democratic Labor Party.

His years in exile had been hard, marked by poverty, by a need to work always in secret, by a revolutionary name that had come to be more natural than his real identity, by constant surveillance by the *shpiks* of the Okhrana, the Tsarist secret police who maintained foreign headquarters in Paris. It had been a life of writing ciphered letters in invisible ink; of coded knocking in the middle of the night by newly arrived comrades, haggard, unshaven, often hungry; of sad news of arrested friends; of endless and often heated polemic in cafés about socialist theory. For Lenin was always engaged in bitter feuds with other revolutionaries about ideology.

The world in which they lived was small, incestuous in character, marked by fierce conflicts between the opposing factions and rigid loyalties within them. Outside these narrow limits of cafés and revolutionary journals, Lenin was virtually unknown.

Even before the war, his group of comrades had been an unhappy, frustrated, homesick circle of people, buoyed up only by the hope inherent in Karl Marx's theory of the inevitability of revolution. After 1914 their feeling of remoteness had grown.

Bronski's astonishing statement, therefore, was a revelation to Lenin and Nadya, a sudden tantalizing glimpse of what they had worked for all their lives. It was too sudden to be absorbed at once or even to be believed. Under Lenin's incredulous questioning, the young Pole insisted that special editions of the Zurich newspapers, only just on the streets, carried brief telegrams from St. Petersburg: Revolution had flared through the streets of Russia's capital city and climaxed in victory for the people. All the Tsar's ministers had been arrested. Twelve members of the Duma—the nearest institution in autocratic Russia to an elected assembly—had assumed power.

They were sparse facts, but they flashed vivid images in the minds of Lenin and Nadya. They had both lived and worked in

Petersburg,* the city built by Peter the Great on a hundred islands in the Neva Delta. It was easy for them to imagine the scenes of revolt: the crowds surging through the streets; the Cossacks lined up to charge; the drawbridges raised over the Neva—the traditional method by which the Tsars had always cut the city into small sectors for easy control.

For Lenin, even though he had spent years studying the forces of revolt, the news was utterly unexpected, even astonishing. He had forecast in January that Europe, torn for three years by the most terrible war in history, was "pregnant with revolution," but he had not thought it would happen so soon. Nor had he expected it to break out in Russia with its millions of peasants—who were unresponsive militant material—and its unprogressive industry which was years behind that of other major countries. Germany and Britain, with their thousands of factories and big capitalist-exploited working-class populations, seemed far more vulnerable to social explosion—especially now that workers, serving as soldiers, were being slaughtered in such profusion in the trenches.

Bronski, having told them what little he knew, rushed off to break the news to the Kharitonovs, who, until Lenin had come to Zurich the previous year, had been the leaders of the small Bolshevik community in the city. Lenin and Nadya "pulled themselves together" and hurried down through the familiar lanes of the "Old Town" that had been their home for the past few months, to Bellevue Platz on the edge of the Lake of Zurich that was glistening that afternoon in winter sunshine.

There, under the disinterested gaze of a line of enormous vulturelike sea gulls that were always perched on the embankment wall, Swiss newspapers were on display beneath an awning. Surrounding the stand was a crowd of excited, barely credulous exiles. Lenin and Nadya elbowed their way through

*Officially, since 1914, St. Petersburg had been named Petrograd because the old name sounded too German for wartime conditions, but to the characters in this book it was always Petersburg or merely "Peter." I follow their lead.

Also, throughout the book, I am employing the Western calendar, still in use today, rather than the Russian calendar that in 1917 was thirteen days behind it.

21]

the throng and, still dazed, confirmed for themselves that what Bronski had told them was true.

Those first press reports made no mention of the Tsar, but it was clear that the revolution, if it achieved nothing else, *must* end the long autocratic rule of the Romanov emperors—*must* mean, too, that the thousands of political exiles in Europe and elsewhere would be able to return home. Home was the overriding thought in the minds of every man and woman in that shocked, elated crowd on the embankment of the Lake of Zurich—and, for that matter, of all the crowds in other Swiss cities who were crowded around newsstands.

Even then, Lenin did not trust the news—"If the Germans are not lying," he wrote in a hastily scribbled note to his friend Inessa Armand that afternoon—nor did he overestimate it. Few members of the Duma were socialists. The pattern of the French Revolution of 1789—in which the first people to take power were aristocrats—would almost certainly be repeated during the early stages. Even Karl Marx had predicted that unlike more developed nations, Russia would need a long period of capitalist parliamentary democracy before progressing to socialism. Under these circumstances, the danger of counterrevolution, even of an attempt to reinstate the Romanovs probably as constitutional monarchs on the British model, was enormous.

Crucial, too, would be the attitude to the war of the new men in power in Petersburg. Lenin was fully conscious that, as all the excited exiles were trying to absorb the news, ministers in the war capitals at that very moment were certain to be engaged in crisis meetings to consider one issue: Would Russia stay in the conflict?

For Britain and France, weakened badly by the appalling Battles of the Somme of 1916 and the attrition of the U-boats, it was vital that the massive German military forces should continue to be divided by the need to maintain armies in the East. For Germany, by contrast, it was equally vital that Russia should conclude a separate peace. The 1,000,000 German and Austrian troops on the vast Eastern Front, which stretched from the Baltic to the Black Sea, could then be withdrawn and thrown in one total effort against the Allies in France.

The revolution that had now broken out in Russia, though very welcome to the men in the Wilhelmstrasse in Berlin, was not enough on its own to achieve the result they wanted. It was unlikely that the new leaders in Petersburg would be socialists, for in revolutions power tended to fall at first into the hands of the people nearest to it under the old order. But even the socialists in Russia, like those elsewhere, had been split into two violently hostile divisions over the whole issue of the war.

Some Russian revolutionaries believed that imperialist Germany must be defeated before progress could be made toward socialism. Others, the internationalists, like Lenin, saw the war as a totally capitalist conflict that, since it exploited the working class on both sides, must be ended.

Clearly, from the rival war capitals, massive campaigns would now be launched to sway the political pendulum in Petersburg, the Germans favoring the pacifist internationalists, the Allies acting against them—in particular those in foreign exile, for these were under their control.

Even in those first few minutes after he had seen the news for himself in print, Lenin had realized that this issue would be critical. For obviously, the Allies would not assist any pacifist socialist to return to Russia where he would work for a peace that would be fatal to their interests—least of all Lenin who, as any inquiry would reveal, had been campaigning bitterly against the war ever since it had begun.

If transit by way of France, Italy or Britain was to be impossible, how was he to get home to Russia? It was vital that he did—to help preserve and direct the revolution. For although his party was small—barely 2,000 members in Petersburg and only 45,000 throughout the whole vastness of Russia—its following was strongest among the proletariat, the industrial masses. It was a base that Lenin knew he could broaden, for he was a brilliant strategist. The prospect that now lay before the people to assume power, to create a socialist society, had never existed before. If it was not grasped very soon before the impact of the inevitable counterrevolution, it might not occur again for a very long time. For Lenin, standing with Nadya, jostled by the crowd on the embankment of the Lake of Zurich, the time had come for which he had been preparing himself and forging his party all his adult life. But his ability to exploit the opportunity depended on his reaching Petersburg without delay. The problem that this posed that March afternoon seemed immense.

Fritz Platten, the secretary of the Swiss Social Democratic Party, pushed his way through the crowd to join Lenin and Nadya. He was a tall, slender, handsome young man with a flamboyant taste for broad-brimmed hats and elaborate scarves that was unusual in a Marxist. Like Bronski, he had gone to the Spiegelgasse with the news of the revolution, and the Kammerers, Lenin's landlords, had told him they had gone to the lake.

Already, Lenin was trying to make plans. The three of them walked to the post office. There, Lenin sent a telegram to Berne to Gregory Zinoviev, his main aide who helped him direct the party, summoning him immediately to Zurich for consultations. He scribbled a postcard to Mikha Tskhakaya, the leader of the Bolshevik group in Geneva. He was already carrying a package, addressed to Inessa Armand, who was then living at Clarens on Lake Geneva. He opened it, wrote a brief note to her and mailed it.

While he waited impatiently for Zinoviev to arrive, he went to look for Bronski and, according to Nadya, asked him about a smuggler he knew. Could he not smuggle him through Germany? It was very much of a confused first thought, for later, when he had considered all aspects, he realized that the political repercussions of this within Russia could be enormous. Whatever method he chose to get back to Russia, it must not be secret. Anyway, it later transpired, Bronski's smuggler could get him only to Berlin.

Zinoviev arrived in Zurich that night, and they did their planning on their feet, too elated to sit down in the Ulyanovs' room in the Spiegelgasse. "Vladimir Ilyich and I wandered about without any purpose," Zinoviev recalled, "still under the impact of those earth-shattering events, making plans." Desperate for more news, they went to the office of the Zurich newspaper *Neue Zürcher Zeitung*, trying to assess what the situation was in Russia from "scraps of information."

There was not much planning they *could* do at that early stage, but they knew much about the characters who would be involved in the events that were taking place in Petersburg, who would shape the future face of Russia. Many of them were exiled, like themselves, in various parts of Europe or America. Others were now taking part in the revolution. Some they knew personally, some only by their records, but all were men they had marked.

For years, Lenin had studied them, analyzing their speeches and their articles, combing every report received through the party network. Two years ago, for instance, he had told Zinoviev to set up a file on Nicholas Chkheidze, one of his socialist opponents who was a member of the Duma in Petersburg, since he detected a swing to "chauvinism." "All documents concerning Chkheidze & Co. [against them] should be carefully collected," he ordered. Time would reveal his instincts to be sound.

For the conflict of the next few months that would change the world, that would transform so fantastically Lenin's position in world affairs, lifting him from poverty and obscurity to the rule of 160,000,000 people, was rooted in the past—in the first years of the century.

Chapter 2

IN 1900, LENIN'S three-year exile in the Siberian village of Shushenskoye came to an end, but Russia was no longer practical as a place for revolutionary work—as he and his friend Julius Martov soon discovered when they paid a visit to St. Petersburg. For they were still formally banned from the city as troublemakers and the police picked them up very quickly.[1]

There was too much unrest in Russia at the turn of the century, too much talk of revolution, too many strikes. So they selected Munich as a base of operation to set up a new project that Lenin had conceived at Shushenskoye—a journal that would form the tactical backbone of a united social democratic party, that would guide and inform members as well as establish a secret underground network of agents.

The agents would distribute it, spread party propaganda through local cells and channel information to the Central Committee. The journal would help create a cohesive party that until then had consisted of a series of independent groups.

The name they selected for it was *Iskra* ("The Spark"), chosen from the motto of the Decembrists, the first of the Russian revolutionaries who had staged an abortive attempt to overthrow the Tsar in 1825: "Out of the spark shall spring the flame." It was printed in close small type on onionskin designed for convenient smuggling.

Lenin was thirty when he crossed the border into Germany. Nine years before, as an extramural student at Petersburg University, he had gained his law degree and begun practicing. About the same time he had become an active revolutionary. At first, he had worked for several small militant groups, but by the time he was arrested he was beginning to realize that no real progress could be made without a formal party organization.

Lenin's brother Sasha, like most revolutionaries of the nineteenth century, had been a Narodnik—a member of the People's Will Party, committed to terror as a technique and to the emerging view that socialism could be built on the structure of the peasant communes that already existed throughout Russia.

At first, Lenin too had been a Narodnik until, like many other young radicals, he began to read Karl Marx. Marx theorized that capitalism—a stage that all industrial nations, including backward Russia, must go through—would inevitably disintegrate because it carried within it the forces of its own destruction. Socialism would then emerge through power being grasped, not by the peasants, but by the proletariat, the workers, the fast-growing numbers of men and women who were exploited by capital.

Social Democracy, based on Marxism, had little use for terror since its whole theory was rooted in social development. Force in the form of an uprising might have to be employed at a final stage of the revolution—when a lingering power might still be held by the old order—but the conditions, the setting, must already have matured. Education of the masses, not assassination of the Tsars, was the keynote of its philosophy—as it was, of course, of *Iskra*.

Lenin had only known Martov a few weeks before his arrest—they had met in Petersburg to discuss a merger of their two very small groups—but he had warmed to him immediately, which was strange, for they were very different types of men.

Martov, with a rather mournful bearded face and glasses that were always clouded and slipping down his nose, was gregarious, fluent, a man for whom all-night cafés were a natural setting.

By contrast, Lenin was far more remote. Privacy was vital to him. Even when he was in company including close comrades, he maintained a reserve. "There was an invisible barrier," wrote Valentinov, "a line dividing Lenin from other party members and I never saw anyone cross it."

Lenin and Martov worked well together and shared a deep mutual respect that, for all their bitter conflict later, they were never to lose. They chose Munich to start *Iskra* partly because the German Social Democrats formed the most vigorous Marxist party in Europe—and had agreed to help produce and distribute the new journal—but also because it was the home of a young radical journalist, a Social Democrat, named Alexander Helphand who wrote under the pseudonym of Parvus. Parvus was to be very important in Lenin's life—so important that in July, 1917, their association would almost destroy him. But that was a very different Parvus—rich and an agent of the Germans, with millions of marks at his disposal. In 1900, as a young man of reputation much respected in revolutionary circles, Parvus lived in the Munich suburb of Schwabing. The first eight issues of *Iskra* were printed in Parvus' home on a special illegal press, fitted with a device that could instantly destroy the printing frame in the event of a police raid.

From the start Lenin knew that if *Iskra* was to gain the major support of Russian Social Democrats, he needed the backing of the three most famous of the older generation of Marxists: George Plekhanov, Paul Alexrod and Vera Zasulich.

While Martov toured Russia recruiting agents, Lenin traveled to Geneva to persuade Plekhanov, whose writings he much admired, to join the *Iskra* board. The *Iskra* board consisted of the three older-generation Marxists and three young men—Lenin, Martov and a comrade who had helped them to conceive the project, Alexander Potresov. It was an explosive partnership, mainly because of the inevitable clashes between Lenin and Plekhanov, the lions of different eras, but it was eased to some extent by the fact that *Iskra* was edited in Munich, far from Geneva.

Nadya became secretary of *Iskra*, maintaining contact with the network of agents. "The odor of burnt paper was almost noticeable in her room," Trotsky was to write later, though he had not met her at this stage.

Nadya came from a similar kind of social background to Lenin's, with parents who were minor nobility. By the time they moved to Schwabing, they had known each other for six years—since they first met in Petersburg at a Pancake Party on Shrove Tuesday. They had worked for the same Social Democrat group, engaged in promoting strikes and unrest, that led to the arrest at different times of both of them—*and* of Martov. Their relationship was strangely passionless. They shared an obsession for revolution and Lenin's letters reveal little emotion at a personal level. Engaged or married couples were permitted to spend their exile together. Lenin needed a secretary and Nadya could write a beautiful copperplate hand—useful for the final copies of manuscripts that Lenin was writing in exile. When she told the authorities she was his fiancée and applied to join him, Lenin confirmed this. She arrived in Shushenskoye, with her mother, who continued to live with them much of the time, even when they had left Siberia. Shortly afterward they married. It was primarily a working relationship—marriage anyway was deprecated by revolutionaries as bourgeois—but they shared a common sense of humor as well as common ideals, and it was not unhappy.

By the end of 1901 the Russian Social Democratic Party, with its focal center of *Iskra*, had become an organization—crude and marked by friction, but a political entity nevertheless. The Okhrana was eyeing it a trifle nervously. At their request, the local police brought pressure on the German Social Democrats. They wanted *Iskra* out of the country. So the editors moved to London.

Lenin and Nadya rented two unfurnished rooms in Holford Square, Finsbury. Martov had gone to live with Vera Zasulich and another comrade in what Lenin referred to as a "commune." Vera did her best to calm the conflicts between Lenin, often sensitive to criticism, and the older Plekhanov, touchy and often heavy-handed.

Relations became even more soured after Trotsky's arrival in London, since Plekhanov loathed the young man. Lenin had been waiting for Trotsky eagerly, for friends in Russia had written that this young revolutionary from the Ukraine, who had escaped from Siberia and joined the *Iskra* organization in Samara, was a "young eagle."

He had knocked loudly on their door early one morning when both of them were still asleep—giving the secret triple knock. Nadya had opened the door in her dressing gown. "Pero is here," she had called to Lenin. "Pero," meaning "Pen," was one of Trotsky's pseudonyms.

He was twenty-three, dark, bespectacled and dramatic. Over tea in the kitchen, Lenin had grilled him about the party in Russia, and Trotsky had warned him of the poor condition of *Iskra*'s frontier organization.

Lenin had taken him for a walk through London and showed him Westminster Abbey—"Their famous Westminster." Trotsky told him that in prison in Moscow he, like other political prisoners, had studied Lenin's first book, *The Development of Capitalism in Russia*, written in Siberia. "We often spoke with astonishment of this colossal work," Trotsky told him.

"Indeed," answered Lenin with a smile, "it was not all done at once."

Lenin tried to promote Trotsky onto the *Iskra* editorial board, but predictably, since it would have strengthened the younger element, Plekhanov checked the move. The friction with Plekhanov, however, was not so important then in 1903 as the conflict that had been growing, at first almost imperceptibly, between Lenin and Martov. It exploded at the party congress in August—the first major conference that was truly representative of party delegates from Russia and all over Europe.

It was at this congress that deliberately, once he found he could not carry it in the way he thought it ought to go, Lenin split the party. It was a conflict that continued for fourteen years until the climax was acted out in November, 1917.

Lenin was a strategist. He was concerned with practical power. As he had detailed in a pamphlet a few months earlier,

What Is to Be Done?, he believed the party should be a tight organization of highly disciplined full-time secret workers, controlled on a semimilitary basis through local cells and area commands, by a small central committee.

Martov was far more of a democrat in the Western sense of the word. He wanted a broad party open to anyone who gave it "regular personal cooperation." To Lenin this was too insipid to achieve successful revolution, too open to compromise, too "soft." He demanded "personal participation" as a requirement for membership, by which he meant full-time dedication.

On the membership question, the voting went with Martov—despite feverish behind-the-scene activity by Lenin. The division colored the whole congress and was reflected in other issues. The delegates split into "hard" and "soft" and eventually into "Bolsheviks" (men of the majority) and "Mensheviks" (men of the minority).

Even the naming was tactical, the "Bolsheviks" being chosen by Lenin on the basis of one issue in which his faction had won a majority vote. The very fact that Martov accepted the minority labeling was evidence of an attitude that was essentially "soft."

The split was permanent. Attempts at sealing the division were made repeatedly over the years, but they never succeeded on any kind of permanent basis. For the two viewpoints were basically in conflict. They represented different philosophies.

In fact, they represented different sorts of people, too. The Mensheviks attracted the Marxist intellectuals and most of the exiles. The Bolsheviks, too, had their intellectuals but they appealed especially to the committee men, the provincial party workers, the professional revolutionaries—"the bacteria of revolution," as Lenin called them. In essence, the "hards" were militants, the "softs" favored debate.

Plekhanov supported Lenin at the congress but later wavered and finally joined Martov. Trotsky tried to stay in middle ground over the issue that was splitting the party, but later he, too, moved toward Martov—though not completely, for Trotsky was an independent.

It caused a personal split between Lenin and Trotsky that,

even by March, 1917, was not healed. To Lenin, Trotsky, like many of his opponents he wished to abuse, was now "Comrade Voroshilov," a character in Turgenev's novel *Smoke.* To Trotsky, Lenin became a "despot." When he spoke of the "victory of the Proletariat," his onetime protégé wrote acidly, he meant victory over the proletariat.

For a few months after the congress, Lenin continued to edit *Iskra*, but Martov refused to participate. Relations with the others became difficult. At last, he resigned, leaving virtually all the previous party leaders with Martov.

Lenin and Nadya went walking in the Swiss mountains, his usual therapy when the strain became too great. Then he returned to Geneva, where they had now gone to live, and with a tiny nucleus of twenty two persons who supported the Bolshevik view and his leadership, he started his own organization.

For more than a year, the conflict between the two groups, fought out in virulent articles, speeches and even personal meetings, was excessively bitter. Lenin, almost like a wounded animal, stood alone with his nucleus of supporters against virtually all the others.

Then, for a brief period, their feuding was dwarfed by 1905—a crisis year after which nothing was ever quite the same again.

To the exile colony in Geneva, the news in January of "Bloody Sunday"—when troops drawn up before the Tsar's Winter Palace in Petersburg had opened fire on an unarmed crowd led by a priest named Father Gapon—had been an emotional shock of extraordinary impact. Lenin and Nadya had gone to the émigré restaurant of Lepeshinsky, where other dazed comrades had assembled. "The people gathered there hardly spoke a word to one another they were so excited," wrote Nadya. "With tense faces they sang the revolutionary Funeral March [for the hundreds of dead in Palace Square]. Everyone was overwhelmed with the thought that the revolution had commenced."

In fact, the revolution had not commenced, though the public outrage that followed the "massacre" had led to strikes, peasant insurrections, even a naval mutiny.

Lenin had flung himself into a study of military tactics for the armed revolt he knew was imminent, pouring through such works as General Cluseret's *On Street Fighting* and Von Clausewitz's celebrated *On War*.

Not that he thought that the revolution would be successful. When a young Bolshevik from Kazan came to see him in Geneva and asked what the Russian Bolsheviks should do, Lenin snapped, "One thing, an armed uprising—an immediate armed uprising."

The Kazan comrade replied that the Bolsheviks within Russia did not think that an uprising at this time could end in victory.

"Victory?" echoed Lenin. "What do we care about victory? . . . We want the uprising to shake the foundations of the autocracy and set the broad masses in motion. Our task will then be to attract those masses to our cause. . . . The uprising is what matters."

In the autumn, as the situation in Russia grew tenser with the humiliation of the nation in the war with Japan, Lenin lashed the comrades in Petersburg for their failure to stimulate action. "I'm appalled . . ." he wrote, "to see that more than half a year has been spent in talk about bombs—and not a single bomb has yet been made. Go to the youth. Or else, by God, you will be too late."

There was talk of a "Soviet" in Russia—a council of delegates from workers' strike committees who could coordinate action—conceived initially on the lines of the Committees of Correspondence and the Continental Congresses of the American Revolution. Trotsky, Parvus and Axelrod all wrote of the need for such a body as a base for joint action by the workers.

In October, in the tense political climate, a small printers' strike flared into a complete nationwide stoppage. By the end of the month a Soviet was being formed in Petersburg to take over the leadership of the strike—with twenty-three-year-old Trotsky playing the dominant role—and other cities were following this lead.

Anxiously, the Tsar bowed to the pressure—and issued a manifesto granting a parliament, elections and freedom of

33]

speech. But the militant revolutionaries did not believe it. The jails, as Trotsky declared, were still full of political prisoners. Dramatically, before a crowd of thousands, he tore the manifesto into pieces and began to exploit further the power of the strike weapon. For one thing had become wonderfully clear: The people were willing to obey the Soviet.

Others, too, read the message. Reaction swept the country in a form that was to be a constant danger to the forces of revolution—and to reach a climax in 1917. Extralegal bands of right-wing extremists, often armed and encouraged by the police, began to stomp the country under the banner of Holy Russia, singing the national anthem, "God Save the Tsar." Their organizations bore such titles as The Black Hundreds. They were to be Lenin's bitterest enemies—especially in 1917.

To combat the violence of these bands, workers in the factories formed fighting companies of armed men. That, also, was to be a pattern repeated in 1917.

In December the Tsar struck. The Izmailovsky Regiment arrested the whole Executive Committee of the Petersburg Soviet. In response, the Moscow Soviet declared a strike. The workers took to the Moscow streets, and the troops sympathized with them. Twice Cossack units refused to charge. And up went the barricades.

The government sent in the crack Semenovsky Guards. They cornered the armed militants in the Presnya workers' district of Moscow—and then shelled the area for three days. Hundreds were killed, including eighty-six children. It was an appropriate end to a year that had started with the massacre in the snow of Palace Square on "Bloody Sunday."

For Lenin, the important aspect was that revolutionaries had been fighting in the streets. It *could* happen—and it could happen again on a much bigger scale. The few hundred dead in Moscow that December were the price of militant experience. "The one who has been whipped is worth two who have not," he commented.

Lenin and Nadya arrived in Petersburg in November, 1905, and typically he insisted that they should live separately under false identities. He was taking no chances. Nineteen hundred and six was a year of repression, of rigorous police activity, of brutal raids, officially approved, by Black Hundreds gangs.

Lenin moved with Nadya to Finland, which, though part of the Russian Empire, had a degree of autonomy and was safer than Petersburg. The Moscow rising in December and the conflicts between the workers and the Black Hundreds had left Lenin with a taste for militancy—*and* a zest for robbing banks as a way of raising party funds. He urged his followers to give top priority to military training. By the end of 1905 an organization of fighting squads had been set up.

By then, faced as they all were with an immediate common aim, even Lenin had urged a move to unity of Bolsheviks and Mensheviks. In 1906 Lenin was once more on the Central Committee of the combined Russian Social Democratic Party, and by careful and characteristic tactics, he won control of its military bureau.

The Mensheviks, who dominated the Central Committee, were strongly opposed to violent tactics, but they did approve Lenin's proposal that defensive actions could be conducted against the Black Hundreds, who were a severe harassment in certain areas.

Exploiting this vote, Lenin set up a secret center and treasury within the party—secret, he insisted, because of the danger of Okhrana infiltration.

His squads mounted a series of bank raids, most of the proceeds of which went into his secret treasury, which he used to finance Bolshevik interests. Several of these were handled by an incredible cross-eyed Caucasian bandit codenamed Kamo, who had been a friend since boyhood of Joseph Stalin,[2] from whom he now took orders.

Kamo's most dramatic raid was the seizure from a carriage on its way to the State Bank at Tiflis of 341,000 rubles that he then smuggled across the Russian border in a hat box. But the notes were all of high denomination—500 rubles—and the changing of them for other currencies without attracting attention in Western Europe would clearly be difficult.

Lenin planned that the notes should be split up and, at the same time of the same December day, should be presented at a range of banks in different cities.

As was to happen so often, one of Lenin's key men was an Okhrana spy. On the day of the operation, local police were waiting.

The bank raid—which was hardly the kind of defensive operation the party had approved—promoted a violent reaction against Lenin from the Mensheviks. Paul Axelrod wrote to Martov: "How can one remain in the same party as the Bolsheviks?" Plekhanov insisted: "The whole affair is so outrageous that it is really high time for us to break off relations with the Bolsheviks." To which Lenin merely commented coolly: "When I see Social Democrats announcing . . . 'We are no anarchists, no thieves . . . we are above that . . .' then I ask myself: Do these people understand what they are saying?"

In 1911, Martov published a long document indicting him. It marked the now irreversible split between the two men—and the two factions.

By then, Lenin and Nadya had been back in Europe for three years and he was heading the new team that would still be with him in November, 1917. In 1908, Gregory Zinoviev had been released from jail in Petersburg and had arrived in Geneva with his wife, Zina. They had been followed a few weeks later by the Kamenevs—Leo and Olga, who was Trotsky's sister.

Gregory Zinoviev and Leo Kamenev helped Lenin edit *Proletarii,* the party journal, and formed with him the operational core of the new Bolshevik organization. Both of them were twenty-five, as compared with Lenin, who was then thirty-eight. Kamenev was the stronger personality. With a beard, a quiet voice and wise-looking eyes behind steel-rimmed spectacles, he gave an impression of authority that was beyond his years. Although Zinoviev had been a revolutionary just as long as Kamenev, he seemed younger and slighter. He had a strangely high-pitched voice, was stocky, a bit plump, with thick curly black hair and a pallid skin that suggested he did not spend enough time out of doors.

The three Bolsheviks—Lenin, Kamenev and Zinoviev—became known as the Troika. From Geneva, they all moved to Paris. With their wives, they formed the nucleus of the Bolshevik community that would often meet in the cafés of the Avenue d'Orléans, near the Lenins' home. Money was always short. Nadya was highly amused when a newcomer to the city asked Lenin the price of veal and goose. "I could have told him the price of horsemeat and lettuce," she remarked.

It was in Paris in 1910 that the Troika was joined by a new comrade—Inessa Armand—whose impact on Lenin was traumatic. She was thirty-one, a striking woman with untidy chestnut hair, dark gray eyes and an electric personality. Like most of the revolutionary women, she wore severe unfeminine clothes. Completely fluent in five languages, she played the piano brilliantly and possessed an intellect that led to a rapport with Lenin he had known with no other woman in his life.

By birth she was French, being the daughter of a Parisian vaudeville comic, but she was married to a Russian industrialist whom she had met as a teen-ager through her grandmother, who had the post of tutor in his family home near Moscow. She had left her husband, together with her five children, to devote herself to revolutionary politics.

Inessa had modeled herself on Vera Pavlovna, the free-living liberated heroine of Nicholas Chernyshevsky's novel *What Is to Be Done?* that had grasped Lenin's imagination when he was still a teen-ager—and, for that matter, that of most of the other revolutionaries of his generation. Deliberately, he had used the same title for his important pamphlet before the split in 1903.

Chernyshevsky's Vera Pavlovna rejected the traditional concept of wife and mother. In their home she had her own room, and her husband had his, so that unquestioned they could entertain their own friends. She took lovers, was gripped by a great need to correct social injustice, and when eventually she deserted her husband and children, she did so without quarrels or agonized hesitation.

By the time she met Lenin, Inessa had done much the same. Finally, she had gone to live with her husband's younger brother, Vladimir—and had been shattered by his death from tuberculosis the year before she met Lenin. By that time she was a veteran revolutionary. She had been arrested three times, jailed, and had even escaped from exile in Archangel in Russia's Arctic north. She was an ardent Bolshevik, having been as struck by Lenin's pamphlet *What Is to Be Done?*, which she had read six years before, as she had been by Chernyshevsky's novel.

To the Troika and the comrades of the Bolshevik community, Lenin's reaction to Inessa was astonishing. He had displayed little interest in women before—except purely as comrades. Yet with Inessa he would go alone to the cafés in the Avenue d'Orléans and behave with her in a way that moved the socialist Charles Rappaport to comment how "Lenin with his little mongol eyes gazes all the time at this little 'Française.' . . ."

She was the only person, outside his family and Martov, whom he ever addressed in letters by the intimate pronoun *ty* instead of the usual polite second-person *vy*. Even Zinoviev and Kamenev, his two closest comrades were *vy*, as indeed were their wives, whom he saw several times a week.

At a party level, he relied on her at times even more than on his comrades in the Troika. When in the summer of 1911, he started a school for revolutionaries in the village of Long-jumeau, near Paris, Inessa was the only woman lecturer, alternating with Lenin himself in the course on political economy.

She handled his translations and traveled on his instructions, often carrying out complex and delicate tasks, for which her languages were an important asset. She attended conferences for him, acting under highly strategical briefings. Sometimes she would resist, and he would beg her—"Consent, do!"—for if he saw a task as necessary, he would employ any method to achieve this end.

When she was not with him, he wrote to her frequently—mostly about politics, for politics were his life—but often anxiously and sometimes with deep personal concern. Repeatedly, he would complain of her silences, when she would leave letter after letter unanswered. Sometimes, this was due to postal delays—especially in the war—but there were clearly times when she was punishing him or possibly just trying to reduce his importance in her life.

He would share with her his triumphs. "Victory! Hurrah! The majority are for us," he wrote from a congress in Brussels.

Her music had an enormous effect on him—especially Beethoven's *Pathétique* and *Appassionata* sonatas. Years later, after Inessa had died of typhus, when he was listening to a recording of the *Appassionata* with Maxim Gorky, Lenin confided that "it is amazing more-than-human music. I want to utter gentle stupidities and stroke the heads of people. . . . who can create such beauty."

Nadya expected him to leave her for Inessa. For this would have conformed with the mores of the revolutionaries, with the philosophy of individual freedom and honesty expounded by Chernyshevsky and also by Turgenev, whom Lenin greatly admired.

Several times, according to Alexandra Kollontai,[3] Nadya told him she was leaving, but on each occasion he asked her to stay—possibly because of a lingering bourgeois past or of a sense that a broken marriage was undesirable in a future statesman, even a revolutionary, or maybe because she provided a stability that at times he lacked.

Nadya agreed to stay with him, but, so Lydia Fotieva, another comrade, reported, she gave up sharing his room and moved in with her mother—at any rate for a while.

For a time, as they moved from city to city, Inessa lived with them both so intimately that the relationship was almost a *ménage-à-trois*—not usually in the same house but always close, either next door or just across the road. In her writings, Nadya refers to her warmly and occasionally in idyllic terms. "We would wander for hours along the forest roads covered with fallen yellow leaves . . ." she wrote about a fine autumn in Berne. "Sometimes we would sit for hours on the sunlit, wooded mountainside, while Ilyich [Lenin] jotted down outlines of his speeches and articles. . . . I would study Italian. . . . Inessa would sew a skirt. . . ."

In 1911 the Tsar changed his policy again and once more permitted the election of a Duma and even a degree of free speech. For a short time, *Pravda* could be published openly, and the Ulyanovs and the Zinovievs moved to Cracow, in Austrian Poland, close to the Russian border, so that they could write articles, help direct the paper and maintain a close contact with the party network. Inessa joined them for periods.

Zina Zinovieva, operating under her maiden name Lilina, helped Nadya with the secret correspondence that, to avoid the censors, was often mailed within Russia by peasant women who came across the border to shop in Cracow markets.

Articles were sent to Petersburg daily by train, being written after a morning editorial conference in the kitchen of the house they shared.

For a time, the exiles could even be optimistic once more. There were Bolshevik delegates in the Duma, but then repression followed on the previous pattern, and there was news of arrests—of Stalin, of Inessa, who had crossed the border on a special mission with another comrade, of George Safarov and eventually of Kamenev, who had returned to Petersburg with his family to take control of *Pravda*.

When war broke out in 1914, they moved back to Switzerland, first to Berne, where they were joined by a returned Inessa, who rented a house across the road, and then to Zurich.

Switzerland became an island of neutrality to which, by choice or necessity, many Russian revolutionaries hurried from the belligerent countries. It was a traditional refuge for Russian political exiles. There was even a Russian library in Geneva. But with Europe gripped in war, and the barriers that this created against the movement both of people and mail, the climate became stifling. Grimly, Lenin worked in this cultural vacuum to prepare for the world that he was sure would emerge from the carnage of the trenches.

Chapter 3

DURING THE WINTER MONTHS before Bronski hammered on their door, the life of Lenin and Nadya declined to a level they had never known before. Nadya's chronic illness—owing to her thyroid—was accompanied by a long spell of bronchitis. Their bare room had no stove, and they shared a narrow kitchen with their landlady, Frau Kammerer. There were three other tenants: an Italian, some Austrian actors who had "a wonderful ginger cat" and a German soldier's wife who lived with her children in one room.[1]

Their life was very uneventful, the letters from Russia rare, routed—with the help of a German agent, who read them carefully—by way of Scandinavia. Every morning Lenin would leave for the library, taking a detour by the lake and the Limmat River for exercise. Always he came home for lunch and then returned to the library in the afternoons.

On Thursdays, if Nadya's health permitted, Lenin would buy "two bars of nut chocolate in blue wrappers at 15 centimes apiece" on his way home at lunchtime, and they would go walking on Zürichberg Mountain.

Lenin planned his life into precise fixed hours—for work, for sleep, for leisure, for meals. He took great care of himself. He did not smoke and rarely drank alcohol—a glass of beer sometimes. Every day he did physical exercises—a habit started in prison in Petersburg before he was exiled to Siberia—and often went for long walks.

His working habits bore the same pattern of precision. When he was working at home, he would start by dusting the table with a special duster and arrange his books and papers in meticulous order. Strangely, although clothes were not important to him and his suits were always creased, he hated them to be in need of repair. He liked to sew on loose buttons himself, unaided by Nadya. When in other cities he had required a bicycle to travel to the libraries, he had kept this, according to Valentinov, "as clean as a surgical instrument."

It was in character that he should be extremely good at chess, a game that at times obsessed him. He could play for hours on end. Once, according to Nadya, he called out in his sleep, "If he moves his knight here, I'll counter with my castle." ,

By that March in Zurich, poverty had become an enormous problem for them. Often for lunch they had only oatmeal that Nadya was always scorching, for she was not a good cook. "We live in grand style, you see," Lenin joked to Frau Kammerer. "We have roasts every day."

Through most of the months since the outbreak of war they had been living on a small inheritance that Nadya had been left by her aunt, supplemented by Lenin's writings and occasional sums from the family in Petersburg. By the end of 1915 their funds were almost exhausted. "We shall soon be coming to the end of our former means of subsistence," Nadya wrote to Lenin's younger sister, Maria, in December, "and the question of earning money will become a serious one."

In January, 1916, when they were still living in Berne, Lenin wrote to M. Kharitonov that he wanted to work in the Zurich Library for two or three weeks. Could he get them cheap accommodation? He did not want to pay more than a franc a day and could, if necessary, share a single bed with Nadya. How much could he get for a lecture?

In fact, Nadya had been having trouble with their landlady in Berne, and since Lenin found the library so much superior in Zurich, they decided to stay in that city.

Toward the end of the year, their financial situation grew far more acute. "I need to earn," Lenin wrote to Alexander Shlyapnikov, the Central Committee member in Petersburg in charge of foreign communication. "Otherwise, we shall simply die of hunger, really and truly!! . . . The cash must be dragged by force out of the publisher of *Letopis*, to whom my two pamphlets have been sent . . . this is absolutely serious, absolutely, absolutely."

Urgently, Lenin sought assignments for articles, pamphlets and lectures. He even urged Mark Elizarov, his brother-in-law, who was a director of a marine insurance company on the Nevsky Prospect in Petersburg, to explore the possibility of finding him a commission for mere translating.

Lenin had an acute, wry sense of humor—often sarcastic both at the expense of himself and of others. His writer friend Anatol Lunacharsky was a "godseeker," a member of a group that became a target for one of his angry campaigns because they saw revolution in poetic terms as "a stage, inevitably tragic, in the world-wide development of the human spirit toward the 'universal soul.'" Once, after hearing Lunacharsky speak in this vein at a public meeting, Lenin approached him with his head bowed in humility and a malicious glint in his eyes. "Bless me, Father Anatol," he whispered.

Lenin's humor was strained that winter. "There are no changes here," he wrote gloomily to Maria in Petersburg. "We live very quietly; Nadya often feels poorly."

In February he received a windfall from Maria—808 francs he had not expected. He was delighted. "Please write and let me know what this money is . . ." he asked. "I cannot understand where so much money comes from; Nadya says jokingly that I must have been 'pensioned off.' Ha, ha! The joke is a merry one, for the cost of living makes one despair and I have desperately little capacity for work because of my shattered nerves."

The émigré colony in Zurich was very small. "We held ourselves, as was our custom, a little apart," Nadya wrote. Often Grisha Ussievich, an ardent young Bolshevik, "dearly loved," would drop in to the Spiegelgasse to see them for a moment after lunch on his way back from the émigré restaurant. They saw a lot, too, of Kharitonov and his wife and another young Bolshevik they admired, Nicholas Boitsov.

For a time, when they had first moved to Zurich, they had been visited every morning by a young nephew of Rosalya

Zalkind, an old comrade. The boy was demented from hunger, wore clothes so dirty and torn that even the libraries would not admit him. Rather sadly, trying to control his impatience—for his time was so limited—Lenin would discuss ideology with him, but the meetings left him with a feeling that "everything in the world ached." Later the young man became insane.

In the evenings sometimes they went to the Café Adler in Rosingasse, just off the Zahringerplatz, where they met the few Russian and Polish Bolsheviks who lived in the city, some Swiss socialists and a few Germans and Italians. Lenin tried giving some lectures there—usually about attitudes to the war—but they were not very successful. On one occasion, a young Swiss comrade argued with him that all their efforts were a waste of time since they could achieve nothing. "You can't break down a wall with your forehead," he told him, so Nadya reported.

It appears to have been a general view. Although forty people attended the first meeting, fewer came to subsequent lecturers. At the fourth, only a handful of Poles and Russians turned up. "They joked together a bit," recalled Nadya sadly, "and went their separate ways home."

It conformed with the mood of their life at the time. Lenin had grown less confident that he would be able to take part in the dramatic social changes for which he had striven so long. "We of the older generation may not live to see the decisive battles of this coming revolution," he told a young audience in January.

That winter had started badly for them, for, apart from their poverty, 1916 had been a year of tragic news. Lenin's mother, Maria Alexandrovna, had died in Russia. She had been living in the apartment on Shirokaya Street in Petersburg that she shared with her daughters, Anna and Maria, Mark Elizarov, Anna's husband, and their foster son, Gora. She had been a remarkable woman, to whom Lenin, like his sisters, had been devoted.

In the same month Anna, now fifty-three, was arrested. She had been sentenced to exile in Astrakhan but, owing to illness, had been released and allowed to spend most of the winter in Shirokaya Street—under very close surveillance. The police had raided the apartment twice and arrested her again in February.

In Switzerland, thousands of miles from Petersburg, Lenin felt trapped and ineffective. In his working life, he suffered the same sense of frustration. The party organization had almost broken down, not only because of the problems of contact between Zurich and Petersburg, but also because internal communications between Russian cities had been badly eroded by Okhrana operations. Worst of all, unlike the years before 1914, no one ever arrived from home with firsthand news.

Lenin continued to edit the party journal, now called *Sotsial Demokrat*, though its distribution was limited. Zinoviev helped him, though he had not moved with Lenin from Berne, where he was a laboratory assistant. Production of the paper was handled by Vyacheslav Karpinsky, a librarian, who lived with his mistress, Olga Ravich, in Geneva.

With hours to himself every day in the library in the Predigerkirche, Lenin wrote articles and pamphlets, often sending them to Inessa, who was then living at Clarens on Lake Geneva, for translation into French. Ever since 1914, he had striven to keep the party together outside Russia and had even worked to create a united all-party socialist front of internationalists—for although Lenin was the frequent cause of splits, he did in fact favor unity, provided it was on his terms.

To exiled revolutionaries, arguing endlessly in the cafés of Swiss cities, these exile politics seemed important, but it was a case of big frogs in very little pools. Lenin was utterly confined and the pressures of his frustration were immense. His letters to Inessa were often marked with urgent alarm over matters which barely merited so much angry emotion.

One day that winter, Lenin and Nadya saw in the street Ernst Nobs, editor of the socialist newspaper *Volksrecht*, with whom Lenin had quarreled. Nobs tried to avoid him, pretending he had to catch a tram, but Lenin, grabbing him firmly by the waistcoat, renewed their old argument.

Nadya, watching, was conscious that in Switzerland there was "no outlet for his colossal energy." The scene reminded her of a visit they had made together to London Zoo.

"I remembered a white northern wolf. . . . We had stood a

long time outside its cage. 'All animals, bears, lions, tigers,' explained the keeper, 'get used to their cages in time. Only the white wolf from the Russian north never becomes accustomed to the cage and day and night bangs his head against the bars.' " To his dedicated wife, Lenin shaking poor Nobs by his waistcoat seemed like the white wolf.

That winter, desperate as he was, Lenin quarreled with almost everyone with whom he had contact in Europe or even in America. Nicholas Bukharin, a Bolshevik with a fine brain whom he normally admired, was given a lashing. "That swine Trotsky," now in New York, came under new and virulent attack. Rosa Luxemburg, a Polish star of the German socialists whom he liked and respected, was sharply criticized. Karl Radek, an Austrian-Polish revolutionary journalist whom he had known for years, was labeled a "huckster who squeezes into the crack of differences between us—the time-honored policy of riffraff and scoundrels."

Even his most fervent and dedicated supporters were smarting after clashes with him—and he had to calm them with his usual technique of expressing surprise at their emotional reaction, by suggesting that they had misunderstood him, by analyzing what had disturbed them to demonstrate how wrong they were to take exception.

He wrote to Zinoviev, who had displayed a sudden unusual flare of rebellion, insisting, "There is no conflict—you are imagining too much really." In one of his many confessions to Inessa, he admitted that he had written "a very excited letter" to Olga Ravich "which Karpinsky called abusive. . . . I shall write her an apology."

In February he exploded at Inessa, who once again was ignoring his letters. "You did not take offense, did you," he queried, "at my writing about your not having gone over the French text? Incredible! . . . Is it conceivable that anyone can 'take offense' at such a thing? Inconceivable! And on the other hand the complete silence . . . is strange. . . ." He knew his lady, and their relationship was changed.

During that awful winter, Lenin's *rages*, as Nadya called

them, using the French word, were much more frequent. They would overwhelm him in an almost childish loss of temper and, certainly if they were provoked by political opponents, would take the form of violent fits of hatred. At these times, according to Valentinov, a comrade of the earlier days, he "wanted to 'smash their faces in' . . . to insult them, to trample them underfoot, to spit on them. . . .

"Following an attack . . . his energy would begin to ebb, and a psychological reaction set in: dullness, loss of strength and fatigue which laid him out. He could neither eat nor sleep. Headaches tormented him. His face became sallow, even dark at times, the light died in his small Mongol eyes."

Many of his *rages* in Switzerland—especially his outbursts of passionate anger against his own Bolsheviks—were provoked by the vital issue of the war.

To Lenin, patriotism was a confidence trick, employed by bourgeois imperalist governments to create a fighting fervor among their people—but he knew it stirred deep emotions. This was why it was dangerous, why he sprang at once to crush any sign of it in his followers. To a Marxist, which Lenin was by definition ("I am still 'in love' with Marx and Engels and cannot calmly stand any abuse of them" he had written Inessa in January), socialism was a world state ideal.

However, the natural love of home could easily create thoughts of defending, of fighting for that home, even in ardent Bolsheviks—for they were for the most part sentimental Russians who missed Russia very badly. In 1914, Lenin had been shattered—more shattered than by anything else since the 1903 split—by the sheer scale of socialist support of the war.

When he read that the German Social Democrats—the very party that had helped him print and distribute the first few issues of *Iskra*—had voted for war credits in the Reichstag, he would not believe it, convinced it was a propaganda lie issued by the German government.

Only two years before, the Second International had drafted a resolution declaring that any kind of war could only mean for the working class "shooting one another for the sake of the capitalists' profits, for the sake of the ambitions of dynasties, for the accomplishment of secret diplomatic treaties." It was the duty of socialists, it had asserted, to take advantage of such a crisis for rousing the people against the capitalist order.

How, Lenin questioned with astonishment, could these men and women have reneged on such a basic issue? But the Germans were soon balanced on the Allied side by Plekhanov, and large numbers of other socialists who were backing the war policies of their governments. When Lenin learned that in Paris Plekhanov, the hero of his youth, had been urging Russian exiles to enlist in the French Army, he despaired: "Can Plekhanov have turned traitor too?"

After a bitter meeting in 1914 with a handful of Bolsheviks in the Bremgarten woods near Berne, an appalled and incredulous Lenin had issued a defiant resolution defining what he saw as the facts:

The war was simply "a struggle for markets and for the freedom to loot foreign countries" between bourgeois governments. It was a means of suppressing the revolutionary movement by "setting the wage slaves of one nation against those of another. . . ."

Patriotism was a "chauvinist sophism" employed by both sides to "fool the masses." It ignored the fundamental truth of socialism stated years ago by Marx and Engels in *The Communist Manifesto* that "the working men have no country."

The defeat of the Tsarist monarchy and its army, he insisted, would be a "lesser evil by far" than its victory, for the ensuing chaos would provide a base for revolution, for civil war throughout the world between the classes.

In the three years that had passed since then, he had not changed his belief.

By March, when he heard the news of the revolution, Lenin's life centered on four places: Berne, where Zinoviev helped him to edit *Sotsial Demokrat* and run the party such as it was; Geneva, where Olga Ravich and Karpinsky handled printing and production for him; Clarens, where Inessa was; and Zurich, where Kharitonov was Lenin's main contact with the small local party.

He also had some communication with the party network in Scandinavia that had long been the route into Russia for secret letters and the Bolshevik journal—often sewn into the soles of shoes of comrades who crossed the border. But the war had made the use of this channel, too, very much more difficult and irregular.

Lenin's key correspondent in Sweden, though he wrote also to Alexandra Kollontai, was a Polish Social Democrat named Jacob Fürstenberg, who was seen even by Lenin's close comrades as a sinister character. Fürstenberg had a range of contacts in the semicriminal underworld, as well as links with the Wilhelmstrasse in Berlin. He was not even a member of Lenin's Russian party, though he handled special tasks that involved party funds. He was to play a critical role in the months that lay ahead.

Lenin wrote very often to those he did not meet—often at least to those in Switzerland—exhorting, complaining, urging speed, lashing comrades and opponents who erred on ideology.

It was this limited, inverted life of bickering conflict and small-scale politics that was transformed on March 15 by the brief news from Petersburg.

During the next few hours, more news began to arrive in the newspaper offices from Russia, and Lenin was able to begin assembling a picture of the situation that was emerging there. He learned how completely unexpected the revolution had been, how it had exploded—under the combined pressures of hunger and poverty and repression and organizational chaos and a war that seemed as though it would never end.

As in 1905, a stoppage in one plant had flared suddenly into a strike of many factories in the city, escalating to a massive demonstration in which tens of thousands of workers had marched in protest to the center of the capital.

Following the usual custom, the government had ordered the raising of the drawbridges over the Neva, but the weather was bitterly cold, and the river was frozen. The angry workers had not needed bridges.

Mutiny had swept through the regiments of the big city garrison, and the troops had joined the demonstrators. Again, as in 1905 in Moscow, the Cossacks had refused to charge. "The pharaohs," the hated whip-carrying mounted police, had been overpowered by the weight of sheer numbers.

The revolt had gusted like a storm, surging to its peak on the third day. Hundreds died in shooting on the streets—to be buried later in the Field of Mars, near the Winter Palace. Buildings were ransacked and set on fire. In army barracks and naval ships, officers were murdered.

Finally, mobs of angry men had broken into the jails and freed the political prisoners. Then they had marched, thousands of workers, soldiers and released revolutionaries, to the cream and gold Tauride Palace—once the home of Prince Potemkin, the lover of Catherine the Great—and demanded that the Duma should grasp the power that until then had been held by Tsar Nicholas II.

It had been the end of Tsardom, the beginning of rule by the people—rule at first, until order was restored, by a "provisional government" of ministers approved by the Duma. Later, everyone was agreed, there would be nationwide elections to a Constituent Assembly—a Parliament.

The chain of events of 1905, broken off so savagely by the slaughter in Moscow, were set in motion again. Delegates from the factories and the regiments—elected secretly as part of the underground activity of various parties before the revolution—began to arrive at the palace, the focal point of the revolution, in search of guidance.

The Soviet "happened"—and it was "happening" in other Russian cities to which the explosion in the capital had soon spread. One after another uncertain men, many unable to read or write or even to articulate the messages of the people who had elected them, stood up in the hall of the west wing of the Tauride Palace and swore allegiance to the revolution.

The Soviet, developing more by a common instinct than by preconceived ideas, was a strange body. In essence, it was a kind of crude instant labor union congress, except that its members did not just come from unions. But they did come from groups of workers, from factories, from the railways, from the docks, from the barracks, from any place where men were employed in large numbers.

Furthermore, the Soviet did not see itself as an instrument of government, but as a supervisor in the interests of the people, as a guardian designed to ensure there was no return to Tsardom, no counterrevolution. From the start, as in 1905, it commanded the complete obedience of the people.

· Scouring the newspapers in Zurich, Lenin was able very quickly to assess the new conditions. Most of the new ministers were members of the liberal Kadet Party (Constitutional Democrats) which was led by an ex-university don named Paul Milyukov, just appointed Foreign Secretary. The Kadets, who had a big following among the middle classes, sought to establish in Russia a capitalist democracy on British lines. Inevitably, they supported the war with the Allies until Germany was defeated.

Lenin was appalled, as indeed were the Bolsheviks in Petersburg, by the new men in power. For what kind of revolution was this? The new Premier was even a prince.

In its very early days, the Soviet, with the ideas of so many of its members rooted in the Parisian mobs, was a very revolutionary body. It howled for the trial of the Tsar with hopes of a dramatic execution. In its first official act, it banned the death sentence in the army, forbade the saluting of officers, ordered all regiments to form committees that were to send delegates to the Soviet in Petersburg. The committees were to set up control over the arms and munitions held by their regiments. For the time being, the Petersburg Soviet was acting as the center of the revolution for the whole of Russia.

Despite this, Lenin did not trust the men in the Soviet, for it was dominated by two socialist parties that dwarfed the extremist Bolsheviks—the Mensheviks and the SR's, the Socialist Revolutionaries. The SR's had taken over and refined the policy of the old terrorist Narodniks, in whose cause Sasha had died. Like the Marxists, they had abandoned terror as a technique—though there were still a few SR militants—but they were the party of the peasants, the biggest section of the Russian population, including many soldiers and sailors who had been called up from the villages to fight.

Lenin knew that the Mensheviks would cooperate with the new ministers, for compromise was in their nature, and he was pretty sure the SR's would, too. In his first letter to Alexandra Kollontai in Norway only hours after he had first heard of the revolt, he insisted that, above all else, he wanted no links with these parties, no talk of unity or combined fronts. Small though they were, the Bolsheviks would stand alone, the party of the workers, the party that would *not* collaborate with capitalists.

In this, Lenin did not trust many of his Bolsheviks either—which was one reason why it was absolutely vital that he should reach Petersburg quickly to set up a firm leadership over the party. At that early moment, though, the obstacles seemed enormous. "We are afraid it will be some time before we succeed in leaving accursed Switzerland," he wrote in another letter to Alexandra Kollontai.

Despite his pessimism, he now left no source untapped in a frenzied effort to find a way of overcoming the difficulties. "Vladimir Ilyich at this time resembled a caged lion," recorded Zinoviev. "We must be on our way. Every minute is precious. But how . . . passions rage. . . ."

He considered going across Germany by plane but realized quickly that this was utterly impractical. During one of his sleepless nights, when he was in bed with Nadya, he said to her suddenly, "You know, I could go on the passport of a dumb Swede." Dumb, of course, so that he would not have to reveal that he could speak no Swedish.

"You'll fall asleep and see Mensheviks in your dreams," she teased, "and you'll start swearing and shout 'scoundrels, scoundrels' and give the whole conspiracy away."

Despite her mockery, he was serious about the idea. He wrote to Jacob Fürstenberg in Stockholm asking if he could produce Swedish identities for him and Gregory Zinoviev.

Meanwhile, he moved on to another possibility. On April 18 he wrote to Inessa asking her to go to England to explore whether there was any possibility of the British granting him a passage. When he followed this up with a phone call the next day to Clarens, Inessa stubbornly refused his request. "I must say," he wrote to her that night, "I am keenly disappointed. In my opinion everybody these days should have a single thought—to rush off. . . . I was certain that you would rush off to England, as only there could you find out how to get through and how great the risk is (they say via Holland, London-Holland-Scandinavia, the risk is slight). . . ."

The same day he investigated yet another plan. "Take out papers in your own name for traveling to France and England," he instructed Karpinsky in Geneva, "and I will use them to travel through England (and Holland) to Russia. I can put on a wig."

Another idea, again among his stream of instructions to Inessa on March 19, was to ask the Germans to allow the passage of a rail coach to Copenhagen—but he was adamant that no one should know the suggestion came from him. Strangely, Julius Martov, his onetime friend, made the same proposal that day at a meeting in Berne of exiles of all parties, urging that this could be given a semblance of legality by the Russian government releasing a number of German prisoners of war equal to that of the people who traveled. When Zinoviev, who attended the conference, reported to Lenin the next day, his leader was delighted. The only problem was that everyone at the meeting had agreed that prior approval for the journey should be awaited from Petersburg. This meant delay, but Lenin conceded that politically it was vital, for the repercussions of accepting cooperation from the hated enemy of Russia could clearly be immense. Since 1914, hundreds of thousands of Russians had died from German bullets and bayonets. Ill-equipped, poorly shod, they were still being slaughtered in the thick mud of the trenches that formed the vast line from the Baltic to the Black Sea. Against that background, how would the ordinary Russian even in a revolution react to the news that Lenin and other exiles had accepted German help? Even with the agreement of the government, it would be a fact that would be easy for a political opponent to exploit. Without this approval, it would be extraordinarily dangerous, for it would be treason. So the exiles waited for the hoped-for cable from the Foreign Ministry in Russia.

While Lenin was exploring these bizarre plans to travel to Russia, Alexandra Kollontai was planning to leave Norway for Petersburg. She had cabled him a request for "directives" ("Just imagine thinking about 'directives' from here," commented Lenin with mock wonder) and now on the nineteenth he wired her the line she was to take in Russia: "Our tactics: No trust in and no support of the new government. Kerensky is especially suspect. No rapprochement with other parties. . . ."

Lenin's comrades found it strange that he should attach such importance to Alexander Kerensky, who was only a junior minister in the new government. Other men seemed far more formidable. But even then Lenin seemed to sense that in the conflict that faced him when eventually he got to Petersburg, Kerensky would be his most critical adversary. It was a belief that was marked with historical irony, for out of all the territory of the Russias, Kerensky also came from the little Volga town of Simbirsk. His father had even taught Lenin in school, and after the death of Lenin's father—according to an assertion by Kerensky—he became the family guardian.

Kerensky, who was ten years younger than Lenin, was in the right wing of the SR party.[2] A lawyer who had won a big popular reputation as a courageous defense counsel for the victims of Tsarist oppression, he was a gripping orator, with a dramatic touch and an obvious belief that he had been selected by destiny for greatness. Perhaps it was his talent that had caused Lenin to single him out, or maybe it was just that, as one of the only two members of the Soviet who were also ministers in the new government, he symbolized the whole issue of compromise— and of chauvinism, for he was firmly behind the war. And it was this aspect of compromise that made the delay, while Martov's proposal to approach the Germans for a train was explored by telegraph with Petersburg, such agony for Lenin.

Never in all his years of exile had he felt so impotent. Every day he scrutinized the papers for news from Russia, often exploding into impotent rages when he read of actions that he had no power to stop. "It's simply shit!" Lenin raged when he read a reported compromising speech of the Menshevik leader Nicholas Chkheidze, according to a visitor.

However, his repeated outbursts of fury did not stop him from working. In his one room in the Spiegelgasse and in the library of the Predigerkirche, he spent hours each day, writing a series of letters for the newly revived *Pravda*, laying down the party aims on a wide range of issues.

Lenin visualized a new type of society. The power that had been held formerly by the Tsar, he contended, had simply been taken by the bourgeoisie, the capitalists, the landowners. What was needed now was the destruction of the whole state apparatus—expecially the old police organization,[3] for this was the base on which counterrevolutionaries always scrambled back to power.

In its place, Lenin's key suggestion was that the whole people of both sexes should be armed. From this mass of gun-carrying workers, a militia would be formed with a wide range of duties, including such aspects as welfare and community sanitation. Members of the militia would take off from work one day in fifteen for their service in the corps on full pay.

The people's militia, which on any one day in Petersburg would amount to 50,000, though this could be fast raised to 750,000 in emergency, would be merged with the bureaucracy, the army and the new police. "Such a militia would guarantee absolute order and a comradely discipline practiced with enthusiasm."

In his concept of an "armed proletariat," Lenin's idea was to end rule from above—from the state and agents of that state—and to replace it with rule from below. Every official should be answerable to the people—and immediately replaceable by them. It was thinking that was highly idealistic, rooted in the mobs of Paris in 1789 and, particularly, in the Paris Commune in 1871, when for a short time the people of the city set up their own government.

It was essential, Lenin declared, for the party to conduct a concentrated campaign to spread the system of the Soviets right down through the nation to villages and city districts. For the bourgeois, he warned, was very well organized and, unless the workers could become equally well organized, they would never be able to hold the power, even if they succeeded in grasping it.

In Zurich, however, as the days went by, Lenin's way of getting to Russia seemed even more obscure than before—largely because, despite his earlier assurances to Inessa, he had begun to express doubts that the Germans would cooperate. "Valya has been told [at the British Embassy] that there is no passage at all through England," he wrote Inessa on March 25. "What if no passage whatever is allowed either by England or by Germany!!! And this is possible!"

In truth, though, as he well knew, this was not possible.

Chapter 4

LENIN KNEW HE WOULD soon hear from Parvus. The approach was not overt. His friend Jacob Fürstenberg cabled him offering him transit for two across Germany.[1]

Lenin was fully aware of the real source of the offer for, while Fürstenberg might have been able to produce such items as the forged Swedish passports he had been asked for, he was certainly in no position to supply railway facilities. But Parvus could.

Cautiously, since at this stage Lenin was leaving any channel open, Zinoviev wired back: "Uncle wants to know more. Official transit for individuals unacceptable." But when Parvus sent an agent to Zurich to explain the offer further, Lenin rejected it outright. Desperate though he was to find a way of crossing Germany, this was too furtive. A train, carrying a large number of political émigrés with the approval of Petersburg, was obviously the ideal plan. And in March, even though Lenin was a bit skeptical, this seemed a possibility.

In any case, there were certain dangers to dealing with Parvus at all. For he had changed beyond all recognition since the days when Lenin had known him in Munich. Then he had been a brilliant young Marxist journalist, as shabbily dressed as the rest of them, the man who had printed the early issues of *Iskra* on a secret press in his home. Now he had become a capitalist. The new Parvus, now grossly fat, was a bizarre, fantastic paradox. In the same flabby body coexisted a flamboyant tycoon, displaying the worst of bourgeois vulgarity, and a brilliant Marxist mind.

After the split of the Russian Social Democrats in 1903,

Parvus had formed a kind of partnership with Trotsky. Together, they had developed a theory of continuous revolution in Russia—which conflicted with the idea of progress by clearly definable stages believed by most Marxists.

At the time Lenin had attacked their arguments fiercely, but even he had regarded Parvus as a revolutionary of stature—especially after the 1905 revolution, in which Parvus, working with Trotsky, had played a prominent role that ended with a sentence to Siberia.

Since then, however, Parvus had made a fortune in Constantinople, though no one knew quite how. Rumors suggested massive and dubious deals in grain and arms.

By the outbreak of war, Parvus had stepped into a new role that made him suspect to everybody—a millionaire Marxist. Though he still had socialist ambitions, he had become a caricature tycoon with an enormous car, a string of blondes, thick cigars and a passion for champagne—often a whole bottle for breakfast.

The European revolutionaries were horrified by him—especially when they learned that his big-business contacts reached into the Wilhelmstrasse in Berlin. Even Trotsky disowned this "Falstaff . . . whom we have now placed on the list of politically deceased."

Lenin had last seen him two years before in 1915, when he had walked into the Student Restaurant in Berne with an ex-mistress and a young Bolshevik, Arthur Siefeldt. It was far too modest an establishment for the new Parvus to patronize in the ordinary way, but he was looking for Lenin.

Lenin was lunching with Nadya, Inessa and another comrade. Parvus stood, his eyes sweeping the crowded room in search of him—so enormous, according to Siefeldt, writing in a Baku journal, that he resembed "an overfilled sack of grain . . . his stomach vibrated." Then, when he had seen Lenin, he moved heavily toward his table.

Lenin had greeted him cordially enough, despite their differences. When Parvus asked for a private meeting, he had taken him back to the rooms that he and Nadya rented.

That discussion is still clouded by mystery, but almost certainly it was extremely important in the history of the world. "Parvus," so Lenin said to Siefeldt later, "ate without salt—meaning he had achieved nothing. Lenin had told him that he did not want to see him again—and, so far as is known, he never did. Parvus, writing of the meeting, limited his record to the fact that they had an argument about the development of revolution.

Neither was telling the truth—at least nothing like the whole truth. Without Parvus and his organization, through which he was to channel millions of gold marks to the Bolsheviks,* Lenin could never have achieved supreme power in Russia two years later in 1917. And the strands of that association—a strangely remote association in the sense that neither had direct contact with the other and both adamantly denied its existence—had already been laid in the early months of 1915 in the Wilhelmstrasse in Berlin.

The relationship between these two men—the wiry, disciplined esthete and the Rabelaisian *bon vivant*—was colored by irony, for they were competitors. Previously, they had competed fiercely as Marxist intellectuals with differing views. Now they were ranged against each other as potential leaders of the socialist revolution—antagonists, but antagonists who needed each other. And the arena was now far larger, for Parvus had begun to gain the support of one of the world's great powers.

He was, in fact, in Berne on that summer day in connection with a massive revolutionary operation that dwarfed anything that Lenin had ever been able to organize. For Parvus' mysterious fortune had given him big resources and contact with powerful men—including the German ambassador in Constantinople.

To the ambassador, Parvus had suggested that the Germans and the Russian Marxists had a common interest in the destruction of the Russian autocracy and explained that he had a

*For evidence of German financing, see page 290.

plan to exploit this. His suggestion was passed to the Foreign Office in Berlin at an ideal time. For by the end of 1914 it was clear that the war was not going to be won with the speed that the Kaiser and his generals had predicted. "Revolutionizing" had just become the new policy, outlined in a paper by Arthur Zimmermann, who was then Undersecretary of State at the Foreign Office. A revolution, so Zimmermann proposed, would force the Tsar to conclude a separate peace that would enable the Germans to concentrate their force on a single front in the West. Parvus was invited to Berlin.

In a high-level meeting in the Wilhelmstrasse, early in 1915, Parvus declared that he could create the revolution that Zimmermann wanted. One of the key points of his plan centered on Lenin. German money, he suggested, should be invested in his network of experienced professionals. Parvus saw this as the spearhead of an operation harnessing the whole force of Social Democracy, believing that the Bolsheviks and the Mensheviks must be united.

Parvus viewed himself as a kingmaker, the power behind a throne that Lenin would occupy. Whether or not his long-term aim was world socialist revolution—to which he had been committed as a young Marxist in Munich—is not clear. Certainly, at that meeting with the officials of the German Foreign Office he was presenting himself as a man who loved Germany—loved it, in fact, to the extent that very soon afterward he took out nationalization papers.

From the German viewpoint, Parvus had one enormous asset. He knew everyone of note in the world of militant socialism. He had lived with them, argued with them in cafés, disputed theory with them in angry articles—and had been respected by them.

The Germans were deeply impressed. As an initial venture they agreed to his proposal that he should stage a nationwide strike in Russia, and the Treasury released to him 1,000,000 gold marks to finance it.

This was the reason for his visit to Switzerland in May, 1915. Typically, complete with girls and champagne, he had moved into the Baur au Lac, Zurich's most luxurious hotel.

To find Lenin he traveled to Berne. The Bolshevik organization with its network in the Russian factories could obviously help him organize his strike. Also, though, he wanted to explore Lenin's reactions to his more ambitious plan for revolution in which the Bolshevik Party was crucial.

In their meeting in his rooms in Distelweg, Lenin clearly rejected the proposal that Parvus put to him, but almost certainly, there were other areas of agreement. After the meeting, Lenin very seriously considered moving to Scandinavia, where—since secret routes to Russia, both for communication and people, had long been established—Parvus' assistance could be far more effectively exploited than in Switzerland. Eventually he decided not to go—and it was a decision he was to regret in 1917, as he cried out in one of his frustrated letters in March to Inessa, for it would have removed his dilemma of how to get home. Far more important at the time, was his clear agreement that his close friend Jacob Fürstenberg should work for Parvus.

When Lenin refused him the cooperation of the Bolsheviks, Parvus set up his own organization under the cover of a commercial company that actually traded. With headquarters in Copenhagen and a network of agents inside and outside Russia, the organization sold German-made products to the Russians and vice versa. Chemicals, medicines, surgical instruments and even contraceptives were handled by what was a careful mixture of an espionage ring and a staff that had no idea of the true nature of the organization.

The appointment of Jacob Fürstenberg as president of this odd multifaceted corporation created a situation that was bizarre indeed.[2] For it meant that Lenin's trusted friend, who carried out for him vital secret assignments, was also the key right-hand man of Parvus, the maverick tycoon, the traitor to the cause despised by all his former revolutionary comrades because of his links with imperial Germany.

This close connection, with its potential element of political danger, was no doubt one reason why Lenin launched a savage attack on Parvus when he set up a socialist newspaper *Die*

Glocke ("The Bell")—backed, of course, with German funds. Parvus' new paper, Lenin charged in *Sotsial Demokrat*, was an "organ of renegades and dirty lackeys" associated with "the cesspool of German chauvinism." Later it was an attack that he was to quote as evidence that he had nothing in common with Parvus.

Parvus delivered his strike to the Germans without Lenin's help—but its scale was disappointing. During January, 1916, 55,000 workers stopped work in various plants in Petersburg. But this was hardly what the men in the Wilhelmstrasse had paid out 1,000,000 marks for. Parvus, who was distrusted by the aristocrats in the Foreign Office anyway, was dropped for a few months—until March, 1917, when the fall of the Tsar opened up an entirely new spectrum of opportunities and his value to the Germans became apparent once more. His new status was reflected in an early invitation to an audience with Arthur Zimmermann, the new German Foreign Secretary.

Zimmermann had an unusual background for the post to which he had been appointed four months before. For he did not come from one of the aristocratic Junker families of which virtually every senior official in Berlin was a member. Unlike all the ambassadors who reported to him, there was no "von" in his name. A man of the middle classes, he had broken through this formidable class barrier through ability. A well-built, ruddy-faced man, who drank a quart of Moselle every day with his lunch, this shrewd statesman enjoyed the respect of the Kaiser.

Possibly, however, the most important factor in March, 1917, was the fact that the whole concept of "revolutionizing" had been his own—and the scope for this had suddenly been broadened by the events in Petersburg to dimensions that had not existed before.

For two years, the Political Section of the Foreign Office had been patiently developing the revolution policy. During this time German agents both inside and outside Russia had been cultivating socialists of all parties—but Lenin had emerged as the man with the most potential from the viewpoint of German interests. Parvus had not been his only advocate. An agent named Alexander Kesküla, an Estonian Bolshevik, recruited b¦ Baron Gisbert von Romberg, German minister in Berne, had also urged that German funds should be concentrated behind the Bolsheviks and, soon after the meeting with Parvus in Berne in 1915, had even discussed with Lenin the terms "on which the Russian revolutionaries would be prepared to conclude peace with us in the event of the revolution being successful"—*i.e.*, with German help. These included an astonishing agreement by Lenin to put a Russian army into India.

In view of the size of the Bolshevik Party, this whole conversation in 1915 had been so academic that it was a joke, and even now in 1917 it would not be long before Lenin's assertion that the Bolsheviks would accept power if it were offered would be greeted with mocking laughter by more than 1,000 delegates to the Congress of Soviets in Petersburg.

But it was not seen as a joke in Berlin. Both Zimmermann and Count Diego von Bergen, the official in charge of political subversion in Russia, knew that money placed behind even a small party could, provided it was well organized, produce big results. At that stage, of course, it was not well organized at all, fragmented as it was by the war and the Okhrana. But its cellular structure, the philosophy of full-time disciplined dedication that Lenin fought for in 1903, and the quality of its leader had led Von Bergen to order special attention to be paid to the exile living in the one room in the Spiegelgasse.

According to the files of the Wilhelmstrasse, Kesküla provided the Bolsheviks with money, though there is some reason to doubt whether Lenin knew this. Kesküla has stated that he arranged this through Arthur Siefeldt, who fed the cash into the party in the guise of subscriptions under various names. By this means it can have been very little, for a substantial sum would have been noticed, even though Kesküla was paid nearly 250,000 marks over a period of two years by the Germans.

He also had Bolshevik literature printed and smuggled into Finland—and helped to ease Lenin's communication problems with Russia, taking care to read the material that passed through his hands. Kesküla, a German official reported to Berlin from

Sweden, had "maintained his extremely useful contact with Lenin and has transmitted to us the contents of the situation reports sent to Lenin by Lenin's confidential agents in Russia. . . ."

By March, 1917, therefore, the principle of German contact with Lenin and his party had been established, albeit on a small scale. By then, too, Parvus' network—and the commercial cover that was built into it—provided a new channel through which funds of a much larger order could be passed.

It took a few days for the news of the revolution to be digested in the Wilhelmstrasse, but a clear policy soon emerged—with the help of Parvus and Count Ulrich von Brockdorff-Rantzau, the German minister in Copenhagen, who had long been a close friend of Zimmermann's and was deeply impressed by the ideas of the strange revolutionary tycoon whose home was now in Denmark.

The policy was cynical but realistic. The German aim, as outlined by Rantzau, should be "to create the greatest possible degree of chaos in Russia" by throwing full German support behind "the extremist revolutionary movement," directed by Lenin. Meanwhile, there should be no German attack on the Eastern Front, for this might fan an undesirable mood of patriotism—at least not for three months, by which time the moral disintegration should have reached a stage where they "could break the power of the Russians by military action."

On April 5, in pursuance of this policy, the Treasury paid more than 5,000,000 gold marks to Parvus for political purposes in Russia.[3] It was far more than it had ever released before, but it was only a fraction of the investment it was going to make.

To the men in the Wilhelmstrasse, if not to Parvus, Lenin was a pawn—and was completely expendable once he had served his purpose. "He's finished," the Kaiser was to write contemptuously on a memorandum from Moscow a year later—six months after his Intelligence Service had financed Lenin's seizure of power and his negotiators had forced the Bolsheviks to relinquish to Germany vast areas of the Tsarist Empire. This brief and acid comment summarized clearly the attitude of the Kaiser and his High Command.

Meanwhile, in March, Arthur Zimmermann was personally supervising arrangements for the first stage of the plan: the transportation of Lenin and the émigré revolutionaries in Switzerland. On March 23 he received a telegram from Baron Gisbert von Romberg, his minister in Berne, who had been informed unofficially that "leading revolutionaries here wish to return to Russia via Germany. . . . Please send instructions in case applications to this effect should be made to me."

Immediately, Zimmermann had referred the request to General Headquarters in the massive castle of Pless near the Polish border urging that "it is in our interests that the influence of the radical wing of the Russian revolutionaries should prevail."

Within three days, the Kaiser and his generals had approved the project and detailed plans were fixed. "Special train will be under military escort," Romberg was informed in Berne on March 26. "Handover at frontier station . . . by responsible official of the consulate. Send information immediately concerning date of journey and list of names. Information must reach here four days before the frontier crossing."

The arrangements for the trip were settled, but in Berne Romberg appeared to be in no hurry. At the legation, he received the negotiator appointed by the all-party committee of émigrés—the leader of the Swiss Social Democrat Party named Robert Grimm—but the minister was not very forthcoming. He urged him to obtain approval to the passage from Petersburg, which had already been requested by cable, and played with him a little. When Grimm began to speak of the conditions that the exiles would have to insist on, Romberg checked him. "Excuse me, Herr Grimm," he said, "I was under the impression that it was not I who was asking permission to travel through Russia but Mr. Ulyanov [Lenin] and others who were asking me for permission to travel through Germany. Surely, we are the ones who have the right to impose conditions."

Of all the German officials, Romberg, who had been running a team of agents since 1914, seemed most concerned about the important aspect of political repercussions to the trip within Russia. For the more these could be reduced, the easier it would be for the Bolsheviks to increase their influence. For this reason, he wanted the travelers to come from all parties and to go, if possible, with the approval of the Russian government.

In Berlin Arthur Zimmermann waited impatiently for a week for Romberg to settle arrangements; then he ordered action. Rantzau, his minister in Copenhagen, had warned him in a cable that day that there were signs "that the English are also in contact with extremist socialist circles"—though, in truth, there seems to have been no grounds for this. More important, probably, was the fact that Germany was now facing a new and powerful enemy. Within hours, in the Capitol in Washington, President Woodrow Wilson would ask Congress "formally to accept the status of a belligerent."

Before they knew that the Tsar would fall in March, Zimmermann and the German High Command had ventured on an enormous speculation in which timing was critical. On the theory that the Allies would collapse very fast if they could create a complete blockade of supplies across the Atlantic, they had ordered their U-boats to sink all shipping bound for enemy ports—including vessels sailing under neutral flags. On March 18, only three days after the news of the Russian Revolution had astonished the world, the U.S. people learned that three American ships had been torpedoed without warning.

The danger that America would declare war had been finely calculated in Berlin. To counter it, Zimmermann planned to bring Mexico and Japan into the war. But the crucial immediate issue on which the whole gamble depended was to weaken the Allied strength in France before U.S. troops could be deployed in Europe.

Against this background, it was even more vital that the Russian Army should collapse, that Lenin and the extremist socialists should reach Russia without delay and start creating the chaos that was central to Zimmermann's plan. On April 2 an urgent telegram was dispatched to Romberg in Berne: "According to information received here, it is desirable that transit of Russian revolutionaries through Germany take place as soon as possible, as the Entente have already begun to work against this move in Switzerland. I therefore recommend all possible speed in your discussions. . . ."

As soon as he received the wire, Romberg abandoned his mood of relaxation and began combing Berne by telephone for Paul Levi, a German journalist who he knew was close to Lenin at this time. He traced him eventually in the Volkshaus Hotel. "I've been looking for you all over town," he said, according to Levi. "How can I get in touch with Lenin? I expect final instructions any moment regarding his transportation."

Three days before, Lenin, too, had made the traumatic decision to wait no longer. No response had been received from Petersburg to the request for government approval—and Lenin knew why. Paul Milyukov, the new Foreign Minister, was a bourgeois liberal patriot. Without question, he would not want Lenin or any of the other antiwar socialists in Russia making trouble.

Also, the news from Russia was disturbing. The government had developed an artful patriotic line, exhorting the people "to defend the republic" that their revolution had just created. This was "swindling the workers," he wrote to Jacob Fürstenberg. Alexander Kerensky was giving his "direct help" in the deception. The Soviet had allowed itself to to be fooled by a trick. For this policy was merely a cover for the old imperialist war policy of the Tsars—that would benefit the bourgeoisie but not the workers.

"The workers must be told the truth," Lenin insisted to Fürstenberg. "For God's sake try to deliver all this to Petersburg and *Pravda*. . . . Do everything in your power."

But he knew it was not enough, knew that unless he personally were there to drum the facts into the workers and soldiers "in a very popular way . . . without learned words," the fraud would continue. Also, he was worried to hear that Kamenev and Stalin had returned to Petersburg, after release from Siberia. Kamenev would be the main party leader until Lenin's return, and by instinct and personality, he was on the right of the party spectrum. Under his control, the danger that the Bolsheviks would collaborate with other parties, especially the Mensheviks, was far greater than it had been before.

On Saturday, March 31, after a tense discussion with Nadya and Zinoviev in his room in the Spiegelgasse, Lenin made the decision to cross Germany without approval from Petersburg. He wired Robert Grimm that the party had decided to accept the offer of a German train—which in fact had still not been made in any definite way. "We earnestly request you to make arrangements immediately. . . ."

Lenin was taking by far the biggest risk of his life, a risk so colossal that even now with all the benefit of hindsight it is astonishing. It was the move of a gambler making one play with enormous stakes. For by committing treason, by accepting help from an enemy who could only benefit from his declared policy of immediate peace, he was laying himself utterly vulnerable to his many enemies, both on the right and the left, in Russia. He would be a collaborator of the Kaiser.

Fully conscious of the immense danger, Lenin did his utmost to reduce the risk. He was a lawyer as well as a politician, and the terms he insisted should be met before he could accept German help were designed around the concept of a "sealed train"—a train that would have the extraterritorial status of a foreign embassy, on which the returning exiles could travel through enemy Germany without contact with enemy Germans. From the moment they boarded the rail coach they would not leave it until the end of the journey. The doors would be sealed.

Fritz Platten, the Swiss Social Democrat, had agreed to travel in the train in charge of the party and would be the go-between. Since he was not Russian, he faced no problems of compromise. If any talking to Germans were necessary on the journey, Platten would do it.

It was an attempt to make acceptable a journey that was in essence unacceptable—for sealed or not, it would still be provided by the Kaiser, the enemy of the Russian nation. As an idea, it was fairly ingenious, but inevitably it would fail. In a sense it would make Lenin's situation even worse, for the "sealed train"—with its sinister undertones—was to become a legend, a symbol of treachery, a jeer to yell at public meetings.

From the moment Lenin sent the wire to Robert Grimm he embarked on a hectic flurry of last-minute preparations. On Sunday he cabled Fürstenberg in Stockholm to "earmark . . . three thousand Kronen for our journey [onward from Sweden]. Intend leave Wednesday minimum ten persons."

The next day he wired his sisters in Petersburg: "Arriving Monday 11 P M Inform *Pravda*." He wrote to the "Zurich group of Bolsheviks," presumably care of Kharitonov, giving instructions that the list of those who wanted to travel with him and how much money they had was to be sent at once to Zinoviev in Berne. The Lausanne group of Bolsheviks, headed by M. Goberman, was to be alerted in the same way. "We already have a fund of over 1,000 francs for the journey," he said.

On Wednesday morning, as soon as he heard that Romberg had been seeking to contact him, he told Nadya to pack. They were taking the first train to Berne. She was accustomed to fast moves, but this scheduling was tight. "Go on your own," she suggested. "I'll leave tomorrow."

"No," Lenin insisted, "we'll go together."

They caught the 3 P M train—together with Zinoviev and Fritz Platten, whom Lenin, who had never trusted Grimm since he was friendly with Martov, had now asked to take over the negotiations with Romberg. When they said good-bye to their sympathetic landlords in the Spiegelgasse, Lenin remarked, "So, Herr Kammerer, now there's going to be peace."

That afternoon Fritz Platten visited Romberg at the German Legation and put to him Lenin's conditions. Now that he had been ordered to expedite the journey, the baron raised no objections. In addition to the "sealed" aspects of the train, Lenin insisted that no names should be given—just a list of numbers of passenger—and that they should pay their own fares.

One important point that Platten demanded from Romberg was that the "safe transit" of the exiles should be guaranteed. For the political repercussions in Russia were not the only danger Lenin foresaw. To him the class war was far more important than the military war, and by traveling on a German train, he was placing himself completely in the hands of his stated enemy, Kaiser Wilhelm II, at a time when revolution had just toppled his cousin, the Tsar. All of Lenin's life had been devoted to overthrowing the system of which Wilhelm was monarch. His articles, like the writings of Marx and Engels, had specified Germany as especially open to revolt, and the danger of infection across the Russian border must now be greater than ever. The value of Lenin and his comrades as campaigning pacifists in Russia was obvious—"live bombs" as Karl Radek called them sarcastically—but was not the other danger greater? Lenin did not discount the possibility of a trap. Owing to "the suspicious nature of the Russians," Romberg warned Berlin, they would not at first believe in "the possibility of safe transit" through Germany.

Lenin's suspicions had some justification. There was considerable fear of the spread of revolution from Russia within Germany. Within hours of the news of the Tsar's fall reaching Berlin, Chancellor Theobald von Bethmann-Hollweg had announced plans to extend the franchise. Less than a year previously three German officers and thirty-two privates had been executed for distributing among front-line troops the internationalist antiwar Kienthal Manifesto, for which Lenin had been partly responsible.

Within a few days, Emperor Karl of Austria was to write to the Kaiser warning that "we are fighting against a new enemy which is more dangerous than the entente—the international revolution. . . . I impore you not to disregard this fateful side of the question. . . ."

For Lenin, the danger from the Germans that was implicit in the trap was a risk he was prepared to accept, though it did add another dimension of menace.

Baron von Romberg assured Platten that there would be no problem in guaranteeing the travelers "safe transit," and in view of Zimmermann's demands for action, he anticipated little trouble over the other conditions. That day he wired Lenin's terms to Berlin for approval.

Chapter 5

IN LONDON THAT WEEK, Lenin's proposed journey was brought to the notice of Arthur Balfour, the British Foreign Secretary. On April 5, in fact, two telegrams that had reached the Foreign Office were causing anxiety.[1]

From Berne, British Ambassador Sir Horace Rumbold reported that negotiations were in progress with the German government to obtain "safe conducts through Germany to Russia of Russian socialiasts and anarchists resident in Switzerland." Since they were in favor of immediate peace with Germany, they would be commissioned to "make violent propaganda among the working classes in Russia and among troops at the front." The first party would be sent through shortly.

That night the Foreign Office cabled the news to Sir George Buchanan, British ambassador in Petersburg, asking him "to enquire whether the Russian Government intended to take any steps to counter this danger."

The other telegram that arrived in London that day was received at the Admiralty. Six socialists had been removed by British naval authorities from the SS *Christiania Fiord*, which had called in at Halifax, Nova Scotia, on her way to Russia from New York. It had been reported that one of them, Trotsky, was "the leader of a movement to start a revolution against the present Russian Government, the funds being subscribed by socialists and Germans." Would London please make discreet inquiries of the Russian government if it would like them to proceed? So yet another telegram was dispatched to Sir George Buchanan in Petersburg.

It was proof, at least, that Lenin was wise to make no attempt to seek British help for his return plans. For ever since the revolution, the British Cabinet—under pressure from Buchanan in Petersburg—had been doing everything it could to please the new Provisional Government in Russia. On the ambassador's urging, messages of goodwill had been sent from the House of Commons and from the leaders of the British labor movement. Still, Milyukov had warned Buchanan, there was disappointment in Russia regarding the warmth of British feeling toward the revolution.

The Russian ministers—uneasily eyeing the uncertain radicals in the Soviet—were frightened men, and so clearly were those in London. Sir Cecil Spring-Rice, British ambassador in Washington, was now urged to arrange for messages to be sent to Petersburg from labor leaders and prominent men in the United States emphasizing the necessity of continuing the war in order to secure the triumph of the principles of freedom and domocracy. "There is real danger," warned the telegram, "of revolutionary pacifists obtaining the upper hand and occupying the position of the Provisional Government."

If there appeared to be an element of panic, it was not strange. The Allies were about to launch a new offensive on the Western Front. It was now scheduled for April 9.

While the telegrams were passing between London, Washington and Petersburg, troops were moving up into position through the mud of northern France, artillery and supplies were being established. The initial strike would be launched at the German position at Arras.

That week Lenin's plan to cross Germany, with the Kaiser's help, was under discussion elsewhere in Petersburg, as well as in the British Embassy and the Foreign Ministry. Across the Neva in Old Petersburg, the Bolshevik Central Committee was also considering it in the mansion it had seized from its prior owner, Kshesinskaya, a prima ballerina who had once been the mistress of the Tsar.

Kamenev and Stalin had taken over control of the party—and the editing of *Pravda*—from Vyacheslav Molotov and Alexander Shlyapnikov, who had been running the Bureau of the Central Committee in the absence, in Siberia or exile, of all the leaders. And precisely as Lenin in Zurich feared, they had toned down the early Bolshevik militancy of the party and even offered its cooperation to the new Soviet. It was the precise opposite of what Lenin had ordered, but Lenin was abroad. From Switzerland, it was argued, he could not judge the mood of a city that was tasting the euphoria of freedom for the first time in its history.

Alexander Shlyapnikov, in charge of foreign communication, had experienced enormous trouble in contacting Lenin at all. At first, he had believed that this was due to chaos in the telegraph system, caused by the revolution. Then he had realized the difficulty was more sinister, resulting from deliberate anti-Bolshevik orders by the new government.

For this reason he had sent a courier, Maria Stetskevich, through the Finnish border to Sweden to communicate with Switzerland from foreign soil. On April 2 she was back in the city with letters from Lenin and Jacob Fürstenberg. So, too, was Alexandra Kollontai.

The Central Committee, therefore, knew of the plans for the train across Germany and was only too conscious of the use to which the "chauvinists" in Petersburg would put it. All the same, deciding like Lenin that the risk was worth it, they wired Fürstenberg: "Ulyanov must come immediately." Then, as Anna and Maria pondered the danger that the Germans might use the train as a trap, they sent a second wire: "Do not force Vladimir to come. Avoid all risk."

Once more, in case the cable was blocked by the censors, Maria Stetskevich set off for the Swedish-Finnish border. This time, in a rigorous search at Tornio, she was stripped naked and her letters seized, but she was allowed to proceed to Sweden. It was an ominous sign of what lay ahead of Lenin. For it was through this border post that he and his comrades would have to pass on their way to Petersburg.

The final approval from Berlin for the train reached the German Legation in Berne on Thursday, April 5—within hours of the telegram from London to Petersburg asking Sir George Buchanan what Miliukov was going to do to stop it. Two second-class carriages, Romberg was instructed, would be waiting at Gottmadingen, a tiny station in the hills on the German side of the Swiss border, on Saturday evening, April 7. A legation official was to accompany the travelers on a regularly scheduled Swiss railway train from Zurich, which stopped at Gottmadingen on the way to Singen, the formal German frontier post where customs and immigration officials were based. There a military officer would take over as escort.

Earlier that day, Arthur Zimmermann had personally requested General Headquarters to provide "a tactful officer with political understanding" to conduct the exiles on their six-hundred-mile journey across the whole of Germany from Gottmadingen to Sassnitz, the port on the Baltic from which a ferry sailed daily for Gothenburg, in the south of Sweden. From there they could travel on by train through Finland to Russia. In fact, General Headquarters decided to send two officers.

Once again, Lenin threw himself into a frenzy of action, wiring the new departure date to Karpinsky, whose duty it was to inform the others, and to Jacob Fürstenberg in Sweden. Now, however, Lenin had suddenly become alarmed that the "sealed" aspect of the train would not provide him with enough cover when he faced the inevitable inquisition in Petersburg. He had good reason for his new anxiety. On Thursday he had heard that the French newspaper *Le Petit Parisien* had reported that Milyukov had threatened to prosecute on charges of high treason against everyone who traveled through Germany.

To strengthen his case, in the face of this new danger, Lenin conceived the idea of drawing up a formal approval of the journey to be signed by a body of international socialists—as eminent as possible. The key signature he wanted was that of Romain Rolland, the celebrated French writer who was in Switzerland—and he asked another Frenchman, Henri Guilbeaux, a newspaper editor, to seek it for him. But Rolland refused to sign, asserting that Lenin was a "dangerous and cynical adventurer" whose plan to return to Russia through

Germany would "cause great damage to the pacifist movement."

Lenin had to be satisfied with lesser men—among them Bronski, signing for Poland, Guilbeaux for France and Fritz Platten, for Switzerland—though he planned to augment the list with prominent Swedish Social Democrats when he got to Stockholm.

They did not leave on Saturday, or on Sunday, the next scheduled date, because Romberg, with his understanding of the problems, was trying desperately to arrange for some exiles of the SR party—the Socialist Revolutionaries—to join Lenin on the train. For Martov and the Mensheviks had been adamant in their opposition to traveling without approval, which in a few days was to be refused formally by Milyukov, and it was obvious that the train journey would be less explosive politically if the travelers were not all Bolsheviks.

Romberg failed to convince the SR's—at any rate in time, and there was clearly a limit to the number of times departure could be postponed. He had to be content with the presence in the party of a few Bundists—Jewish Marxists who had their own Social Democrat group affiliated with the Russian party—which presumably was better than no outsiders at all.

Early on Monday, April 9—only a few hours after the Allies had launched their new offensive on the German line at Arras—the travelers assembled at the Volkshaus in Berne. Those that came from other Swiss towns had arrived the day before—such comrades as Goberman from Lausanne, A. Abramovich and A. Linde from Chaux-de-Fonds and a group of five from Geneva. Heading this last section was sixty-year-old Mikha Tskhakaya, who had so terrified the Ulyanov's landlady when he had first called on them years ago when they, too, were living in Geneva that she slammed the door in his face. For he had been wearing Caucasian costume, and, with his thick gray beard, he had looked like a brigand.

Twelve months before, during an all-night talk in Lenin's room in Zurich, the two men had promised each other in jest that in a year they would go back to Russia together. On the day the news arrived from Petersburg Lenin had sent his cohort a postcard: "Congratulations on the revolution in Russia. Your optimism justified. . . . I am preparing to leave, packing, what are you doing?"

"My suitcase has been ready since last year," Tskhakaya wrote back.

Among the five from Geneva were Olga Ravich, who was very much a last-minute addition to the party—Lenin in his letters had assumed she would be staying with Karpinsky—and a young comrade, David Souliashvili. Before they left from Geneva Station, one of the farewell crowd on the platform had thrust a red handkerchief through the window of the carriage into Souliashvili's hands—to serve as a revolutionary flag. Like an eighteenth-century standard-bearer, he was clutching it still.

G. Sokolnikov was among the Geneva contingent. He worked for the French journal *Nashe Slovo*, which Martov and Trotsky had once edited together until it was suppressed in 1916. He had not been a Bolshevik long, but Lenin's letters to Inessa indicated he regarded him as a man of talent. He was to play an important part in Lenin's rise to power during the months ahead.

Inessa had joined Lenin in Berne a few days before from Clarens to help with the last-minute arrangements. Zinoviev was there, of course, with Zina and Stepan, their nine-year-old son, who had been born only a few months after they had first joined Lenin in Geneva in 1908. Among the party, too, was George Safarov, a young engineer Lenin often sent on foreign trips, and his wife, Valentina.

Others such as Kharitonov, young Gregory Ussievich and his wife, Helen Kon, daughter of the well-known Polish socialist Felix Kon, would join them in Zurich.

The youngest member of the party was Robert, a four-year-old Jewish boy from Geneva, who appealed to Nadya so much that he features almost as prominently as Lenin in her account of the journey.

That morning Lenin, usually so calm at times like this, was taut and flustered, mopping his forehead with a handkerchief. There had been so much to organize. On Saturday he had wired

Kharitonov in Zurich warning that Platten must get permission to take provisions with him. He had cabled Furstenberg that they would be leaving Sunday, instructing him to call "Belenin"—the code name for Alexander Shlyapnikov—and Kamenev to Finland for discussions before he reached Russia. Then, as the plan was changed once more, he wired again: "Final departure date Monday—forty people," though the numbers were to be an overestimate, for in fact there were only thirty-two, including two children.[2]

Nadya was cool enough. She congratulated them all on the speed with which they had assembled. "True Bolshevik discipline," she commented according to Olga Ravich.

The Ulyanovs' luggage consisted of three baskets—one for their personal clothes, one filled with books and one packed with old newspapers—and two boxes, crammed with newspaper cuttings and party documents. They also had a portable Swedish kerosene stove that would be useful on the journey.

They took the train from Berne to Zurich, where they all had lunch with some of their Swiss comrades at the Zahringerhof Hotel in the Zahringerplatz, near the library in the old church where Lenin had spent so many hours.

Here, at the lunch table, they all signed a statement, accepting the leadership of Fritz Platten, confirming that they knew of Milyukov's threat that they would be arrested and agreeing on their own responsibility to the conditions that had been negotiated with the Germans.

During lunch Lenin read a letter "to Swiss workers." It was a significant speech because it indicated, only hours before he left Switzerland, his concept of long-term socialist revolution—a concept that was to change on the Sealed Train. "Russia is peasant country," he declared, "it is one of the most backward of European countries. Socialism cannot triumph there immediately."

After lunch, they all walked from the Zahringerplatz across the Limmat to Zurich Station—a crowd of men and women and children in threadbare clothes, the men in black hats, the women in long skirts, ankle boots, their heads under varying types of covering ranging from scarves to Olga Ravich's big broad-brimmed "chapeau." They carried blankets and pillows. Presumably their baskets, their main luggage—Romberg had warned Berlin that there would be three baskets per person—had already been left at the station.

On the platform, where the train that was to take them to Gottmadingen was waiting, a crowd of "about a hundred Russians," mainly hostile, had gathered to demonstrate against Lenin's decision to go through Germany without approval from Petersburg.

"The farewell was rather stormy," caustically commented an observer from the German Legation, "a typically Russian-Polish little scene of enchantment." Somewhat loftily, he interpreted it as a sign of the lack of discipline and harmony among the workers' parties of the world.

The catcalls were shrill: "Provocateurs! Spies! Pigs! Traitors!" the protesters yelled. "The Kaiser is paying for the journey," taunted one. "They're going to hang you . . . like German spies," shouted another.

One jeer of "Traitor" brought an immediate response from a member of the train's Geneva contingent. "Traitor!" he yelled back. "And what are you? . . . I know for a fact that you get two hundred francs a month at the [German] consulate!"

They beat on the side of the carriage with sticks, shouting and whistling all the time. At one point D. B. Ryazanov, a close friend of Trotsky's, ran onto the platform, and seeing Zinoviev at the window, he pleaded with him: "Lenin's got carried away! He doesn't realize what a dangerous situation it is. You're more level-headed. Tell Vladimir Ilyich to stop this mad journey through Germany!"

Zinoviev shrugged his shoulders and grinned. Zina, his wife, was watching Lenin, who "stood listening to them and smiled sardonically. 'Hiss as much as you like,' he said, 'we Bolsheviks will shuffle your cards and spoil your game.'"

Fritz Platten was involved in a fight with a "practically insane Social Democrat," and eventually even Lenin was provoked to physical violence. Someone told him that a Social Democrat named Oscar Blum had boarded the train and taken a seat in the carriage.

Blum, author of a book, *The Brains of the Russian Revolution,* had been present at the lunch at the Zahringerhof. According to one report, when he asked if he could join the party, Lenin put the issue to a vote, which resulted in a decided turndown.

A German diplomat reported that Lenin suspected Blum was a Russian agent, though it is more likely that if he was a spy at all, he was working for the French or the British. Certainly he was determined. Despite the adverse vote, he had climbed cautiously onto the train. Incensed, Lenin stalked to the compartment where he was sitting, grabbed him by the collar and thrust him out of the carriage onto the platform—which truly he had no right to do, for this, unlike the train that was to collect them at Gottmadingen, was public transport.

At 3:10 P.M., to the accompaniment of jeers and cheers, the train moved out of Zurich Station. "Ilyich," shouted one supporter, "take care of yourself. You're the only one we have." Some of the others began to sing the "Internationale." Defiantly, David Souliashvili streamed the red handkerchief he had been given on the platform in Geneva, like a flag from the window.

As the train steamed through the Zurich suburbs and began to climb into the hills, Fritz Platten distributed pieces of paper marked with numbers, ranging from one to thirty-two, to serve in lieu of passports. He briefed the travelers on the terms of his agreement with the Germans, the main point being that they were not to leave the sealed carriage or to speak to anyone. The instructions seem hardly to have been necessary, but they contained a vital point.

It was the reason, in fact, why Romberg had sent a telegram to Berlin at 1 A.M. that morning. Arthur Zimmermann had accepted all of Lenin's terms except one: The insistence that no German should have any contact with the travelers. As late as Saturday, a wire from Berlin had reached the legation in Berne insisting that Wilhelm Janson, a German trade union leader, should join the train. It was part of Parvus' vast plan to link the German

Social Democrats into the operation that would bring about Lenin's return to Russia.

Romberg understood the political danger in which Lenin stood better than did Parvus and was convinced that the proposal to have Janson join the party could prejudice the whole German aim. "The émigrés expect to encounter extreme difficulties, even legal prosecution, from the Russian government because of their travel through enemy territory," he explained by telegram. "It is therefore essential to their interests that they be able to guarantee not to have spoke to any German in Germany."

At Schaffhausen, the Swiss border town on the banks of the wide, curving waters of the Rhine, Customs ordered the party to get out of the carriage onto Platform 3. They were party to no German agreement to allow the travelers through without formality. They combed the luggage and confiscated much of the food that Platten had assembled for the journey. In wartime Switzerland, there were strict limits on what food could be taken out of the country. Even so, to the distressed passengers, they seemed overmeticulous. For although the Germans had said they would provide them with what food they could, Romberg had warned Platten to take a basic supply. The Swiss action could well leave them hungry. "It was obvious that they were against us," recalled Souliashvili.

It was not to be their last experience with Swiss officialdom. At Thayngen, the last halt on Swiss soil, new officials insisted on yet another examination.

Furiously, Platten complained at their treatment and sent an angry telegram to the government about these petty obstructions by Swiss bureaucrats. But his fury made little impression. Perversely, the uniformed officials continued to carry out their duties to the letter.[3]

At last the Swiss customs officials were finished with them, and they cross the border into Germany. Despite the uncertainty that lay before them, it was a relief. Certainly Olga was pleased, not only to be going home, but to be leaving the deadening "calm of bourgeois Switzerland with its measured tranquility."

"Some people need battles," she wrote in her account of the

journey, "some people need storms." She would not be lacking in storms or battles during the months ahead.

In a few minutes they could see ahead the tall hill, topped by a wood, that dominated Gottmadingen. The train slowed as it approached the village which lay to the right of the tracks. The old Bahnhof Hotel, with its curving roof and faded cracked plaster, moved past the windows followed by the station building. They came to a steaming halt at the single platform—empty except for two German officers, in high boots and green-gray uniforms, who awaited them.

The sight of the officers, stiff and upright, caused acute anxiety among the revolutionaries peering out of the windows of the train. Nearly all of them had been in jail, had been in illegal situations, had been pursued, had been called in to local police posts in foreign cities for interrogation. Suspicion was rooted in them.

The two officers had, in fact, been briefed in person by General Erich Ludendorff, Chief of Staff of the German Eighth Army on the Eastern Front. According to Soviet historian A. Ivanov,[4] Lieutenant von Buhring, the junior of the two officers, could speak fluent Russian but was under orders not to reveal this fact. If true, it was the one note of political caution in what was otherwise a totally cynical military operation.

At the request of the officers, the travelers clambered down from the train and unloaded their baggage onto the platform. Uneasily, at the direction of Captain von Planetz, the senior of the two Germans, they filed slowly into the third-class waiting room.

The atmosphere in that bare waiting room was as tense as if the officers had been in the service of the Okhrana. The entire party had the suspicion in the back of their minds that they might have walked into a trap. "We expected any kind of disaster on this journey," Mikha Tskhakaya, the veteran Caucasian, explained later.

When Captain von Planetz asked them to separate into two groups—men and women—the unease grew. They had lived too long under the threat of arrest to be herded by uniformed officials without becoming alarmed. Instinctively, Lenin backed against a wall, and the rest of the men surrounded him—a ring of grim-faced figures in black hats and overcoats. "We didn't want them to look too closely at him," recorded Karl Radek. "It was very unpleasant."

There was a dramatic silence broken only by a loud exclamation from Robert, the four-year-old boy from Geneva, whose mother had stood him on a table. "Mamele," he asked, "what's happening?" In a whisper, she tried to quiet him.[5]

The other child, nine-year-old Stepan Zinoviev, stood silently beside his slim dark mother. He had often known anxiety in his parents.

As quickly as they could, the officers completed their formalities, checked the passengers, collected the payment of fares that Lenin had insisted on during the negotiations. Then Captain von Planetz invited them to board the train that now stood at the platform.

It was not much of a train—just a green carriage, with eight compartments, three second-class and five third-class, and a baggage wagon. It had been necessary for Lenin's concept of sealing the travelers off from German contact to be eased slightly to accommodate the two officers, for clearly the travelers could not cross wartime Germany without an escort. However, the Germans had attempted to conform with the theory by allocating the end third-class compartment to themselves and drawing a white chalk line across the floor of the corridor. No one was permitted to cross this line except the Swiss Fritz Platten. Fortunately, there was a toilet at each end of the coach so that the officers had no reason to move into "Russian territory."

Once all the passengers were aboard, three of the four external doors to the carriage were locked. The fourth, opposite the officers' compartment, was left unlocked, but this was on the German side of the white line, so lip service at least was paid to the idea of the Russian confinement within the coach until they reached the Baltic. According to Kharitonov,[6] no one bothered to lock the doors on the other side of the carriage, which opened directly from the compartments—either because these were forgotten or because it was felt that the principle had already been met.

One of Platten's accounts suggest that the blinds were drawn, though it is quite clear from some versions of the journey that at times they were not. Probably, since it was now late afternoon anyway, they were pulled down for the start of the journey.

The single men in the party accepted the hard wooden benches of the third-class, relinquishing the more comfortable second-class compartment with their brown padded upholstery to the women travelers—together, of course, with their husbands and children.

Lenin and Nadya, at the insistence of the comrades, had the end second-class compartment to themselves. As soon as the train moved off from Gottmadingen Station, the gloom of the travelers lifted. Spirits soared. There was laughter and joking. "Robert's cheerful voice," recorded Nadya, "could be heard through the whole coach." The excited little boy ran up and down the corridor, stopping to clamber onto the lap of Sokolnikov, whom he appeared to have adopted. He "did not want to talk to the women."

Some of the younger ones in third-class began to sing the "Marseillaise." It was taken up in other compartments. The sound of elated voices, shouting out the battle chorus of the French Revolution, echoed through the woods beside the track as the train clattered north into Germany.

In the Wilhelmstrasse, in Berlin, Arthur Zimmermann was following the progress of the party with very close interest. Telegrams had come in from various ministers. In particular Romberg warned that transit facilities for the party to pass through Sweden, already requested by the German minister in Stockholm, had still not been granted. From Copenhagen, Count von Brockdorff-Rantzau had wired: "Dr. Helphand [Parvus] has requested to be informed immediately of the arrival in Malmo or Sassnitz of the Russian refugees traveling from Switzerland through Germany. Helphand wishes to meet them in Malmo."

Zimmermann had wired Stockholm urging action—and sent an answering telegram to Copenhagen: "Russian émigrés from Switzerland will arrive Sassnitz at noon Wednesday."

In the British Foreign Office in Whitehall, a telegram arrived during the day from Sir George Buchanan in Petersburg. He had discussed the question of the train carrying Lenin and his party with Mr. Milyukov, the Foreign Minister. "All that can be done," the minister had told him, "was to publish their names and the fact that they had come through Germany and this would be sufficient to discredit them in Russia."

Later in the day another wire had arrived from Buchanan, this time about Trotsky and his comrade socialists in detention in Halifax. The minister, Buchanan reported, had asked that "they should be allowed to proceed at once [to Russia]. There were so many extreme socialists already here that he did not so much object to others coming who had lived abroad as their experience of other countries inclined them sometimes to take a more reasonable view of things and to exercise a moderating influence on their Russian colleagues."

Accordingly, the next morning, Foreign Secretary Arthur Balfour gave orders for their release—only to cancel them on receipt of yet another telegram from Petersburg. Mr. Milyukov had had second thoughts and would now like to know the Christian names of the detained socialists and the "reason which led them [the British naval authorities] to suppose that these persons have been paid by Germany to upset the Provisional Government."

The reasons were not very sound, for they were not the result of anything so dramatic as espionage. The naval commander in Halifax had read a report in a newspaper.

As the little train, drawn by a long black engine, with smoke streaming from a squat funnel, moved through the wooded hills, "Lenin," recalled Zina Zinovieva, "did not leave the window." Standing, as always, with his thumbs stuck in the armholes of his waistcoat, he would not have seen much in the dusk light—just the passing firs and the beeches that grew thickly beside the tracks.

They did not have far to go that night. For it had been arranged that they should spend the night at Singen, a colorless little town on the junction of two main rail lines that reached north into the body of Germany. Here the carriage and the baggage wagon were shunted into a siding, and the escort officers passed beer and sandwiches across the white chalk line in the corridor.

For all the comrades' insistence that he should have the compartment to himself with Nadya so that he could have peace in which to work, Lenin did not get much that evening. In addition to the noise in that coach, lying motionless in the darkness of the Singen siding, the problems that must inevitably emerge among thirty-two people forced to spend several days in in the limited space of a rail coach appeared very early—marring the excited good humor.

One of the earliest difficulties concerned smoking, which Lenin detested. He had ruled at the start that those who wished to do so must retire to the toilet. A queue formed in the corridor, and eventually a quarrel broke out between the smokers and the comrades who wanted to use the toilet for its intended purpose.

With a sigh, Lenin decided the issue. He wrote out passes in two categories of priority: smokers, who ranked as second priority, and the others. It eased the tension, though a lighthearted argument soon developed among the men standing in the corridor about the importance of their varying needs. "It's a pity Comrade Bukharin isn't with us," joked Karl Radek, for Bukharin, one of the most brilliant thinkers in the party, was an expert in the theories of Ben Baverk,[7] who had tabulated the levels of human necessity.

One way or another, Radek caused Lenin a lot of trouble that first evening. He was not with the other single men in third-class—though why has not been explained—but he was certainly the main cause of the noise and shrieks of laughter in the second-class compartment next to Lenin's. Radek was sharing this with Olga Ravich, George Safarov and his wife,

Valentina, and Inessa. With his ruddy face and glasses and thick gray curly hair, he was an amusing companion. He had a great gift for anecdote, for mimicry, for singing. He did not even spare Lenin from his clowning. Several times, according to Olga, when Ilyich looked in at the door, Radek challenged him, "whether he wanted to or not, to assume the leadership of the revolutionary government. Vladimir Ilyich frowned but indicated that he would not refuse."

Olga wrote her two accounts of the journey after Lenin's death, and she treats this scene seriously. In fact, in the rowdy high spirits of that compartment, where they were joined occasionally by Kharitonov and the buoyant Ussievich, Radek was clearly mocking the Bolshevik leader—mocking him sympathetically, for Radek was an ardent revolutionary, but mocking him nevertheless.

He had selected a sensitive issue, for while Lenin knew that he must lead the revolution, which was why he was returning at such enormous risk to Russia, he was fully conscious of the immense problems that lay ahead of him and, only too aware how little support the Bolsheviks could yet command—as indeed was Radek.

Lenin's relationship with Radek had been erratic. He had known him for years, had even gone openly to his defense when the German Social Democrats, in one of the conflicts that so often flared through the revolutionary parties, were subjecting him to a bitter attack that climaxed in his expulsion for no less a crime than theft. Since the outbreak of war, when they had both been living in Switzerland, there had been ructions between them—primarily because Radek and his Polish friends had not conformed with Lenin's line. It was only a few months since Lenin had described him angrily to Inessa as "impudent, insolent, stupid." Since then, they had settled their differences, and Radek, who as an Austrian had no right of entry into Russia, had agreed to carry out an important assignment for Lenin in Sweden.

Lenin must have found Radek's extrovert exclamations very irritating, must have had to fight to control that instinct for withdrawal that certain kinds of human contact seemed to induce in him. But clearly he concealed his feelings and responded good-naturedly.

There were limits, though. Olga had a very high-pitched laugh, and, as the evening wore on, he could stand her cries of mirth no longer. He got up from his seat, strode into the corridor and opened the door of the next compartment. He did not speak but, grasping Olga firmly by the hand, led her down the corridor to another compartment farther from him. Possibly, he took her to the only second-class compartment that was still available—with Zina Zinovieva and Ussievich's wife, Helen Kon—though this was still a little close to him and, for that matter, to Radek. More likely he pushed through the swing door in the corridor, which divided the two sections of the carriage, and deposited her in one of the hard wooden seats of the third class.

Unlike Radek, Olga never mentioned the incident in either of her accounts, in which she blamed Safarov, Kharitonov and Ussievich for the noise. But she was writing in later days when Lenin was being deified, and the event lacked a certain dignity. However, there is little doubt that at the time she accepted her chastening without complaint. She had been a party member and a close friend of Lenin's for a long time. In fact, she had been one of the comrades assigned by him to cash the 500 ruble notes from the Tiflis bank raid. She had been arrested with the bills in her possession in a Munich bank by waiting German police. Soon afterward, because of a letter she had written to Geneva, Swiss police had taken Karpinsky into custody.

In that noisy compartment with Radek, Inessa appears to have been unusually subdued. The accounts of the journey written by Safarov and Radek and Olga barely mention her other than to note that she was with them. The omission is strange, especially that of Safarov who worked very closely with her, crossed the border into Russia with her from Cracow in 1912, was arrested and may have been her lover. For she was a vivid personality, not easily ignored. The impression that remains is one of her sitting a bit quietly, almost an outsider to her elated companions and the giggling Olga.

The fact that she was not next door with Lenin and Nadya was in itself significant, being one more indication of the change in her relations with him. She had, after all, lived closely with them—until the end of 1915, when she had left them in Berne.

She had gone before—when they were living in Cracow, for example. She had become restless in the little provincial town and had missed Paris. But her departure from Berne was marked by clear signs of strain. In Lenin's first letter to her, after she had left, he did not use the intimate pronoun *ty* which had colored his earlier letters and he referred to Nadya coolly as "my wife." Possibly this was due to French censorship, for Inessa had gone back again to Paris, but if so, it did not fool them, for within weeks the Sûreté reported to the Okhrana that she was his mistress. But the letter also contained a clear appeal that had a strong romantic element. He and his "wife" had taken a walk "along the road to Frauen-Kapellan where the three of us—you remember?—had that lovely stroll one day. I kept thinking of you and was sorry you were not here."

Lenin was uneasy about her—especially since she appeared once more to be ignoring his letters. Had she taken offense because he had not seen her off on the day she had left Berne? "I did think that, I must confess," he told her in a second letter, "but I dismiss the unworthy thought from my mind."

Four days later she had still not replied, and Lenin was deeply worried. "How are you getting on?" he asked. "Are you content? Don't you feel lonely? Are you very busy? You are causing me great anxiety by not giving any news about yourself. Where are you living? Where do you eat?"

She returned to Berne only for a short while in July, 1916, when she was trying to get a passport to go to Norway. It was the end of the affair, but he continued to write to her. Not very often at that time and usually only about work she was doing for him. By October he was writing more frequent letters that were very practical with none of his lighthearted foreign farewells. His "wife," however, was now "Nadya."

In November there was another crisis in their relations for he wrote to her: "Of course, I also want to correspond. Let's continue our correspondence," as though the question of continuing had been in issue.

Certainly, he continued writing—and more frequently than he had before, often several times a week. Apparently, Inessa worked for him willingly enough but did not choose to live where he did. She left Paris for Switzerland and moved from Hertenstein and Sorenberg to Clarens. But she avoided Zurich where he was. And she still failed to answer his letters sometimes—which still exasperated him.

Returning to Russia now, an attractive woman in her early forties, she had much to ponder. During the last few weeks, Lenin had leaned on her heavily, had been as demanding as in the past, as was his right, for it was in the cause of the party. It would have been strange if there had been no sadness in her, for it was the end of a period in her life. By the end of the journey, perhaps even *on* the journey, she had decided not to stay near Lenin in Petersburg, where clearly so much was going to happen. Instead she was going home to Moscow.*

Separating Olga Ravich from Karl Radek did not stop the noise in the carriage, and when later in the evening the travelers still showed no sign of settling down, Lenin decided that his tolerance had reached the limit. "When the time for sleeping has come, no one wants to be quiet," recorded George Safarov, writing as Russians often do in the present tense. "Ilyich assumes the role of a monitor. He tries to be very severe. Alas, the severity does not produce an impression on anyone."

Finally, Lenin insisted that they go to sleep "as an order of party discipline." Normally, this would have produced immediate obedience, but for once even this failed to achieve results.

---

*Alexandra Kollontai, who knew them both very well, wrote a novel, *A Great Love*, based on the relationship—about an affair between a revolutionary leader living in exile and a girl called Natasha. Like Lenin, he had a wife who was often ill, wore a beard and sometimes an old cap. Like Inessa, she had had other lovers, enjoyed a private income, worked for the party and was a fluent linguist. Eventually, in the story, she left him for underground work in Russia. Her reasons for breaking off the affair were that her lover did not rate highly enough her talents as a revolutionary—which would hardly seem to apply to Lenin—and that their passion had begun to fade, which might well have been Inessa's reason. Certainly, it would have conformed with the philosophy of clean breaks advocated by Chernyshevsky and Turgenev, whom Lenin admired greatly.

Chapter 6

AT 5:10 A.M. IN THE EARLY LIGHT of the next morning, Tuesday, April 10, the sealed carriage and its baggage wagon were connected to a train and drawn backward toward Switzerland out of Singen, for the line ahead led to Radolfzell and Ulm, then curved onto the branch track that would take them to Stuttgart.[1]

Tea made on Nadya's portable Swedish kerosene cooker had eased some of the discomfort of a night of sleeping in their clothes in the carriage. The Swiss frontier authorities had permitted them to keep the rolls they had brought with them—though they were growing a little stale by morning—so breakfast had not proved too much of a problem.

Through the windows, the travelers peered sleepily at picturesque hilly country: sloping meadows, thick with clumps of trees, fir woods, village after village that were almost identical with Gottmadingen, groups of houses with stylistic curving roofs cloistered around a little church. All the time the train was gaining height as it ran through ever-higher hills.

Their journey across Germany—attached to various trains—would take them over four different state railways, and each time they crossed from one system to another, a new engine would take over. Owing to military restrictions on the lines to the front, they would at times move out of one state railway for a few miles and then return to it. At present, they were in Baden on the Baden State Railway.

Arrangements to feed the travelers would be somewhat unsatisfactory until they reached Frankfurt, where, it would seem from Nadya's reference to "the cook," a restaurant car was part of the train that took them on the long haul to Berlin. Until then they would have to make do with what food they had brought and with sandwiches obtained for them at the stations.

In his end compartment, Lenin was absorbed in work, writing in an exercise book, according to Radek, in his small narrow-nibbed scrawl. Almost certainly, 1905 was in his mind—in fact, he spoke of it to the comrades—for it was the last time he had made this journey.

There were similarities between the two trips. As on this occasion, he had been traveling to revolution, had written letters urging the arming of the people, had cursed the distance between Switzerland and Russia which made judgment of the revolutionary situation so much harder. And, as he had this time, he had left his papers with Karpinsky.

The pattern, of course, was only repeated at a very superficial level, for now there was no Tsar to order in the Semenovskys. This time there was an unprecedented crisis of history, a period of opportunity, when a correct assessment of the strength of the forces of revolution, of sheer timing, was vital.

Zina Zinovieva, with nine-year-old Stepan, was in a second-class compartment, next to one that was occupied by Lenin and Nadya. Almost certainly she was sharing this with Helen Kon, Ussievich's dark wife, young Robert and his mother and Gregory.[2] Zina had first met Lenin fourteen years before in 1903, when she went to hear him speak at a café in Berne. The Okhrana was tailing Gregory, and it had seemed wise to leave Russia for a while. At this time, although Lenin was well known in revolutionary circles, his photograph was rarely published, and few of the young Marxists knew what he looked like.

The café had been packed with people when she arrived breathless a little after the time the lecture was due to start. "You're late," a man standing near the entrance reproved her gently—so she recalled in *Leningradskaya Pravda*. He was short, bald, his head fringed with red hair. His eyes were small and round and almost disappeared into slits when he smiled.

Zina laughed. She was very young, barely out of her teens. "This charming man wouldn't start without me," she answered cheerfully.

"Are you sure?" he asked quietly.

"Certainly, I'm sure," she said brightly.

"Then now you have arrived," he asked with overelaborate courtesy, his eyes lightening with amusement, "may I please have your permission to begin?"

"My blood ran cold," Zina wrote. Lenin still teased her about the occurrence on occasions.

It was during the conflicts with the Mensheviks, soon after the split at the party conference in London when, as Gregory put it, "Martov had begun to sing flat." Gregory was then only twenty. They had gone to see Lenin with a few other young Berne Bolsheviks.

They were deeply impressed with his informality, with the fact that he listened to them intently and explained with great simplicity these idological problems they did not understand.

They had also gone to see Plekhanov and been struck by the contrast. Plekhanov had treated them with polite formality, offering tea in delicate china in his drawing room. Instead of china cups, Lenin had drunk tea with them out of mugs, sitting around the kitchen table. They had not seen him for another five years until, once more, they had come out of Russia, this time to exile.

As Zina gazed out of the window of the carriage, for once in her life with little to do, her thoughts must have lingered on the nine years of exile she was leaving behind her. She later wrote a lot about their life with Lenin, revealing facets of his personality that other contemporaries have largely ignored—such as his enjoyment of bicycling. When they all were living in the village of Longjumeau near Paris, they worked hard for the party school all week, but the four of them—Lenin, Nadya, Gregory and Zina—would go bicycling all day on Sundays, starting off early in the morning. "The condition laid down by Vladimir Ilyich," wrote Zina, "was: Not a word about politics." He was a "wonderful bicyclist"—and thoughtful, too, watching

Nadya and Zina carefully and often taking them in tow on the hills.[3]

Lenin was fond of young Stepan—"Why is he crying?" he asked on the day of his birth—and when they were sharing a house in Cracow when the little boy was four, he had often played games with him, even wrestling with him on the floor. He carried him on his shoulders, scrambled under furniture to retrieve his ball, carried out his "orders."

"Sometimes," wrote Zina, "Vladimir Ilyich and Styopka knocked over everything in the room. When it became very noisy, I would try to stop them. But Ilyich always insisted: 'Don't interfere! We're playing!' "

Once, as they were walking along a Cracow street with the little boy running ahead of them, Lenin mused in sudden melancholy: "It's a pity we haven't got a Styopka like that."

Lenin's affection for the boy had remained as he grew older. In July, 1916, only nine months before they boarded the Sealed Train, Lenin ended a letter to Zina from the mountains where they had gone for a trip for Nadya's health: "Beste Grüsse, especially to Styopka who must have grown so that I won't be able to toss him up to the ceiling."

The track curved down into Rottweil. The passengers could see the three spires of the medieval town set behind a wall of high old red-brick houses. The train passed through the station, crossed the waters of the Neckar over two bridges as the river twisted through the valley and penetrated a long tunnel, cutting through the hills.

After the darkness of the tunnel, the day seemed unusually bright as the train emerged into a narrow valley with the hills steep and high on either side, very close to the track, thick with firs.

As the valley broadened, the line ran alongside the Neckar again. The stream was turbulent with small rapids and boulders that jutted up from the waters.

The route they were taking by way of Stuttgart involved a slight detour. For the direct line to Frankfurt had forked west a few miles back, at Tuttlingen, where they had halted to change the engine as they moved onto the Württemberg State Railway. But this would have taken them onto one of the main rail supply routes to the German front in France, where at that moment, as the Sealed Train steamed north, the Kaiser's troops were striving desperately to check the new Allied offensive. Military traffic was permitted only on the rail line that stretched south from Karlsruhe through Offenburg.

The carriage bearing the Russians across Germany and its baggage wagon would have to travel through Karlsruhe, but by diverting through Stuttgart, they would approach from the east, where they would not hamper the military trains.

Soon, as the train clattered through the wide valley of the Neckar, they could see Horb with its high complex of old buildings dominated by an ancient square stone watch tower and a high spire. The river, streaming over a small waterfall, divided the town, then turned sharply under the rail track. The valley narrowed here so that there was no view from the train windows—just the close grassy sides of steep banks reaching upward from both sides of the line.

And suddenly they were running down out of the hills, and on both sides there was open country, gently undulating, the monotony offset here and there by a tree or a hill.

To the travelers, it seemed depressing—"I remember the painful impression left by the frozen countryside," commented Zinoviev, even though it was spring. To all of them the most remarkable fact was the absence of "adult men," as Nadya put it—just women, very old men and children.

"The fields," wrote Olga, "gave an impression of having been allowed to go to waste, abandoned for a long time."

"The stations," recorded Zina, "were empty."

Germany presented a picture of a country that had long been at war, and the travelers realized that the same weary picture would be repeated in Russia, where most of the men of fighting age were at the front—possibly facing the men from the villages through which the train was now continuously passing.

Life in Switzerland had been hard for the exiles because most of them were poor, but Switzerland had not been a country at war. The difference was harshly emphasized to Sokolnikov, who, sitting by the window on the hard wooden seat of one of the third-class compartments, was puzzled by the stares of the few people they had seen in the stations as they slowed or stopped—in particular probably, though he did not specify the place in his story of the journey, at Tuttlingen, where they had changed engines.

Sokolnikov's perplexity was strange. For he had suffered true hardship. Like so many others, he had been arrested after 1905—though only seventeen at the time—and exiled to Siberia. There, at one stage, he had been shackled because he had refused to take his hat off to the settlement governor. He knew the agony of solitary confinement which he had eased by playing chess through the wall with the prisoner in the next cell, using pieces of bread as chessmen.

For weeks, after his escape from Siberia, he had been on the run, making his way across Russia to the Prussian border.

Even so, despite his experience in suffering, he had not recognized the look in those German eyes staring at him in his compartment. At last he realized the reason why he was attracting such incredulous attention! A white bread roll that they had brought from Switzerland lay on the small table by the window. White bread in wartime Germany was clearly unheard of.

From Vailingen, the engineer began to apply the air brakes, vibrating through the train, as the train cut down through woods toward the old city of Stuttgart. At moments, the trees and grassy banks that lined the track cleared to reveal the town way below them for a few seconds before closing in once more like a screen—until eventually they were running just above red-tiled curving roofs and beyond them a range of church steeples.

It was the first big station in Germany at which they had stopped. No one, of course, was permitted to leave the carriage, but they stared out of the windows at the platform. Even this major station appeared strangely quiet and dead.

Fritz Platten was impressed that the two German officers

traveling with them were conducting themselves precisely according to the arrangement he had discussed at such length at the German Embassy in Berne. At no time had either of them attempted to cross the chalk line on the floor of the corridor.

While the train was standing in Stuttgart Station, Captain von Planetz summoned him. Wilhelm Janson, the trade union leader whom the telegram from Berlin had been so insistent that Lenin should meet, had boarded the train and requested a meeting with Platten.

The Swiss socialist agreed and crossed the white chalk mark in the corridor, as only he was permitted to do. From the past, he knew the trade union leader whom he now met in the German officers' compartment. Janson told him that he brought greetings from the General Commission of the German trade unions and would like to pass them personally to the comrades.

Platten explained the travelers were passing through Germany on an extraterritorial basis and were unwilling to see anyone. However, he promised he would talk to them and give Janson an answer in the morning. The union leader left the wagon and returned to his carriage in another part of the train.

Platten had a strong sense of the dramatic, and he must have guessed what Lenin's reaction would be when he told him of Janson's request. "If he enters the carriage, we'll beat him up," exploded Lenin, so Platten recalled. "Tell him to go to the devil."

Janson, a member of the German Social Democrat Party that had destroyed the Second International, had no hope of seeing Lenin, quite apart from the fact that such a meeting would have compromised the Russians. Certainly, he had not chosen his moment well. For Stuttgart was the site of the conference where the International had been born.

Janson's presence on the train made Lenin concerned about Radek, whom Janson knew from the days of the scandal when the Austrian was expelled from the German Social Democratic party for theft. Radek, traveling "like a hare" (incognito), was vulnerable. Janson might well catch a glimpse of him in one of the stations and might even report him out of malice since he had failed in his mission to talk to Lenin.

Radek was ordered into the baggage wagon for safety. "They gave me a survival kit of about fifty newspapers so that I should be quiet and not cause any disturbance"—which the emotional and fervent Radek was often tempted to do.

The train continued its journey across the nondescript countryside of Württemberg, pausing at Bretten to change the engine again, for the sealed carriage and its baggage wagon were back once more on the Baden State Railway which it had left at Tuttlingen.

The train ran on into Karlsruhe. The grim station, in the heart of the industrial area, made no impression on the travelers—despite the fact that military supply trains must have been thundering south toward Offenburg while they waited at the platform.

The section of the track that connected Karlsruhe to Mannheim crossed the Baden plains—bare, flat, open country across which the travelers could see for miles.

As they neared Mannheim, some of the comrades in the third-class compartments were singing again—revolutionary songs in French. As the train crossed the Rhine and slowed to a halt in the big station, they began to sing louder. Probably, others took up the songs, maybe in other compartments. For it became oppressive to the two Germans in the end third-class compartment—conscious that the songs could be heard on the platform.

Once again Captain von Planetz asked Fritz Platten to cross the white chalk line. This time the German was furious, asserting that the singing of such French songs within his country was an insult to the German nation.

Platten apologized for his comrades and hurriedly quelled the offensive noise.

Once again, the engine was changed as they were now on the Prussian-Hessian State Railway and they moved off from Mannheim across the bare plains toward Frankfurt.

In the Wilhelmstrasse in Berlin, Arthur Zimmermann kept in touch with the journey. A telegram arrived from the German minister in Stockholm. The Swedish government would permit the revolutionary party to travel through Sweden on their way to Finland.

In fact, although Zimmermann did not know this, the ambassadors of the Allied powers in Stockholm had met to consider if they should apply pressure on the Swedish government to refuse transit or to take some other action "to hold up the arch-revolutionary on the way through"—according to Lord Esme Howard, the British minister in Sweden. "But the plan seemed impossible. It looked as if it might make the situation worse. Indeed, so far had the Revolution gone in Russia at that time that it appeared wiser to let things take their course rather than interfere in matters of which we were then practically ignorant."

Howard had not been slow to realize that Germany might help Russian socialists, dedicated as they were to peace, to return home. Seventeen days before, he had alerted London to the security risk at the Swedish-Finnish border. "Several very doubtful characters have left for the frontier as there seems to be no control whatever and anybody can enter Finland and Russia without inspection. This is a great danger and it is most likely that the Germans will now send in agents of all kinds to blow up munitions factories etc. as well as to work for a separate peace."

The British vice-consul at Haparanda on the Swedish frontier, Howard reported, was assisting the British and French military control officers at Tornio, the Finnish border town. "Owing to the present unrest, Russian officers commanding are practically useless for control and all the work is being done by British and French officers." This, of course, explained why Maria Stetskevich, Shlyapnikov's courier from Petersburg, had encountered such trouble and why every effort would be made to block Lenin's entry though, as Howard knew, the means to accomplish this were limited.

Howard and his fellow ambassadors were not the only men pondering how they could check Lenin's passage to Russia. In Petersburg, just after the March Revolution, a tough, militaristic colonel named B. V. Nikitin had been appointed head of counterespionage with an office on Znamenskaya Street. His Tsarist predecessors had been dragged off to the Duma during the uprising and had been charged with being agents of the secret police. As a result, the counterespionage network had eroded rapidly, since clearly it was not too healthy a form of employment in the new conditions.

Nikitin, however, was a determined man, and he gradually reassembled it. He was concerned only with detecting German espionage, but since, with good reason, he suspected enemy spies of causing trouble and dissension in the chaotic city, this took him into the domestic political area.

The left-wing socialists, especially the Bolsheviks, were demanding an end to the "predatory war." Since the Germans also wanted to end the war on the Eastern Front, the colonel concluded that the Bolsheviks must be German agents. He had already set himself the task of proving this by the early April morning that a Major Alley of the British Embassy called on him with the news that Lenin and a party of thirty "internationalists" were traveling through Germany by train on their way to Russia. The major even supplied him with a list of the travelers.

Appalled, Nikitin called on General Lavr Kornilov, commander of troops in the Petersburg area, and demanded that he should bar Lenin's entry at the border. Kornilov, a regular officer with dictatorial ambitions, was to become an important figure at a most critical time for Lenin later in the year. Now in April, however, with Russia in chaos, a few more left-wing revolutionaries did not strike the general as of overwhelming significance.

Kornilov agreed to do what he could, as did other equally weary authorities, but the formal answers were all the same. The Executive Committee of the Soviet insisted that the returning exiles should be allowed to enter the country. Even though the Mensheviks and the SR's who dominated the Soviet were scarcely friends of Lenin, freedom, in those early weeks after the revolution, was highly valued in the new Russia. Nikitin, however, was a resolute man—and he was to prove a deadly adversary for Lenin.

Chapter 7

AS THE TRAIN STEAMED into the Frankfurt Station, it was the evening rush hour. Men and women workers were streaming along the platforms toward their homebound trains. "Thin tired people with weary eyes were moving in a long procession past our train," recorded Fritz Platten. "We did not see a single smile. The depressing scene from the train gave the exiles high hopes that the German hour for revolution against the ruling class could not be far away."[1]

Platten—interpreting rather liberally his right to freedom of movement—left the train to visit a girlfriend in the town. The two German officers also departed from the carriage—presumably to have a drink.

The station was full of German troops, some of whom were drawn up in ranks at the head of the platform.

On his way out of the station, Platten dropped in to the buffet, ordered some beer and sandwiches and newspapers for his party—and tipped some soldiers to take them to the carriage.

Presumably, he told them that in the carriage was a party of Russian revolutionaries who were determined to stop the war, for Radek—who had refused to stay in the baggage wagon any longer—saw the troops suddenly break ranks and coming running toward the train. "Each one held in both hands a mug of beer. They flung themselves on us . . . asking would there be peace and when." Radek, always eager for converts, harangued them until their alarmed officers hurried them off the train.

Still, the attitude of the soldiers encouraged the revolutionaries—especially since they were all "patriots" and could be expected to be nationalistic and belligerent.

The journey to Frankfurt had taken longer than expected, and by the time they arrived at the city they had missed their scheduled connection to Berlin. The sealed carriage and its baggage wagon were shunted onto a siding for the night. Early the next morning, Wednesday, they were on the move again—for Berlin.

Meanwhile, that day at Trelleborg, the port in southern Sweden where the ferryboats arrived from Sassnitz, Jacob Fürstenberg was waiting. After the stream of telegrams from Lenin in Zurich, he had checked into an hotel in nearby Malmo the day before, Tuesday, and had met the afternoon ferry from Germany. There was, of course, no sign of Lenin and his party. On Wednesday, when the train was still between Frankfurt and Berlin, Fürstenberg returned to Trelleborg and once more watched the passengers descend the gangway from the ferry from Sassnitz.

The sinister Pole was a strange character for Lenin to rely on to the extent that he did though Lenin was to do so to a far greater extent during the coming months. For in theory Fürstenberg was everything that the Bolshevik leader abhorred. The organization he managed for Parvus was engaged in war profiteering—and the worst kind at that. For it prospered by dealing in the basic necessities that were in short supply: medicines and drugs for the wounded, contraceptives for troops in need of women. Hospitals and brothels were his customers. His business methods, too, were disreputable, much of his trading being in smuggled goods—and indeed he was now living in Sweden because he had been deported from Denmark.

Even in his tastes, Fürstenberg seemed the last type of man to appeal to Lenin. He was elegant and debonair and never without a flower in his buttonhole—the traces perhaps of his upbringing in the bourgeois home of his wealthy parents in Warsaw.

At one time he had been among the leading Polish Social Democrats, but like the Russians, the Polish Social Democrat Party had been splintered by dissension. Because of the distrust of him by the top Bolshevik hierarchy, Lenin later had to fight very hard for his friend, who, as he insisted to the Central Committee in December that year, "has worked for the party for over ten years."

Even though Fürstenberg was still not technically a Bolshevik—as Lenin was quick to point out in July, when he was dissociating himself from him as far as possible—the two men had known each other for a very long time since they had met at the traumatic 1903 conference in London when Lenin split the party. Even without being Bolshevik, Fürstenberg had been one of the tribunal in 1913 with Lenin and Zinoviev that had "tried" one of the leading Bolsheviks, Roman Malinovsky, on charges that he was an Okhrana agent—and acquitted him, wrongly it transpired.

On that Wednesday afternoon, when he realized that once again Lenin and his companions were not among the passengers on the ferry from Sassnitz, Fürstenberg began to fear that they had encountered trouble within Germany. Anxiously, he wired Switzerland for information.

All Wednesday morning the train drawing the sealed carriage and its baggage wagon sped toward Berlin. At first, it seemed, the men in the Wilhelmstrasse hoped that the travelers could make up the delay at Frankfurt and still reach Sassnitz in time to catch the afternoon ferry to Trelleborg, for the train was given top priority over all other traffic. At Halle, where it was diverted from the Saxony Line to the Prussian Line, even the private train of the German crown prince was held up for two hours to allow it to pass. But soon it became clear that the carriage would not reach the coast before the ferry sailed and the Foreign Office officials began replanning the schedule for the party to leave Sassnitz on Thursday, the following day.

As the train traveled through the Berlin suburbs, the exiles were appalled by the signs of war in the city, which had been the target of Allied air raids. Radek commented on the barbed wire on the platform of the Potsdam Station. To Zinoviev, Berlin seemed "like a cemetery," and the usually buoyant Olga found it "deathly still."

The restrictions at the station were the most rigorous they had encountered so far. Even Platten was not permitted to leave the carriage. A staff officer from the Wilhelmstrasse, clad tactfully in civilian clothes, arrived to inquire if their journey had been satisfactory so far, and Platten was warm in his appreciation of German cooperation.

The travelers had been served a good lunch—presumably from a restaurant car on the train—of cutlets and peas with milk for the children.

They discovered that more German Social Democrats had boarded the train, but according to Nadya, the only contact the visitors managed to establish with the Russian revolutionaries was young Robert, who asked them in French what the train guard did. Nadya did not explain how Robert obtained access to them, but presumably the rules about not leaving the coach were not applied too strictly to four-year-old boys—possibly on the platforms of stations when the train stopped or even perhaps when the door linking the carriage to the rest of the train was unlocked to allow lunch to be passed through to the revolutionaries from the dining car.

The sealed carriage remained in Berlin for a considerable time—possibly some twenty hours—and the reason for the stay is both obscure and tantalizing. German Foreign Office records indicate clearly that the revised plan, made when it was obvious that the travelers could not reach the coast in time to catch the ferry, provided for them to travel on to Sassnitz that afternoon. Arrangements were made for them to spend the night there in a locked room.

Almost certainly the plan was never executed, and the train stayed overnight in Berlin. None of the personal accounts refer to a stopover in Sassnitz, as could be expected if it had happened. Several mention their arrival in the port. There are other indications that the train was in Berlin at least until late in the evening.

If the train did not proceed as scheduled, what was the reason for yet another change of plan? The question has to be posed in a setting of two important facts: first, the Wilhelmstrasse was only a few minutes from Potsdam Station. Secondly, Lenin was so crucial to German war policy that the German government would shortly invest more than 40,000,000 gold marks in him—by modern standards hundreds of millions of dollars.*

Under these circumstances, it is hardly conceivable that the opportunity for a meeting between Lenin and top German officials, possibly even Arthur Zimmermann himself, should have been missed when it could be arranged so easily.

Fritz Platten specifically denied that any such meeting took place in Berlin—as indeed Lenin did himself in more general terms covering the whole journey. Yet clearly it was vital that no suspicion of such a meeting should leak out, for this truly would have compromised Lenin fatally. But was this a real danger? A carriage waiting in a siding in darkness, with military guards and barbed-wire barriers to keep away outsiders, provided the possibility of the utmost security.

The most intriguing question of all centers on the result of any discussion that may have occurred, for this places it in a context of immense historical importance: Was information obtained at a secret meeting the reason that Lenin changed his mind on the strategy of the revolution?

For although the events of that night in Berlin can only be the object of speculation, there is no doubt whatever that on the journey from Zurich to Petersburg, Lenin altered his whole tactical plan.[2] The scheme he was to outline within hours of arriving in the Russian capital was quite different from that he described at lunch at the Zahringerhof in Zurich just before boarding the train to Gottmadingen and which he had previously detailed in his long policy letters.

No historian—Soviet or Western—has yet been able to give an adequate explanation of his change of plan. Lenin had been thinking and reading of revolution all his life. He was a confirmed and avid Marxist, yet his new tactics were to trample on a Marxian precept that was accepted by all Russian Social Democrats—including Lenin himself until he boarded the Sealed

*For elaboration of sources of this fact, see page 290.

Train. He was not a man to change his mind on so basic an issue unless changed conditions demanded it. And there is no doubt at all that his altered tactics conformed completely with Arthur Zimmermann's policies.

This is not to suggest that Lenin was a German agent in the sense that he was carrying out the Kaiser's policy for money or even for personal power. Without question, as a revolutionary, Lenin had great integrity. His aim never changed for one moment. He sought world socialist revolution on the lines predicted by Marx. But Lenin was always practical. As Nadya emphasized, he would patch up quarrels with men who had been his enemies for years if political considerations demanded this. Equally, he would break with friends if he thought it necessary. When he said in Zurich that he would make a deal with the devil to get back to Russia, he truly meant it. It is clearly possible, even probable, that he did make a deal with the devil in a Berlin siding for something far bigger even than his return to Russia.

For one factor existed after the journey across Germany in the Sealed Train that was not present when Lenin was in Switzerland: massive German financing, enough to publish party newspapers throughout Russia, to spread propaganda on a scale that Lenin had never conceived before.

An indication during a secret meeting of the sheer size of the funds that were available to him would have made possible goals that might have seemed impossible before he left Zurich.

The key aspect in Lenin's change of strategy was in the timing. One Marxist theory that was accepted by virtually all revolutionaries except the anarchists was his concept of two stages of revolution: Because Russia was so backward, by comparison with the Western nations, it must go through a period of capitalist Western-style government before progressing eventually to the second stage of socialism.

In his speech during lunch at the Zahringerhof in Zurich on the day of departure, Lenin had confirmed that he was still thinking on these lines. Yet by the end of his journey to Russia, only one week later, he had abandoned this concept. He had conceived a new program to propel Russia into an *immediate* gigantic leap into the second stage. The means he selected to accomplish this was a campaign demanding the placing of all power in the hands of the Petersburg Soviet which would be linked to other Soviets throughout the nation. And *now*, not later.

From Switzerland, he had urged the arming of the people, demanded a kind of controlled mob rule by the masses. He had associated this with the Soviet, but he had not proposed that the Soviet should rule as a government. This new proposal, crystallized on the rail coach as it traveled north—probably after the long stay over in Berlin—was to astonish everyone in Russia, not least of all his own followers, because it seemed utterly impractical.

His new time schedule seemed to ignore the fact that Russian industry was not developed enough to serve as a springboard for the workers to grasp power. And the whole proposal for the Soviet—an institution that resembled a federation of labor unions and was completely unequipped to govern—was to seem absurd.

It would lead to chaos—but then chaos was almost certainly Lenin's aim, a kind of controlled chaos that would not reach its ultimate stage until the masses were sufficiently educated to see the Bolshevik program for a new society as the answer to all their problems. Chaos, of course, was also the German aim.

In April, as Lenin was traveling toward Russia, the Russian masses did not rate the Bolsheviks very highly—as was reflected in their minority within the Soviet. But Lenin planned to change this with a propaganda campaign that would put the masses behind him. He intended to do this, partly by keeping the Bolsheviks independent from all other parties whom he could charge with compromising with capitalists, but mainly by promoting his program to the people on a platform of a very few, very simple, very attractive party aims that anyone could understand, that his agitators could repeat and repeat.

This would have been Lenin's plan without any help from the Germans. But a secret meeting in Berlin could have revealed to him an entirely new capacity for impact. It could have shown him the difference between a relatively limited promotional effort and an enormous nationwide campaign. For one thing was certain: The Bolsheviks could not gain power until the majority of the Russian masses supported them. What German finance on a large scale could do in hands as capable as Lenin's was to bring forward the time when that situation could exist.

Although the train remained in Berlin for a long time, it did not remain at the Potsdam Station, for this was not the terminal for the line north to Sassnitz. The two German officers—singing sentimental songs, according to the Soviet historian A. Ivanov—left the carriage to have dinner. To their surprise, when they returned, it had gone—which would suggest that the decision to move it was sudden, the result possibly of top-level orders. Perhaps Stettin Station, where eventually the anxious escort caught up with it, was a more convenient or more suitable venue for a meeting than the Potsdam.

People traveled between these two mainline stations under normal circumstances by cab—impossible for the revolutionaries since it would mean leaving the carriage. However, the rail journey gave them a fascinating glimpse of the imperial German capital. "We passed along a circular track through the whole city," wrote Zina. "Berlin produced a more shocking impression on us than the villages. Ilyich lifted up the blind by a corner and . . . studied the destruction of war."

The next day, Thursday April 12, they arrived at Sassnitz and boarded the Swedish ferry *Queen Victoria*. The Germans, who checked them off the train at the port, were content with no more formalities than the numbered tickets provided at the Swiss border. But the Swedish authorities insisted on a passenger list before they could pass up the gangway onto the ship. Almost by habit, for there could be little to fear from the Swedes, they all gave false names.

For the third day running, Fürstenberg was waiting at Trelleborg to meet the ferry. This time, knowing he had to book tickets for them on the night train to Stockholm, he persuaded the harbor master to radio the ship to inquire if the party was aboard.

Meanwhile, in the Wilhelmstrasse, a telegram had arrived from the Kaiser in headquarters at Pless. At breakfast he had suggested to his officers that the Russian socialists should be given literature, such as his Easter Message and the Chancellor's recent speech in the Reichstag (in which, with an eye on the revolution, Bethmann-Hollweg had promised to extend the franchise), "so that they may be able to enlighten others in their own country." His Majesty had also made the point that if Sweden refused transit, "the High Command, would be prepared to get them into Russia through the German lines."
It was an interesting thought but, by now, academic.

The Baltic, as the *Queen Victoria* headed for Trelleborg, was rough. At first, most of the party stayed on deck but many of them, upset by the rolling and heaving of the ship, went below. Others, to keep their minds occupied, stood together in the bows singing songs—such songs, according to Soviet historians P. V. Moskovsky and V. G. Semenov, as "Don't cry over the bodies of fallen fighters" and Lenin's favorite, "They didn't marry us in church." One, in particular, is quoted:

> Our song can be heard far away;
> It will spread and spread;
> Our banner is flying throughout the world.

Once a wave broke onto the bows and splashed Lenin. "The first revolutionary wave from the shores of Russia," said someone, laughing. Lenin smiled, so David Souliashvili reported, and dried himself with his handkerchief.
Lenin walked the deck with Mikha Tskhakaya, the old Caucasian. Mikha had attended the London Conference of Social Democrats in 1905. Together, they had visited the grave of Karl Marx in Highgate Cemetery.

"At the gateway . . ." Mikha recalled, "stood a senior official wearing a tall top hat. The cemetery was an enormous park with narrow alleyways with a mass of . . . expensive monuments—even down to the memorial to a little dog belonging to some lord or lady.

"But the grave of the great thinker of the 19th century, the creator of scientific communism . . . could not be found without the help of stonemasons working in the cemetery. . . .

"For a long time, we sat round the grave in no hurry to leave. Ilyich remarked sarcastically that the official [at the gate] was probably getting worried that we were staying so long here by the grave of, to him, an unknown person.

"That unfortunate bourgeois cannot guess that we are carrying away with us everything that is immortal and deathless in Marx and Engels and are going to embody them even in backward Tsarist Russia to the horror of the bourgeoisie of all countries." It was a prediction that seemed far more possible that afternoon on the ferryboat crossing the Baltic than it had then, twelve years ago, in London.

Once an officer approached the two men on deck. "Which one is Mr. Ulyanov?" he inquired. There was, of course, no "Ulyanov" on the passenger list. "Ilyich and I exchanged glances," reported Mikha.

After a pause, Lenin answered carefully, "It's me." The officer gave him Fürstenberg's radio message from Trelleborg. Relieved, Lenin requested that a reply be sent: "Mr. Ulyanov greets Mr. Ganetsky [one of Fürstenberg's names] and asks him to prepare the tickets."[3]

It was already dark as the *Queen Victoria* steamed past Trelleborg's flashing lighthouse. On the quay a warm welcome awaited the revolutionaries—not only from Fürstenberg but also from Swedish socialists and the mayor of Trelleborg. "There were warm welcomes, questions, noise, shouting of children," recorded Fürstenberg, "but there was no time to lose. In a quarter of an hour the train would be leaving for Malmo."

In a Malmo hotel a table was laden with smorgasbord—or *zakuski* as the Russians call it. "We who in Switzerland had got used to being satisfied with a herring for dinner," wrote Karl Radek, "saw this tremendous table laid with endless *zakuski* and threw ourselves on it like locusts. . . . Vladimir Ilyich did not eat anything. He 'dragged the soul' from Ganetsky, trying to discover from him everything about the Russian Revolution. . . ."

They caught the night train to Stockholm, with Lenin sharing a compartment with Fürstenberg, Zinoviev and Radek and talking endlessly about the "hard battle of the proletariat that lay before us . . ." so the Pole reported, "about the future dangers that were threatening from Kerensky although, at that time, this latter figure was not yet playing much of a part. . . . Vladimir Ilyich pointed out the necessity of setting up party cells abroad . . . 'just to be on the safe side.' "

Lenin planned that an overseas Bureau of the Central Committee should be set up in Stockholm. Fürstenberg and Radek, who, being Austrian, would not yet be permitted into Russia, should be members. Important though they were to be, neither of them was a member of the party.

They did not stop talking until four o'clock in the morning only to be awakened at eight by a crowd of newspaper reporters, alerted from Malmo, who boarded the train at a country station. Lenin refused to see them—he would have problems enough in Russia without any misreporting—and said that a communiqué would be issued in Stockholm.

An hour later they arrived at Stockholm to be met by the mayor and other Socialist leaders. Reporters, photographers joined the melee on the platform. There was even a newsreel camera.

It was a hectic day for Lenin: meetings with Swedish socialists, finalizing plans for the Foreign Bureau that he had discussed on the train and allocating to it the funds that the Bolsheviks had long held in Sweden—and even some shopping.

"Probably," wrote Radek, "the formal look of the Swedish comrades developed in us a strong desire that Ilyich should look more like an ordinary person. We tried to persuade him at least to buy a new pair of boots. He had been traveling in mountain boots with enormous studs.''

Lenin was cajoled into a trip to the Stockholm stores where he met demands that he should buy a lot more clothes than boots. "He defended himself as best he could, asking us whether we thought that on his arrival in Petersburg he was going to open a ready-to-wear shop, but all the same we managed to persuade him to buy a pair of trousers. . . .''

That day Parvus was in Stockholm. He had asked Jacob Fürstenberg to set up a meeting with Lenin. But whatever may have transpired in Berlin, Lenin was far too conscious of the dangers of compromise to risk a meeting with a man who was not only discredited by the whole socialist movement, but was also known to have financial links with the Germans. He refused the invitation—and carefully ordered Radek to record his refusal. His caution was to be rewarded later.

A frigid exchange of messages through Fürstenberg, acting as go-between, followed Lenin's answer. Parvus inquired about Lenin's political plans. Lenin sent back a message that he "was not concerned with diplomacy; his task was social revolutionary agitation." He told Fürstenberg to tell Lenin that he "may go on agitating; but if he is not interested in statesmanship, then he will become a tool in my hands."

Parvus was offended by Lenin's rebuff, but he could not operate without him, for Lenin was central to his whole plan. Also, he was aware that it was not vital for them to meet. Instead, he had a long session with Karl Radek, whom he knew well from the past. And it is certain that this meeting would not have taken place without Lenin's permission. In any event, it was enough to allow Parvus to report to Berlin that he had negotiated with "the Russian émigrés from Switzerland."

Almost certainly, at that long meeting between Parvus and Karl Radek, the details of the financing operation that was to help Lenin seize power were worked out. For Parvus left Stockholm immediately, returned to Copenhagen for a brief meeting with his friend, Count von Brockdorff-Rantzau, the German minister there, then traveled quickly on to Berlin for a personal conference with Arthur Zimmermann which was so secret apparently that no notes or minutes of the meeting were taken.

Then he returned to Stockholm where he was constantly in the company of the only Bolshevik Bureau outside Russia. Fürstenberg had large cash resources in Petersburg—as Colonel Nikitin of counterintelligence discovered by checking the bank accounts of one of his agents. Almost certainly, some of this came from the Germans through Parvus, who owned half the business that Fürstenberg directed, but this has never been adequately proved, and since the firm did trade in Russia, there could be a commercial reason for at least some of the cash.

Astonishingly, through contacts in the Russian Mission in Stockholm, Fürstenberg also used the Russian diplomatic bag. He had established this communication route in April when he wrote to Alexander Shlyapnikov: "On the 4th of this month was dispatched through the mission packet no. 6839 to the Ministry of Foreign Affairs. . . . Confirm without fail by telegraph— though cautiously—the receipt of my packets. The mission [in Stockholm] does not examine packets, I hand them over sealed. If you collect them in time, that is, at the same time as they arrive at the Ministry of Foreign Affairs, I hope you will receive them unopened." According to Fürstenberg himself, he continued using this communication route among others until July.

Parvus was almost certainly the main source, though not the only one, of the funds that the Germans supplied to the Bolsheviks—"almost certainly" because the routes by which German funds reached Lenin's party are far more difficult to establish with any certainty than the basic fact that they did.

The Soviet authorities have always denied the allegations of the "Kaiser millions," and even to this day Communist historians insist that it is all a bourgeois smear. Presumably their reason is that they feel it reflects on Lenin's integrity. Actually, though, Lenin's acceptance of these German funds did not conflict with his ideals as a revolutionary. They did not cause him to change his goals—merely the tactics he employed in achieving those goals. In fact, it can be argued that, since timing was vital during those few months of 1917, he would never have achieved it without this finance.

Lenin's attitude toward his benefactors was very similar to their attitude toward him. To them he would be expendable once he had served his purpose. Lenin did not believe they would exist once they had served theirs. For he believed implicitly in Marx's concept of world revolution, was convinced that a proletarian revolution in Russia would roar like fire through Europe—consuming Germany at a very early stage. The war would end by the transformation of the imperialist conflict into a class civil war, with the workers and soldiers of all the belligerent nations on the same side. So the fact that he had used German money to create this movement—which was inevitable in due course anyway—was truly irrelevant. Just as the Germans believed that Lenin had no hope of retaining the power they might help him to win, equally he was convinced that the Kaiser was merely contributing to his own downfall.

There can, however, be no doubt about this vast financing of the Bolsheviks by the Germans *unless* it is assumed that their Foreign Secretary lied in secret communications to his monarch—which truly does not seem to be a supportable hypothesis, especially considered in the setting of other evidence.

On December 3, 1917, Richard von Kühlmann, who had replaced Zimmermann as Foreign Secretary, sent a telegram to his liaison officer at General Headquarters for the attention of the Kaiser, stating that "it was not until the Bolsheviks had received from us a steady flow of funds through various channels that they were in a position to build up their main organ *Pravda*, to conduct energetic propaganda and appreciably to extend the originally narrow basis of their party."

Three months earlier, in September, he had asserted in another telegram that "the Bolshevik movement could never have attained the scale or the influence which it has today without our continual support."

The extent of the funds that the Germans invested in Russia

113]

during these critical months is revealed clearly in an analysis of the Foreign Office budget for propaganda and special purposes in various countries that is among the department's secret files that were opened after the Second World War. Under a covering note dated February 5, 1918, it indicates that the funds allocated for use in Russia amounted to 40,580,997 marks, of which 26,566,122 marks had actually been spent by January 31, 1918.

Of this, according to other documents in the files, 15,000,000 marks were released by the Treasury the day after Lenin assumed power in November. This means that 11,500,000 were invested in Russia *before* November.

By any standard, this 11,500,000 was a colossal outlay for propaganda. In 1917, at current exchange rates, it was the equivalent of more than $2,000,000 or nearly £600,000 sterling. It would be useful for comparison purposes to convert these sums to modern values but it is hard to find an adequate basis. One writer,[4] after discussion with a German currency expert, has valued 1 mark in 1917 at 40 modern Deutschmarks—which would put the expenditure at a fantastic $130,000,000 or £60,000,000 sterling. But even if a more conservative estimate is used, one that assumed, for example, that $10 today would buy what $1 could purchase in 1917, it would still reflect an enormous expenditure for promotion.

When it is considered that a budget of nearly four times this figure was actually allocated, that the total investment through 1918 may have been nearly eight times as great, the full extent of Lenin's financial backing can be appreciated. Almost certainly, by the time he reached Russia, he knew that whatever finance he needed was available—an astonishing situation for the leader of a relatively small party to find himself in.

There is, however, nothing in the Foreign Office cost analysis of overseas propaganda to indicate that these funds were passed to Lenin and his party—and certainly every Bolshevik source has always rigorously denied it. Could it not therefore have been supplied for propaganda in other ways or to other organizations? Although some minor funds may have been passed elsewhere, the broad answer is no. For the Secretary of State's secret telegrams to headquarters—the crux of the mosaic of evidence—assert definitely that the Bolsheviks were recipients of German finance, and his use of such words as "a steady flow of funds" and "continual support" indicates a substantial volume. Provided the Secretary of State is regarded as a reliable source of the expenditure by his own department, then this is proof that Lenin's party received a large part of the German funds invested in Russia.

In fact, of course, the Bolsheviks were the logical organization for the Germans to support, for apart from the anarchists, whose lack of discipline and structure made them less reliable, theirs was the only party that campaigned consistently and unequivocally for peace as a prime aim.

Furthermore, when seen from the receiving end, the fact is clear that the Bolshevik operation during the spring and summer of 1917 was so massive that, as Professor Leonard Schapiro put it in *The Communist Party of the Soviet Union*, the funds "could not have come from the official source of party revenue—the ten per cent of their income which local organizations were bound to forward to the Central Committee, since revenue from this source was admittedly negligible." Nor could public subscription have accounted for more than a fraction, for many of the party journals were given away free. Certainly, during the early weeks after the March Revolution, *Pravda* was so short of money that it was running emotional appeals for funds. It was soon to have all the money it needed.

In two dramatic articles, published in the Berlin journal *Vorwärts*, Eduard Bernstein, a prominent German Social Democrat who had actually served in the Treasury, put the sums supplied to the Bolsheviks at "more than 50 million marks" though, in fact, if the German investment in maintaining Lenin in power is added to the cost of helping him win it, then Bernstein's sensational assessment can now be seen from the Foreign Office papers to be conservative. By then, of course, the support had to be very major indeed, for the Allies were pouring money into the White Russian opposition.

At any rate, there are grounds to believe, though little hard proof, that Parvus provided the channel through Fürstenberg by which most of the funds in the spring and summer of 1917 were passed to the Bolsheviks. Despite the personal conflict between Parvus and Lenin, it would seem that neither permitted this to interfere with the aims of the socialist revolution.

At 6:30 P.M. on Easter Friday, the travelers boarded yet another train that would take them north 600 miles to the Swedish-Finnish border. The platform in Stockholm Station was crowded with more than 100 people who had assembled to dispatch the revolutionaries on their way. "There was a wonderful mood everywhere," reported the Swedish newspaper *Politiken*. "Everyone wore red revolutionary emblems. . . . In one of the windows was seen the distinctive head of Lenin."

Poor Karl Radek, condemned to be left behind for his "sinful Austrian nationality," watched the scene sadly. One man, whom Radek did not know, stepped forward to make a speech. "Dear leader," he said, "take care that in Petersburg they do not do any terrible things." Lenin responded with an enigmatic smile.

Dramatic as ever, Radek recorded: "The train moved off and for a moment longer we continued to see that smile."

David Souliashvili had helped Lenin with his baggage on the Stockholm Station platform and had been invited to share his compartment with Nadya and Inessa Armand.[5] It was a sleeper, evidently already prepared for the night, for Lenin and Souliashvili took the top bunks, leaving the lower ones for the two women.

Lenin removed his jacket—despite reproaches from Nadya that he would be cold—and pulled from his pocket some Russian newspapers, which he had obtained in Sweden, and began to read intently. Every now and then, he would let out a loud and angry exclamation: "Oh the swine! The traitors!"

Souliashvili presumed that Lenin was reading about the Menshevik leaders in the Soviet—especially Chkheidze—who were cooperating with the Provisional Government.

"Social Democrats!" sneered Lenin suddenly. "That title has

become idiotic. It's shameful to carry such a name now. We must call ourselves Communists. . . ."[6]

The next morning, as the train sped north through the pine forest, the four breakfasted in the compartment on sandwiches and tea brewed by Nadya on her kerosene stove. Then Lenin asked Souliashvili to tell everyone to gather in the corridor since he wanted to speak to them.

When the party was crowded in the corridor, Lenin briefed them on what they should do if they were arrested at the border on the orders of the Provisional Government. On no account were they to offer any kind of defense for traveling through Germany. Instead, they must attack the government for not helping them return from exile and, in particular, for not bringing pressure on the Allied powers on this point.

It was mid-April, but Haparanda, the Swedish border town, which they reached on Saturday evening, was still snowbound. Wearily, for they had been on the move now for five days, the travelers clambered down onto the platform and unloaded their baggage.

Tornio, the Finnish border town was across the broad frozen mouth of the Torniojoki River, which marked the frontier.

To reach the town, the revolutionaries had to travel over the ice in horse-drawn sledges called *veiki*.

"I remember that it was night," recorded Zinoviev. "There was a long thin ribbon of sledges. On each sledge there were two people. Tension as they approached the Finnish border reached its maximum. The most uninhibited of the young people— Ussievich—was unusually taut. Vladimir Ilyich was outwardly calm. He was most of all interested in what was happening in far-off Petersburg. . . . Across the frozen bay with its deep snowdrifts . . . fifteen hundred versts ahead. . . ."

When they reached Tornio, "the young people threw themselves on the frontier guards" and began to bombard them with questions.

The fear that they might be arrested at the border was eased by the warm greetings of the Russian soldiers on duty—but the

British officers, present under the Allied Command arrangements, were so hostile that the travelers' fears were immediately renewed. Officiously, in the wooden frontier hut, the officers conducted a rigorous and lengthy investigation of each member of the party. One of them, it would seem from Lord Howard's report to London, could even have been the British vice-consul from Haparanda.

"'Our Allies,' someone groaned," according to Olga Ravich, "'are making themselves at home.'"

"We were undressed to the skin," recorded Zina Zinovieva. "My son and I were forced to take off our stockings. I don't know what they were looking for. All the documents and even the children's books and toys my son had brought with him were taken."

Lenin himself was closely questioned. Why had he left Russia? What was he going to do in Finland? What was his profession? Tautly, he told the investigating officer that he had left Russia illegally as a political refugee. His religion, he said presumably because he thought they expected him to have a religion, was Russian Orthodox. He did not propose to remain in Finland. In Petersburg he would be staying in his sister's apartment on Shirokaya Street. By profession, he declared, he was a journalist.

He was searched, and his baggage was combed. But although the British officers could make trouble, they could not prevent Russians from entering a Russian province.

Emerging after his vigorous examination, Lenin "observed that the officers were disappointed at having found nothing," recorded Mikha Tskhakaya. "Ilyich broke into happy laughter and, embracing me, he said: 'Our trials, Comrade Mikha, have ended. We're on native land and we'll show them'—and he clenched his fist—'that we are worthy masters of the future.'"

This must have been a spontaneous reaction at having surmounted the first hurdle, for Lenin still feared they might be arrested on arrival in Petersburg. When he discovered that a military guard had been sent up from the capital to accompany the train, he queried Zinoviev, "To take us to jail?"

Nadya, however, was not worrying. She was too pleased to be on Russian soil: "The awful third-class carriages, the Russian soldiers, everything was terribly good." Quite apart from the escort, the train was full of soldiers on their way south.

The only casualty was Fritz Platten, who, despite Lenin's strong support, was refused entry on the grounds that he was not Russian.

Most of that Easter Sunday must have been spent at Tornio, for it was after six in the evening that Lenin's telegram to his sisters was dispatched from the town: "Arriving Monday 11 P.M. Inform Pravda—Ulyanov."

In Stockholm, Lord Esme Howard, the British ambassador, had watched Lenin's progress through Sweden with angry frustration. On Saturday, when Lenin was on the train to Haparanda, he wired home that "a Russian socialist, Lenin, with some others has been allowed by the German Government to pass through Germany on the way to Russia."

Dagens Nyheter, a Stockholm newspaper, Howard reported, had published a bitter attack by Lenin on Britain in which he emphasized that the British government had refused them right of passage while the German government had given them special facilities.

In London, however, as Lenin's journey was watched from the Foreign Office in Whitehall, the situation in Russia seemed better. On Tuesday, while the Sealed Train was on its way from Singen to Frankfurt, Sir George Buchanan had reported cheerfully that the Petersburg garrison had declared the need to continue the war "until the new won freedom is secured," adding that this was "the most hopeful sign since the first days of the revolution."

Five days later, when Lenin and his party were at Tornio, Buchanan wrote that order and discipline had been reestablished in the Baltic Fleet, where the revolutionary fervor had been most violent, and followed this up the next day with a telegram recording that General Michael Alexeyev, the Russian Chief of Staff, was "far more optimistic about the military situation. A conference at headquarters have unanimously decided that the state of the army admits of its taking the offensive.''

It was a swing to the right—part of the erratic moods that characterized Petersburg and other major Russian cities during these critical months, that made an instinctive sense of timing vital to any politician with ideas of achieving power.

Across the Neva in Old Petersburg, news of Lenin's imminent arrival reached Bolshevik headquarters in the Kshesinskaya Mansion only after the train had been traveling for some hours along the rail track that led down the long reach of the west coast of Finland toward Helsinki.

According to Shlyapnikov, a telegram dispatched by Jacob Fürstenberg from Malmo on Friday did not reach him until Easter Sunday. It asked him to take steps to ensure that frontier difficulties were reduced to a minimum—which he did, but by then, of course, Lenin was through the border. Still, the Central Committee did not know his time of arrival.

Late on Sunday night, Nicholas Podvoisky, one of the commanders of the Bolshevik Military Organization, was on duty in the Kshesinskaya Mansion when Lenin's sister Maria brought in the wire that he had sent from Tornio.

Promptly, Podvoisky awoke the members of the Central Committee to plan how they could give their leader a suitable welcome. There were only a few hours to plan it—and the fact that it was Easter, with no one in the factories and no newspapers published, made the task of communication more difficult. However, clearly it was vital for the party to present Lenin with a massive demonstration of working-class support on his homecoming—and make it visible to the Soviet leaders.

Chapter 8

WHILE THE OTHERS in the train peered into the Sunday-evening dusk as the snow-covered pine trees flashed past the windows, Lenin studied some copies of *Pravda* that soldiers traveling on the train had given him. "He shook his head and threw up his hands in despair," recorded Zinoviev as Lenin read about Milyukov and his obvious determination to continue telling the Russian people that the war was in their interest. What angered him even more was the attitude taken by *Pravda* now that Kamenev and Stalin had taken over its direction—in direct disobedience to his order.[1]

Kamenev had set a policy in the columns of the party newspaper that tacitly supported the war. "It would be the most stupid policy," he had written, "when an army faces the enemy, to urge it to lay down arms and go home. That would be a policy, not of peace but of serfdom, a policy to be contemptuously rejected by the free nation."

Meanwhile, young Robert, still watched closely by Nadya, perched himself on the lap of a veteran soldier, put his arms around his neck and babbled in French to him. The soldier shared his *paskha*, the traditional cheesecake that Russians eat at Easter, with him.

"Our people," recorded Nadya, "were glued to the windows. On the platforms of the stations through which we passed, soldiers stood about in bunches. Ussievich put his head out of the window and yelled: 'Long live the world revolution!' The troops looked in amazement at us travelers."

Lenin, seeking some quiet in which to work, moved with Krupskaya into the end seats of an open carriage. The train was third-class, the only lighting "a spluttering candle." But again he did not get much chance. First a lieutenant, walking through the train, stopped and started a conversation, fiercely opposing Lenin's view that the war must be ended. And then gradually soldiers gathered, listened to the argument and entered into it. Eventually the crowd in the carriage became so great that men even climbed into the luggage racks.

Lenin was very skilled at talking to young or uneducated people, starting always by asking them their opinions, making them talk, often displaying his own opinions by putting very short, even one-word questions. Invariably when the soldiers pressed him, so Zina reported, he would say, "No, you speak first."

George Safarov found one soldier who was a regular reader of *Pravda* and "took him as a trophy to Ilyich." Probably it was this man who agreed with Lenin that they should end the war by "sticking their bayonets into the ground."

It was another, however, who reflected the views of most of the men gathered in the carriage. "How," he asked skeptically, "is it possible to finish the war by sticking your bayonet into the ground?"

Lenin took careful note, for he realized that his questioner was typical, that there were millions who thought as he did—millions whom the Bolsheviks would have to swing to their viewpoint by "patiently explaining."[2]

Lenin had told the soldiers, according to Zina, that they were tired of the war, which was no doubt true. But they were not so tired of it that they were prepared to give up all that they had been fighting for. Lenin realized, Zinoviev recalled, that "the defensist view is still a strength to be reckoned with."

It was another reason to fear that the travelers would be arrested on their arrival in Russia. For the Sealed Train would be much easier to explain away to men who wanted to end the war than to those who wanted to continue it, who regarded the Germans as hated enemies.

All Monday the train ran on through Finland, gradually

curving east as it approached the south of the country. By the evening they were approaching the frontier of the Russian homeland.

Beloostrov, the little Russian-Finnish border town, was the first danger point, an obvious place for a unit of Cossacks or Junkers, the elite officer cadet corps, to be waiting to arrest them.

There were no troops at Beloostrov, as the comrades peering anxiously out of the train windows as it approached the border town, would soon realize. But there was a large crowd of workers who, alerted by Bolshevik agitators, had walked "several versts" from the Sestroretsk munitions plant.

It was already dark—and drizzling—as the party welcoming committee of "about 20" waited under cover in the station. Maria, Lenin's younger sister, who had not seen her brother and sister-in-law since she had stayed with them in Paris before the war, was there—together with Kamenev and Shlyapnikov and Ludmilla Stahl, an old friend of the Ulyanovs, and Theodor Raskolnikov, a young midshipman who was the main Bolshevik leader at Kronstadt, the nearest naval base to Petersburg.[3]

On the journey to Beloostrov from Petersburg, Kamenev had said to Raskolnikov, "You have to know Ilyich to realize how much he hates festive occasions." The two men had laughed, for a festive occasion was certainly awaiting him that night.

"At last," recalled Raskolnikov, "we saw three blinding lights [on the engine] and, after that, the illuminated carriage windows moving slower . . . slower . . . slower. . . ."

Lenin stared in astonishment at the cheering crowd on the platform. As he stepped down from the carriage, he was grabbed, lifted shoulder high and carried to the Bolshevik welcoming committee. He had never experienced this kind of exuberant treatment, and he did not like it. "Careful, comrades," he said, according to one of them. "Gently there, comrades."

But his anxiety was only momentary. He was overwhelmed

by his welcome. When the workers put him down, he embraced his sister and his friends and even the delighted Raskolnikov, whom he had never met.

To the Bolshevik leader's surprise, the commander of the town, appointed by the Provisional Government, even approached him and welcomed him with stiff but friendly formality.

"We had barely had time to greet Ilyich," recalled Raskolnikov, "when Kamenev came into the hall with Zinoviev, beaming and excited." He introduced Raskolnikov to Gregory. Since the militant midshipman had thousands of sailors he could fast mobilize whenever required, the two men would soon know each other very well.

Responding to the demands of the crowd, Lenin climbed onto a chair to address them. He was wearing his old gray overcoat, but he had changed the brimmed hat in which he had left Switzerland for a peaked worker's cap. According to engine driver Elmsted, who had not realized until he had stopped his train at Beloostrov who was aboard it, the Bolshevik leader was in an aggressive mood, despite his happiness to be back in Russia. "Russian workers," he asked, "to whom did you give the power you took from the Tsar? You gave it to the landowners and capitalists!"

"It's only for the time being," shouted someone from the crowd.

When Lenin had stepped down, Ludmilla Stahl urged Nadya to say a few words to the women workers in the crowd, but she declined, too overwhelmed by the scene around her. "All words had left me; I could say nothing."

The bell on the train summoned the passengers back aboard. As soon as they were in the carriage, Lenin rounded on Kamenev. "What have you been writing in *Pravda*?" he demanded. "We've seen a few numbers and called you all sorts of names." But he said it with a smile—without "offense," as Raskolnikov described it—knowing that Kamenev of all people was loyal to him, that there must have been a sound reason, perhaps even then realizing that the mood in the city would have made the exact execution of his orders dangerous for the party.

He was to find, however, that Kamenev was not quite as malleable as he had been. Perhaps his long exile had hardened him and reinforced his natural inclination toward the right wing of the party. It was fourteen years since Lev Borisovich, then only twenty-one, had first written to him in Geneva from the Caucasus. They had never met, but Lenin had been pleased, remarking in his reply how "rarely do people write to us, not in 'duty bound' but to exchange ideas. Please write more often. . . . I would say that your article is unquestionable evidence of your literary ability. . . ." Since Kamenev had become one of the Troika, Lenin had often been angry with him—usually on account of his "carelessness" which Lenin would either attack him for directly or complain about to his friend Zinoviev. "I am furious with you . . ." he had written from Cracow, for example, in 1912 when Kamenev was still in Paris. "You did not arrange for letters from the Congress. . . . You made Koba [Stalin] lose most precious time."

But this April evening, in the border station packed with a welcoming crowd, was not the time to harangue his big bearded friend who had plenty of surprises awaiting him that night.

Lenin bombarded him with questions—so intensely that when someone interrupted him to ask him to speak again to the crowd, he snapped, "Let Gregory go and say a few words." Which he did from the platform of the carriage before the train pulled out of the station with the crowd roaring.

One question Lenin asked Kamenev was: "Are we going to be arrested in Petersburg?" "Our friends who had come to meet us," wrote Zinoviev, "did not give a precise answer. They only smiled mysteriously."

Once the train halted at a small station that, like Beloostrov, was crowded with workers from the Sestroretsk plant. Hands were thrust through the windows, and Lenin made a short speech before, to the clanging of the bell, the train moved on toward Petersburg.

Meanwhile, the news of Lenin's imminent arrival was under

consideration in the Ministry of Foreign Affairs in Petersburg. Nuratov, Milyukov's deputy, read three long notes about it from the British and French ambassadors.

All three emphasized that Lenin had traveled through Germany and stressed the danger that he represented. Buchanan, in particular, made much of the threat of his potential influence within the Soviet. Nuratov, however, was not too bothered. He reflected the view of Milyukov, his minister, who was blithely conducting a foreign policy almost exactly the same as that of the Tsar. None of the other ministers was very concerned as to the damage that Lenin might cause to the fragile government that the revolution had set up—except Kerensky, whom Lenin had already singled out from Switzerland as his main potential adversary and who did not now underrate the Bolshevik leader. Already, at a Cabinet discussion about extremists, according to Minister Nabokov, Kerensky had declared "with his usual hysterical giggle: 'Just you wait, Lenin is coming, then the real thing will begin!' "

Despite the warning, the ministers refused to be alarmed. Calmly, Nuratov attached a note to the file of memoranda, scribbling in pencil: "All the information from these three sources should appear in the newspapers tomorrow without fail, with no mention of the sources, and the cooperation of the German Government should be stressed." It was the first move to turn the Sealed Train journey into a national scandal.

"The throng in front of the Finland Station blocked the whole square, making movement almost impossible and scarcely letting the trams through," recorded N. N. Sukhanov of that momentous night. "Troops with bands were drawn up under red flags near the side entrance, in the former imperial waiting rooms.

"There was a throbbing of many motorcars. In two or three places the awe-inspiring outlines of armored cars thrust up from the crowd. And from one of the side streets there moved out onto the square, startling the mob and cutting through it, a strange monster—a mounted searchlight. . . ."

Within the station, triumphal arches in red and gold, erected every few yards, stretched the length of the platform above the heads of the mass of waiting people. Banners, bearing "every possible welcoming inscription and revolutionary slogan," hung above several divisions of guards of honor—soldiers from various barracks, sailors and the Bolshevik armed civilian Red Guards.

At the end of the platform was a band and a small group of Bolsheviks that included Alexandra Kollontai, holding a bouquet of flowers, and Vladimir Bonch-Bruevich, who had lived intimately in Geneva with Lenin and Nadya and was now in charge of producing the party literature. He was a broad, cheerful man, with a beard and steel-rimmed glasses.

All day, from early in the morning, Bolshevik agitators had been touring the barracks and the working-class areas of the city displaying streamers and pasting posters on the walls bearing the curt message: "Lenin arrives today. Meet him." Because it was Easter Monday, the factories were closed. No newspapers were on sale. Many troops were off duty, but by evening the news had spread through the capital, and long processions, banners flying, were on their way to the Finland Station.

During those early weeks, it was the custom to greet returning revolutionary leaders with a parade. Only a few days before, Plekhanov had arrived at the Finland Station to be welcomed by a large crowd, but Sukhanov, who was a Menshevik, was deeply impressed by the arrangements to meet Lenin. "The Bolsheviks, who shone at organization and always aimed at . . . putting on a good show had dispensed with any superfluous modesty and were plainly preparing a real triumphal entry.

"This time, however, they had special reason for making a point of presenting Lenin to the Petersburg masses as a real hero. Lenin was traveling to Russia via Germany in a Sealed Train by the special favor of the enemy government . . . it was clear that the bourgeoisie and all its hangers-on would make appropriate use of it. And something had to be done to counterbalance the repulsive campaign that was already under way."

The train was late, and in what was once the Tsar's private

room two men waited with resigned impatience to greet the Bolshevik leader formally on behalf of the Petersburg Soviet. Ironically, one of them, the chairman of the Soviet, was the grizzled Georgian Nicholas Chkheidze, whom Lenin had long characterized as a dangerous opportunist. The other was another senior member of the Soviet's Executive Committee, M. I. Skobelev.

Sukhanov, also a member of the Executive Committee but present unofficially, was amused by the scene in the Tsar's waiting room, knowing how both men felt about Lenin. "A dejected Chkheidze sat, weary of the long wait and reacting sluggishly to Skobelev's witticisms," he wrote.

At ten minutes past eleven the train steamed into the crowded station, and Lenin and his party stared through the windows at the almost unbelievable sight before them. "Only now," commented Zinoviev later, "did we understand the mysterious smiles of our friends."

With wonder, Nadya watched the scene on the platform and recalled that only a few hours back, after the train had left Tornio, she and Lenin had been discussing the problems of arriving so late at the Finland Station: At that time of night on Easter Monday would they be able to get a droshky to take them to Mark and Anna's apartment in Shirokaya Street?

As soon as the train came to a stop, Bonch-Bruevich recorded, the reception committee "rushed up to the carriages. Vladimir Ilyich followed by Nadezhda Konstantinovna alighted from the fifth coach from the head of the train."

The bands, both inside and outside the station, blared the "Marseillaise"—since, so it emerged later, the muscians had not been free of Tsarist rule long enough yet to learn the "Internationale." Alexandra Kollontai thrust her large bouquet of flowers into Lenin's hands. The waiting officers rapped out their commands, and the guards of honor presented arms.

"That very instant." reported Bonch-Bruevich, "the hubbub died down. All that could be heard was the blare of trumpets. Then suddenly, as if everything had come into motion, there thundered forth such a powerful, stirring and hearty 'Hurrah' as I have never heard in all my life.

"We approached the sailors. Observing the full ceremonial parade procedure the ensign in command reported to Vladimir Ilyich who looked at him perplexed. . . .

"I whispered to him that the sailors wanted to hear him speak. Vladimir Ilyich walked past the guard of honor. . . . He took several steps back along the front rank of this guard of honor . . . halted, took off his hat."

"Sailors, comrades," said Lenin, "as I greet you, I still don't know whether you have faith in all the promises of the Provisional Government. What I know for certain though is that when sweet promises are made, you are being deceived in the same way that the entire Russian people are being deceived. . . . Sailors, comrades, we have to fight for a socialist revolution, to fight until the proletariat wins full victory! Long live the worldwide socialist revolution!"

When Lenin had finished speaking, he found himself facing a young man he knew very well—Ivan Chugurin, who had been a student at the party school in Longjumeau. Chugurin, "his face wet with tears," as Nadya put it, wearing a broad red sash across his shoulders, presented him formally with a Bolshevik party card "in honor of your return home. . . . The Bolsheviks of the Vyborg district regard you as a member of their district organization."

Lenin was deeply moved, for the industrial district of Vyborg, whose workers had sparked off the March Revolution, was the most militant of all the Bolshevik area organizations.

He moved along the platform, under the triumphal arches, between the rows of welcoming troops and workers.

In the Tsar's rooms, "the gloomy Chkheidze," as Sukhanov called him, waited to receive him. At the head of a group of people, Lenin "came or rather ran into the room . . . he stopped in front of Chkheidze as though colliding with a completely unexpected obstacle."

Speaking in a monotone as if delivering a sermon, Chkheidze greeted him in the name of the Petersburg Soviet. "Comrade Lenin . . . we welcome you to Russia . . . but"—Sukhanov described it as a "delicious 'but' "—" 'we think that the principal task of the revolutionary democracy is now the defense of the revolution. . . . We consider that what this goal requires is not disunion, but a closing of the democratic ranks. We hope you will pursue these goals together with us."

Lenin stood there "as though nothing taking place had the slightest connection with him—looking about him, examining the persons round him and even the ceiling of the imperial waiting room, adjusting his bouquet (rather out of tune with his whole appearance)."

He did not even reply to Chkheidze but instead addressed the group of people who had followed him into the waiting room. His theme was exactly as Chkheidze had feared. He congratulated them as "the vanguard of the worldwide proletarian army. . . . The predatory imperialist war is the beginning of civil war throughout Europe. . . . The worldwide socialist revolution has already dawned. . . . Germany is seething. . . . Any day now the whole of European capitalism may crash. . . . Long live the worldwide socialist revolution!"

The people outside the doors were hammering on the glass, demanding that Lenin leave the privacy of the imperial waiting room. He moved out into the square, packed tight with tens of thousands of people, illuminated by the harsh white beam of the searchlight. He still seemed overwhelmed by the gigantic reception, still uncertain what exactly he was supposed to do.

He tried to get into a car that was waiting for him, but the workers around it refused to let him. He clambered onto the hood and made another short speech. Sukhanov could only catch a few words: ". . . Shameful imperialist slaughter . . . lies and frauds . . . capitalist pirates. . . ."

Nicholas Podvoisky, one of the commanders of the Bolshevik Military Organization, had by now taken charge of his leader. At first, they got into the car from which Lenin had spoken, but they could not move forward because of the human crush. So Podvoisky suggested that they should travel on one of the armored cars that was nearby and elbowed a way for Lenin through the milling people.

From the turret, Lenin made yet another short speech addressing the expanse of faces—dark beneath the glare of the searchlight—and again the crowd cried its welcome.

The roar as the engine of the armored car was revved helped to clear a path, and very slowly the heavy vehicle moved across the square. From the turret, Lenin, still clad in peaked cap and overcoat—for the April night was cold—surveyed the incredible scene around him, the thousands of people, the banners with revolutionary slogans, the flaming torches that many were carrying.

The adjoining streets were crowded with the overflow from the square, and the noise of the armored car, as it proceeded, attracted others from the nearby houses.

At every street intersection the vehicle halted, and Lenin had to make another speech, ending each time, according to Podvoisky with the defiant shout: "Long live the socialist revolution! Down with the compromisers!"

After stopping some fifteen times, Lenin arrived eventually at the white brick Kshesinskaya Mansion, where yet another crowd in the Alexandrovsky Park that bordered the house awaited a speech—this time from the first-floor balcony, from which Lenin could see the nearby lights of the Peter and Paul Fortress, where Sasha had been held until he was executed.

The city's reception had been a magnificent demonstration of the party's skill at stage management, for only a handful of that vast crowd had been Bolsheviks, and a large proportion of those cheering people did not agree with many of Lenin's views— especially about the war. "Ought to stick our bayonets into a fellow like that," commented one angry soldier listening to Lenin speaking from the Kshesinskaya balcony as Sukhanov stood near, "must be a German . . . or he ought to be." It was the way a large number of soldiers would be thinking during the next few days when the significance—or even the as yet largely unknown facts—of the Sealed Train journey began to be fully appreciated.

"Supper," recorded Podvoisky, "was laid in one of the first floor rooms. There, gathered at the long table around Lenin, were some sixty activists from the Petersburg Bolshevik organization."

Inevitably, the ubiquitous Sukhanov was present, despite the fact that he was not a Bolshevik, though his wife was. He was

131]

editor of *Letopis* ("Chronicle"), a newspaper owned by Maxim Gorky, to which Lenin had contributed from exile. For a few minutes he sat next to Lenin, talking about the leading members of the Soviet, until Kamenev called out to him from the other end of the table, "Nikolai Nikolayevich, that's enough. You can finish later. You're taking Ilyich away from us."

Kamenev did not get much chance to talk to his leader, for a crowd of sailors from Kronstadt had arrived outside the mansion and wanted to extend a formal welcome. Once more Lenin went onto the balcony, where Simon Roshal greeted him on behalf of the men. To the sailors gathered below him in the Alexandrovsky Park, Lenin declared, "The words 'Socialist Revolution' could not be closer to the hearts of the comrades at Kronstadt!" and a great cheer roared in response.

Lenin was barely given a chance to eat that night, for other rooms in the mansion were crowded with party workers who wanted to hear him. "Someone suggested that the talk be given in the grand hall where only recently the ballerina Kshesinskaya had given sumptuous banquets," wrote Podvoisky.

This was a big room on the ground floor, with enormous plate-glass windows hung with heavy velvet curtains. White silk-upholstered furniture was ranged along the walls. One end of the room, which opened onto the lawn, was curved. It featured an indoor winter garden with big palm trees and a stream that cascaded over rocks.

A table was was brought for Lenin, and he took his place at it with Nadya and his two sisters. His audience sat on chairs facing him.

There were a number of welcoming speeches by members from various Bolshevik district committees. Of all of them, Zina Zinovieva was most moved by that of Vladimir Nevsky, a veteran Bolshevik who with Podvoisky ran the military arm of the party. He was a brilliant agitator whom Zina had heard addressing audiences of thousands, yet in the emotion of the moment, "he delivered a speech stammering and stuttering."

"What was the matter with you, Comrade Vladimir?" she asked him afterward. "Did you forget how to speak?"

"I lost myself," he conceded briefly.

At last, after Kamenev gave the final speech of formal welcome, Lenin stood up and began his speech. For two hours, without notes, he told the Bolsheviks what he planned the party's new policy would be. "I shall never forget that thunderlike speech," recalled Sukhanov, "which startled and amazed not only me, a heretic who had accidentally dropped in, but all the true believers. I am certain that no one had expected anything of the sort."

"The fundamental impression made by Lenin's speech even among those nearest him," wrote Trotsky, "was one of fright. All the accepted formulas, which with innumerable repetition had acquired in the course of a month a seemingly unshakable permanence, were exploded one after another before the eyes of that audience."

Lenin was not a dramatic speaker. He did not have the same ability to grab his audiences from the start as Trotsky had. He rarely used wit or pathos or even overt emotion. Nevertheless, he was an orator of enormous intellectual impact, "breaking down complicated systems into the simplest and most generally accessible element," as Sukhanov put it, "and hammering, hammering, hammering them into the heads of his audience until he took them captive."

He told his listeners that the war could not help turning into a civil class war. He attacked the existing leaders of the Soviet as "opportunists" and "instruments of the bourgeoisie" and even mocked the celebrated manifesto, issued on March 14, which had called for "worldwide socialist revolution." "Revolutions are not called for," he sneered. "They arise out of historically established conditions, revolutions mature and grow."

His attack on the Soviet leaders and policies was "alone enough to make his listeners' heads spin," as Sukhanov observed, because they were creations of the revolution. Kamenev had pledged them the party's cooperation. The ruling mood, as Chkheidze had indicated in his greeting at the station, was one of all parties working together for the revolution.

Lenin emphasized that he at least was not in favor of working together. He was for revolution, for power in the hands of the people, not the control of the bourgeoisie which had it now. He announced his new concept, crystallized almost certainly during those long hours on the Sealed Train probably after a meeting with the Germans in Berlin, his plan for an immediate leap into socialism, which all Marxists knew was impossible. And he proposed to call for "all power to the Soviets," which seemed to his listeners equally impractical. The Soviet was a loose federation of strike committees. How could its 2,000 or 3,000 members, inevitably torn by political differences, ever rule a nation?

The interesting question is whether Lenin ever intended it to? Was the proposal entirely tactical, designed to produce a situation in which the party could seize power? "All power to the Soviet" was an appealing slogan which the Bolsheviks could promote without being charged with self-interest, since they were at present only a minority within it. But it was a slogan he had not mentioned before the journey on the Sealed Train. Now with the fact of the availability of German funds Lenin knew he could put it across.

There is no doubt that in practice in the months that followed, both before and after November, Lenin always put power for the party before power for the Soviet.

In any event, even if he was truly considering the ideologically appealing concept of an all-powerful Soviet at this moment, he was far ahead of his shocked listeners.

For they were intent on protecting the revolution which they had helped create—and in this, Lenin believed, they were pursuing an illusion sold them by the bourgeois. Lenin was preparing for the next revolution.

Certainly, in his speech that night, Lenin insisted that his plan for Soviet power was sound. "We don't need a parliamentary republic," he declared, denouncing this basic Marxist tenet. "We don't need a bourgeois democracy, we don't need any government except the Soviet of Workers, Soldiers and Peasants Deputies."

After this, his demand for "organized seizure" of the land,

though startling as a first stage of bourgeois democracy, seemed relatively mild.

The astounded Sukhanov watched the Bolsheviks applaud their leader at the end of his speech. "On the faces of the majority, there was nothing but rapture . . . but the literate ones, clapping loud and long, seemed to stare strangely in front of them. . . ."

Heavily, Kamenev rose to his feet. "Comrades," he said, "maybe we agree or disagree with the speech of Comrade Lenin. Maybe we disagree with him on his view of this or that situation; but in any case . . . Comrade Lenin has returned to Russia, our brilliant and recognized leader of our party, and together we will go forward to meet socialism."

"Comrade Kamenev," commented Raskolnikov somewhat inaccurately, "had found a unifying formula even for those who were still wavering. . . ."

Sukhanov, his journalist's instincts aroused, did not think he had. After the meeting, he "looked for Kamenev . . . but in answer to my question as to what he had to say about all this, he merely shrugged his shoulders: 'Wait, just wait!'

"As an infidel, I turned to another and then to a third of the faithful. . . . The people I talked to grinned and shook their heads, without the slightest idea of what to say.

"I went out into the street. I felt as though I had been beaten about the head that night with flails."

As dawn lightened the Petersburg sky, Lenin and his family walked to the apartment on Shirokaya Street where Anna, Mark Timofeyevich and Maria lived. He and Nadya were to sleep in the room that had been occupied by his mother until she had died the previous year.

Gora, Anna and Mark's adopted son, though long asleep, had left a greeting. Draped across the pillow on each bed was a hand-scrawled notice: "Workers of the world unite!"

"I hardly spoke to Ilyich that night," recalled Nadya, "there were really no words to express the experience, everything was understood without words."

Chapter 9

WHEN LENIN AWOKE EARLY next morning, the sky was leaden gray—a suitable setting for the events that lay ahead. Shirokaya Street, where the Elizarov apartment was situated, was a broad, nondescript thoroughfare of tall, gray and rather gloomy apartment buildings in the middle of Petersburg Island. This was the oldest section of the city in which Peter the Great himself had lived and built his golden-spired fortress complex of Sts. Peter and Paul.[1]

Number 52 Shirokaya, in which the Elizarov apartment was on the sixth floor, had been constructed on a sharp street corner. As a result, the flat was triangular in shape, and the living room, since it was in the apex, gave an impression of a salon on a ship. There were windows on both sides of the room which narrowed at one end to french doors. Beyond was a balcony that came to a point, like a prow.

The flat was large and comfortable. Mark Elizarov's position as a director of a marine insurance company enabled the family to keep a maid. Both Anna and Maria worked on the staff of *Pravda*. Anna, at fifty-four, was the more reserved of the two sisters. As a young girl she had been striking with dark eyes and long hair, but now in middle age she had become thinner and her face had tautened, sharpening the contours of nose and cheeks. She was a highly disciplined woman, controlled and severe—and looked it.

Maria, by contrast, was far warmer and more spontaneous. Plumper than her married sister and ten years younger, she had a wide Mongol-looking face with a broad nose and dark eyes that resembled her elder brother's. Even as a girl she had been plain, but she had always been Lenin's favorite—possibly because she was the closest in age but also because his role in her life had been that of a father as well as a brother.

Mark Elizarov was an elegant still-handsome man in his early fifties with an ample black beard. Anna had met him in a revolutionary situation, for he had been a close friend and fellow student of Sasha's at Petersburg University. In fact, he had proposed to her during the period after Sasha's arrest when the Ulyanov family was ostracized, an act of courage that must have removed any doubts that might have lingered in Anna's mind.

The arrival of Lenin and Nadya had required a change in the family's living arrangements. Maria had moved into the same room as her sister. Mark had a bed set up in his study. This was to be Lenin's home for some weeks—until it was no longer safe for him to remain in the city.

In the living room was a chess table, fitted with a secret drawer which had long been a hiding place for the more incriminating documents and which had survived many police raids.

Now the police—in the two forms that they had existed in Tsarist days—had been broken up, but many of their members had entered the new militia that had been set up to replace them. Lenin refused to recognize the difference—seeing it as one more aspect of the duping of the masses—and continued to refer to "the police" as though the Okhrana still existed.

Early that Tuesday morning a deputation from the party arrived at the apartment to see him because, in the trauma that followed Lenin's shocking speech the previous evening, they had quite forgotten to tell him that an important meeting was scheduled that day—to discuss with the Mensheviks once again the question of merging the two factions of the Russian Social Democratic Party. In his speech Lenin had, of course, attacked the Menshevik leaders as "compromisers," and even from Zurich, he had insisted that there should be no alliance with other parties. It was, therefore, with some trepidation that the Bolsheviks broke the news to their leader that his orders had been disobeyed.

He could hardly complain. The Bolshevik organization was not a dictatorship, and the decision to open merger talks had been made constitutionally by a party conference. It was also a fact that a close degree of cooperation already existed. In some cities the two factions were working together, even sharing premises.

It is doubtful if Lenin made an issue of this any more than he had of Kamenev's compromising line in *Pravda*. The revolution had been a dazing emotional experience, one hardly conducive to clear thought. It was precisely because of this that Lenin had known it was vital for him to get to Petersburg without delay. Now that he had arrived, he could start giving the party the intellectual guidance that it so obviously needed—and he was going to get his first opportunity that morning. For Bolsheviks from all over Russia were in Petersburg for a conference that had ended the previous evening. They wanted to hear him before they left the city to return home, since only the more important among them had attended his reception in the Kshesinskaya Mansion.

Together with the party deputation, Lenin traveled to his friend Vladimir Bonch-Bruevich's apartment on Khersonskaya in the center of the city for a short meeting with Zinoviev and the party leaders. From the Troitsky Bridge, as they crossed the Neva, which bends in a big U through the city, Lenin would have seen for the first time for more than a decade the Petersburg that he had come to know so well during the years when he was young, first as a student and then as a radical young lawyer with revolutionary plans. On the north side of the river, beyond the golden-spired Fortress of Peter and Paul, was the big Exchange building on Vasilevsky Island. On the south bank was the long façade of the Hermitage and the Winter Palace; behind them, the famous pillared tower of the Admiralty at the head of the Nevsky Prospect and the great golden dome of St. Isaac's Cathedral.

The car moved off the bridge into the center of modern Petersburg, passed through the Field of Mars—those symbolic gardens where a month ago the hundreds of dead had been lowered into the ground one by one, each coffin marked by a boom from the cannon in Peter and Paul—and turned into Nevsky.

The Nevsky cut straight and wide across the heart of the city. Lined with the most expensive shops and the finest apartments, it was the core of the bourgeoisie in the capital—which was why it had been the scene of much of the shooting in March.

To Lenin that morning, there was little sign of revolution on the Nevsky. The men in their neat suits and bowler hats and the women in their long and ample dresses still thronged the pavements. The carriages and automobiles of the rich were still proceeding slowly through the traffic congestion of the fashionable thoroughfare. Commissionaires still stood outside the big hotels, wearing sashes of green, gold or scarlet and peacock feathers in round Chinese-looking caps.

Bourgeois babies were still pushed in big prams by nursemaids dressed in traditional costume—blue if the children were boys, pink if they were girls—their heads covered by white *kokoshniks* decorated with silver tassels and encrusted with imitation pearls.

However, even if the revolution was not too apparent on that cloudy April morning, it had in fact produced enormous changes. Petersburg, like much of Russia, was still on the brink of social and organizational collapse. During the few weeks that had passed since those traumatic March days the entire nation—as Kerensky put it—had been swept by "a sense of unlimited freedom, a liberation from the most elementary restraints essential to every human society."

Crime had soared. In the factories, people had stopped working. For all of Sir George Buchanan's optimism, discipline had vanished in the army and the navy. In the streets soldiers forcibly relieved officers of their swords.

Throughout Russia, in plants, military camps and villages, the newly formed committees were in session. There was endless talk, but little constructive action.

The one factor that prevented a complete breakdown was the Soviet. The government ruled in name, but the Soviet made it possible.

Because chaos was so close, the early extremism, with its undertones of the French Revolution, had now been replaced by an almost universal belief within the Soviet that order must be preserved. Many party aims had been shelved temporarily in the cause of stability. In this sense, they had almost all become "compromisers." Certainly the leading Bolsheviks subscribed to this view of the revolution.

Among the socialist intellectuals, this common attitude was logical and consistent with Marxist theory. It was the first stage of revolution. Autocracy and feudalism had been overthrown.

To the ordinary worker and soldier, the revolution had brought a keen sense of personal achievement. Everyone was "comrade." In the restaurants, a notice on each table declared: "Just because a man must make his living by being a waiter, do not insult him by offering him a tip." Everywhere there were red flags, symbolizing the victory of the revolution. Everywhere the imperial insignia had been ripped from the buildings, leaving crude, bare patches torn in the stone and plaster.

The mood of the city to which Lenin returned for the first time since the 1905 uprising was, therefore, one of intense pride. It was a mood, colored by complacency, that Lenin planned that day to shatter.

First, though, he had a personal visit to make. In Bonch-Bruevich's car he drove to the cemetery where his mother had been buried the previous year. For a few minutes he stood, his head bared, beside her grave. Then he strode away through the memorial stones to start a new revolution.

An hour later in the gallery of the Tauride Palace, Lenin addressed his Bolsheviks—and his speech shook the organization he had created to its roots. Most of it, of course, echoed what he had said the previous night in the Kshesinskaya Mansion, but that had been an intimate explanation of his views to close comrades. Now he was the head of the party demanding that its members face up to their responsibilities, attacking them for betraying socialist principles. And, although they did not know it, he was doing so as the director of a political organization that, though relatively small at present, had as great potential financial resources as any other party in Russia—including the big bourgeois Kadet Party. That knowledge must have provided Lenin with an immense source of extra strength, extra confidence, and it is intriguing to ponder whether he would have been quite so dogmatic, quite so scathing, if it had not existed.

In ten clear points—the April Theses—he laid down the structure of his dramatic new program intended to catapult 160,000,000 Russians toward socialism. They included: no support of the Provisional Government; a complete break with capitalism and an end to the predatory war; the establishment of a republic of Soviets and workers and peasants that would control production and distribution of goods; the nationalizing of all banks under Soviet control; the confiscation of all private lands; a rebuilding of the revolutionary international; and the destruction of the bourgeois state establishment (army, police, bureaucracy) which would be replaced by Soviet organs, consisting of officials who would be elected by the people and replaceable at any time—rule from below, as he was to repeat so often, not from above.

Possibly the most important aim of all, for it was tactical, was his guidelines for the party. In the Soviet the Bolsheviks were a minority, so they must "patiently explain" to the masses how they were being misled—especially to the frontline troops who should be encouraged to fraternize with the German troops who faced them. For this was the start of a world revolution, the transformation of an imperialist conflict into civil class war, and Germany was the first area into which it would spread.

This was his message, but as he delivered it, he taunted the Bolsheviks with duping themselves, with being dazed by the heady atmosphere of the March Revolution.

"Why didn't you seize power?" he challenged them, rocking back on his heels, his thumbs in the armpits of his waistcoat. Then gave them the answer. The bourgeoisie were organized and conscious of the class war. The workers were not.

"We must . . . frankly admit it," he admonished his

listeners, "and tell the people that we have failed to assume power because we are not class-conscious and not organized."

And because they had failed—the people, the party—an imperialist war was continuing. Thousands of men were dying. And astonishing though it was, the masses, "trustingly ignorant," still had faith in the ministers.

It was not only the masses who were misled. "Even our own Bolsheviks," he jeered at them in apparent amazement, "show confidence in the government. . . . *You comrades* have faith in the government." Then, jutting his head forward, he warned them: "If that is your position, our ways must part. I'd rather be in a minority. . . ."

Rounding on the party journal, he taunted: "*Pravda* demands that the government renounce annexations [i.e., foreign territory]. To demand that a government of capitalists renounce annexations . . . is crying mockery. . . ."

Lenin knew there were secret treaties between the Allies— they had appalled Kerensky when he learned of them. Under these, Russia was to gain Constantinople, the Dardanelles and much of Mesopotamia as spoils of victory.

"The fundamental question is: Which class is waging the war?" cried Lenin. "The capitalist class, tied to the banks, cannot wage any but an imperialist war. . . . We must make it clear to the masses that the soviet is the only possible government, a government of a kind that, barring the [Paris] Commune, the world has never seen."

An hour later, as the result of urging from Mensheviks who had entered the gallery as he was speaking, Lenin repeated his speech before a much larger audience in the Grand Hall of the Tauride Palace—with Chkheidze, his main target, acting as chairman.

This was the conference which had been called to discuss once more the merging of Mensheviks and Bolsheviks into a combined Social Democratic Party and end their fourteen years of feuding.

It was because of this that Lenin, as he walked onto the platform, was given a tremendous ovation by an audience that included men and women who had known him for years—*and* known the astringent contempt of his articles and his speeches. If they expected him to reinforce Kamenev's merger pleas, it was partly because of the euphoria of the revolution and partly because at the time of the last revolution in 1905, Lenin himself had pressed for a united front. Even so, Chkheidze, after Lenin's surly response to his welcome at the Finland Station, must at least have been apprehensive.

As Lenin waited for the clapping to stop, he pulled down his jacket, smoothed the hair at the back of his head and studied his audience.

They soon realized that they were not listening to a man who was intent on achieving unity. This was the same disruptive Lenin—but a Lenin who astonishingly, seemed to have discarded Marx.

The murmuring began early in his speech, but when he asserted that the revolution must produce "a Soviet Republic" and defined this as "a state for which the Paris Commune served as prototype," there was a howl from his audience. They stamped their feet, banged their desks, catcalled and whistled. Desperately, Chkheidze tried to restore order, but it was minutes before he could even make himself heard.

Lenin's whole program seemed wildly impractical to his audience, but his mention of the Paris Commune of 1871 appeared totally absurd. The people of Paris had set up the Commune by elections in defiance of the government. It had been an experiment in crude socialism, and it had featured Lenin's concept of rule from below. Even the officers of the National Guard, a kind of people's militia, had been elected.

The French government, frightened by the effect of the commune on the loyalties of the regular troops, had withdrawn from the capital with the army—only to return to smash the experiment in a two-day massacre of some 30,000 citizens.

The few weeks the Commune survived were hardly enough to permit any practical achievement, but even if it had lasted longer, the experience within the limits of a city could hardly be applied to a vast nation like Russia, already tottering dangerously near collapse.

"This is the raving of a madman," someone yelled. "Sheer

anarchy," asserted I. P. Goldenberg, a Bolshevik from *Iskra* days who had defected. Steklov, one of the editors of *Izvestia*, the Soviet's official newspaper, insisted that the Russian Revolution had "passed him by." "After Lenin becomes acquainted with the state of affairs in Russia, he himself will reject all these constructions of his." This was also the view of most of the Bolsheviks. "On that day," wrote V. I. Zalezhsky, a member of the Petersburg Bolshevik City Committee and one of the organizers of Lenin's welcome the previous night, "Comrade Lenin could not find open sympathizers even in our own ranks." Skobelev, who twenty-four hours before had formally greeted him with Chkheidze on behalf of the Soviet at the Finland Station, described him contemptuously as "a man completely played out."

Happily, British Ambassador Sir George Buchanan reported to London that "all Lenin's proposals have been rejected."

In a Cabinet meeting in the Mariinsky Palace Minister of Justice Kerensky declared he was going to visit Lenin. "He is living in a completely isolated atmosphere," he explained to the other ministers. "He knows nothing, sees everything through the glasses of his fanaticism." But he did not go.

Had any of these critics known of the enormous funds that were ranged behind Lenin or realized the scale on which he would be able to promote his new policy line across the nation, they would not have dismissed his ideas so airily. Certainly, it would have made Alexander Kerensky, who saw himself as the potential leader of the new Russia, anxious indeed.

In Germany, the news of the outraged reactions to Lenin's speech was received with as much satisfaction as in London. But unlike Buchanan, who saw Lenin merely as a dangerous demagogue preaching pacifism, the German officials knew better. From Imperial Headquarters, Zimmermann's liaison officer wrote that "Lenin is working exactly as we would wish. . . ."

Chapter 10

DURING THAT FIRST WEEK after his return to Russia, Lenin was facing enormous problems. Until he surmounted them, he could make no progress with his plans to gain the public support he needed for his workers' revolution. He could not start to use the vast sums of cash that were available to him.[1]

His position was precarious in the extreme. The party leaders, ranged around Kamenev, were violently opposed to his policy. The revelation of the Sealed Train, of which few of the thousands who had welcomed him at the Finland Station had known, produced so violent a reaction that his very life was in danger.

For his new ideas were a propaganda gift to the right wing—in particular to Paul Milyukov, the Foreign Minister and head of the big Kadet Party.

The Kadets, backed by a powerful newspaper, *Rech* ("Speech"), had the support of most of the bourgeoisie—civil servants, shopkeepers, military officers, the professions. In addition, many right-wing reactionaries, deeming it wise in revolutionary Russia to conceal their real views, had now joined the party.

Milyukov was a liberal and a patriot who wanted to restore to Russia the dignity and glory that had been badly frayed by the humiliation of the war's lost battles. He was determined to destroy the Soviet and its socialist menace, and he favored an imperialist war policy that even included the ancient Russian aim of Constantinople, but he had to move warily. The masses—and the troops in particular—desperately wanted an end to the war, but they were prepared to continue fighting to defend Russian territory and their revolution.

For Milyukov, Lenin arrived in Petersburg at an ideal moment. For he enabled Milyukov to promote the idea that all pacifists were in league with the Germans and, by pillorying Lenin as a friend of the Kaiser, to lay the groundwork for a strike against the Soviet.

It is highly doubtful if Milyukov truly believed that Lenin was in the pay of the Germans, and certainly he would have been astonished to learn the sheer scale of the financial backing they had provided. But the Foreign Minister was concerned not with truth, but with tactics.

The Sealed Train offered undisputed proof that Lenin had accepted help from the Germans. Naturally, the Kadet newspaper and agitators implied, Lenin wanted an end to the war, naturally he demanded fraternization between the troops at the front, naturally he preached anarchy in his speech in the Tauride Palace, for this was what the Kaiser wanted.

Milyukov's plan, conceived in liaison with General Lavr Kornilov, commander of the city's garrison of a quarter of a million troops, was based on classic techniques that the Tsars had employed for centuries. At least, this was the charge later made by Trotsky and suspected by many of Lenin's rivals in the Soviet. Certainly it was simple: Milyukov's Kadets would provide disorder in the streets. Lenin and the Bolsheviks would be blamed. And the troops, if their resentment against Lenin as a German agent was strong enough, would agree to repress the troublemakers. The counterrevolution would then be in full swing, and the socialists in the Soviet would be vulnerable.

The first stage of Milyukov's plan was brilliantly successful. Lenin had fully calculated the danger of the Sealed Train. Because of this, he had appeared with Zinoviev before the Executive Committee of the Soviet—which was noncommittal but did publish in the official *Izvestia* his explanation of the journey with its emphasis on the role played by the non-Russian Fritz Platten, the "sealing" of the train against any contact with the Germans and the protocol of approval signed by the international socialists.

Lenin had hoped that this would answer much of the criticism. But his statement made hardly any impact at all against the howls of anger against him both in the press and in the streets. Throughout the bourgeois newspapers he was attacked for traveling with the aid of the Kaiser and even, for good measure, for the life of luxury he was leading in the Kshesinskaya "Palace." Mobs paraded through the city bearing placards demanding his arrest. Large hooting crowds gathered in the Alexandrovsky Park outside the Kshesinskaya Mansion, yelling, "Down with Lenin—Back to Germany!"

In several regiments, motions demanding his arrest were carried by big votes in the committees. The Petersburg High School students mounted their own bitterly critical demonstration. The Soldiers' Executive Commission of the Moscow Soldiers' Soviet passed a resolution calling for protection from Lenin and his propaganda. " 'Arrest Lenin' and 'Down with the Bolsheviks' were heard at every street corner," recorded Sukhanov.

In the war zone, hundreds of miles from Petersburg, the Fourth Front Line Sanitary Ambulance unit branded the travelers on the Sealed Train as "traitors."

Even the sailors, the most revolutionary element in Russia, turned angrily against Lenin. The men who had formed the naval Guard of Honor on the platform at the Finland Station were so appalled to learn about the journey that they issued a public statement: "Having learned that Comrade Lenin came back to us in Russia with the consent of His Majesty the German Emperor and King of Prussia, we express our profound regret at our participation in his triumphal welcome to Petersburg."

Maximov, the young ensign who had commanded the guard of honor at the Finland Station, dissociated himself from the Bolshevik leader in a public letter, insisting that he had been completely unaware of the German train.

Day by day, during that first week after Lenin's return, the reaction to the campaign became more violent and extreme. "Not a single Bolshevik," recorded Podvoisky, "was able to enter the barracks without risking arrest or even death." Soldiers who were members of the party were beaten up by their comrades, "who had been poisoned against the Bolsheviks," and were sent to the front out of turn. Special orders banned *Pravda* from military buildings.

Lenin made an attempt to stem the wave of hostility in the army by addressing the soldiers' section of the Soviet, but at that stage his action had little impact. "Go and preach your ideas in Germany," they cried.

Even the anarchists, concerned by the attacks on Lenin for preaching anarchy, disowned him firmly, declaring him "completely alien to the present formation of anarchism. . . . His demagogical speeches are unacceptable to us . . . anarchists condemn Lenin's journey through Germany. . . ."

Strangely, he had a defender in the most right-wing quarter of the capital, presumably because it feared the backlash. *Birzhevye Vedomosti* ("The Stock Exchange News") urged tolerance. "Citizens, calls for the death of Lenin are as criminal and as dangerous for free Russia as the fury of his speeches. . . ."

Because of the obvious danger, Lenin was given a bodyguard in addition to the armed driver of his car, and thirteen rifle-carrying workers from a factory in the Vyborg provided twenty-four-hour-a-day protection at the Elizarov apartment on Shirokaya.

From a narrow room in the *Pravda* offices, Lenin defended himself as well as he could through the pages of the Bolshevik newspaper. He attacked *Rech*, which had alleged that in effect "the Lenin crew is working for Bethmann-Hollweg and Wilhelm II" for failing even to publish the findings of the Executive Committee of the Soviet which had investigated the Sealed Train. He accused the Kadet paper of "inciting ignorant people to violence."

Charging the right-wing press with provoking "a pogrom" that had resulted in "threats of violence and bombing," he appealed to the "sense of honor of the revolutionary workers and soldiers of Petersburg."

Throughout his articles, he accused Milyukov and the bourgeoisie of "shameless lying," of preparing secretly to carry out "threats against the Soviets," of deceiving the masses. "If you gentlemen have the majority of the people with you . . ." he taunted in one article, "what do you fear, gentlemen, why do you lie?" All we want to do is to make clear to the workers and the poorest peasants the errors of their tactics. . . . Why then are you afraid . . .? It is the truth you fear. You lie in order to suppress with the aid of pogrom makers, slander, violence and filth any chance of expounding the truth."

Lenin's cries of outrage in *Pravda* had little impact in face of the onslaught against him—as Alexander Kerensky noted with satisfaction. Over dinner at the British embassy, he told Sir George Buchanan that "the communistic doctrines preached by Lenin," far from being dangerous, "have made the [extremist] socialists lose ground." The Mensheviks and SR's were as nervous of his new program, which *they* saw as sheer anarchism even if the anarchists did not, as the government was.

Kerensky was a leading member of the Soviet—as well as a minister—but his ideas of the kind of government Russia needed were closer to those of Milyukov than of his Soviet colleagues. He felt passionately about the revolution and regarded it as a kind of holy trust given to him by God, but he was becoming very disillusioned about the Soviet—especially its extreme wing that Lenin was now trying to strengthen. For Kerensky, the planned Constituent Assembly, the Parliament, was a far better and proved ideal than the Soviet.

By now, Kerensky had been alerted to the fact that Lenin might have closer links to the Wilhelmstrasse than the mere fact of the Sealed Train suggested. On the very day that Lenin had reached Russia, another visitor had arrived at the Finland Station by an earlier train. He was Albert Thomas, French Minister of Military Supplies, and he had noted the banners and decorations in the station with interest—for he had information about the man they were erected to honor.

A few days later Prince Lvov had sent for Kerensky and two other ministers. The French secret service, he said, had proof which Thomas had confided to him that Lenin was in communication with several German agents. The prince instructed Kerensky as Minister of Justice and the other two ministers to conduct a secret investigation into the truth of the French intelligence reports.

Kerensky does not report exactly what Thomas told them about Lenin's links with Germany—but other indications suggest that it was the alleged Parvus-Fürstenberg channel. Certainly, large sums of money were soon being passed on Fürstenberg's orders to Petersburg contacts with whom he had extensive business dealings. One was a lawyer, Mecheslav Kozlovsky, a friend who was Polish like Fürstenberg himself, and a Bolshevik delegate on the Executive Committee of the Petersburg Soviet.

If at that stage, the government investigators were able to monitor any of Lenin's letters to Fürstenberg—that were probably sent by courier—they would have seemed to confirm Thomas' tip. On April 25, Lenin wrote an angry note to Fürstenberg and Karl Radek: "Up to now we have received nothing, absolutely nothing from you—no letters, no packets, no money." Nine days later, however, he was happier. "The money from Kozlovsky (2 thousand) has been received," he confirmed. The figure is small, and the Soviet editors of Lenin's works explain that these were party funds that had been left abroad. During the next few weeks, however, Mecheslav Kozlovsky was to receive money in far greater quantity from Fürstenberg's sources.

Meanwhile, in April, as the Kadet processions paraded daily through the streets of the city with banners campaigning against Bolshevik German agents, Lenin himself was deeply engrossed in his other conflict. In one sense, his struggle within his own organization, even if it did not carry the physical dangers of the right-wing menace, was the more serious. For without the party as a nucleus that he could expand, Lenin could neither develop his plans for a socialist world nor deploy his new resources.

His situation was strange, for he was not challenged as a leader. Even Kamenev, the keenest of his critics, completely acknowledged him as his chief. The senior Bolsheviks just thought he was crazily wrong, that he had not been in revolutionary Russia long enough to understand the problems.

The day after Lenin's speeches in the Tauride Palace, Kamenev mounted a major attack on the new policy proposals in the Central Committee.

With almost unanimous support, he demanded that the committee should reject the policy outlined in the theses. In the public columns of *Pravda*, he insisted that Lenin's plan was impractical if the Bolsheviks wanted "to remain the party of the proletarian masses." Lenin's assumption that Marx's first stage of revolution was over was "unacceptable." Stalin was among those who supported Kamenev.

So, too, was the important Petersburg City Committee,* which ran the party within the capital. It rejected Lenin's new line by an overwhelming majority vote.

With *Pravda* engaged in fighting off external assaults from the right-wing press and torn by the internal conflict of the party, it was not strange that behind the scenes in the newspaper's offices, the atmosphere was strained. Lenin and Zinoviev had joined Kamenev and Stalin as editors, and according to Vladimir Bonch-Bruevich, "it was enough for one of them to read a scrap from an article he had just written for a violent quarrel to break out . . . in that little narrow room," which the four of them shared. After the quarrels, "a deadly silence would follow in the editorial room . . . and everyone would bury himself in his work." Zinoviev was torn between loyalty to the man he had worked with so closely for years and his friend Kamenev, whose moderate views he tended to share.

It is interesting to consider whether at this stage Kamenev knew that German funds were available or whether Lenin kept the knowledge to himself. It is hard to believe that the leaders were not aware of the general fact—especially Zinoviev, who had been on the Sealed Train and in Stockholm—even though

---

*The Bolshevik organization was structured on a hierarchy of committees. Each city or area had its own committee. So, lower down, did each small district and, lower still, each factory or regiment. At the head of the pyramid was the Central Committee of the party.

Of all areas in Russia in 1917, Petersburg was unique because it was the focus of most of the important events. The Petersburg Committee, responsible for the party within the city, played an unusually vital role alongside the Central Committee that also operated from the Kshesinskaya Mansion. Naturally, their activities overlapped at this time.

Lenin may not have discussed his detailed strategy with them. Certainly, they would have found out as soon as "special funds" began to flow in, for these would presumably have had to be explained, and although a few cover stories were developed, they were inevitably inadequate for the scale of the financing. In any event, even if Kamenev knew, it would not have affected his view that Lenin's policy was ideologically wrong—and would be seen to be wrong by the masses. No amount of money would overcome this basic fact.

Clearly, Lenin did not win all these "tense arguments" in the *Pravda* office, though he probably won most of them. He wrote a series of "Letters on Tactics" which argued out his conflict with Kamenev point by point. He justified the change in policy he was demanding and defended himself against the charge that he had forsaken Marx.

"A Marxist," he wrote, "must take cognizance of living life, of the true facts of reality . . . not continue clinging to the theory of yesterday, which like every theory at best only outlines the main and the general. . . . Theory, my friend, is gray but green is the eternal tree of life."

Lenin was under great strain, but he was standing up to it well. His writing was firm. All the reports of his contemporaries indicate a cool confidence. There were no *rages* when he was in the throes of a conflict—only when he was in a situation in which he was frustrated by inaction, as he had been in Zurich and would soon be again. All the same, his stomach—always his weak point—was causing him trouble, and he was not sleeping well.

Every evening he would cross the Neva from the *Pravda* office on Moika Street and return to the Elizarov apartment on Shirokaya. For Nadya, those early days after their arrival were trying. Anna and Maria fussed over their brother, concerning themselves with the food he ate and the clothes he wore—which Nadya had been doing for two decades. And even though she had for years been secretary of the party and was one of the most experienced revolutionary women among the Bolsheviks, she was given no definite role in the Kshesinskaya Mansion.

She helped in the secretariat which was run by Elena Stasova, whom she had known even before she married Lenin. But Elena already had four assistants in the bathroom that served as an office and seems to have regarded Nadya, whom she did not even mention in her accounts of this period, as potential competition. "I talked to the workers who came there," recalled Nadya, implying she had nothing else to do. "No special duties were assigned to me and the absence of definite work bored me."

It is strange that Lenin did not appear to exercise his influence on her behalf, for she outranked Elena in party seniority, and she could have been useful in his struggle to establish his new policy. But perhaps he did not want to disturb the machine that was operating as smoothly as it could under the circumstances. He had trouble enough.

In fact, Lenin, though isolated among the Bolshevik leaders and under continual attack from outside the party, was not as alone as he seemed. Many of the ordinary party workers below the top hierarchy were as extreme revolutionaries as he was. In the factories in the Vyborg area were Bolsheviks as rabid as any sans-culottes of the French Revolution, and they had, indeed, made some attempt at emulating their atrocities during the violent days of March.

Also, since then, the party membership throughout Russia had grown rapidly—especially in Petersburg, the vortex of the revolution, where there were now 15,000 card-carrying Bolsheviks.

Few of these new party members were intellectuals or even understood the ideological conflicts that were always engrossing the leaders, but they were radical revolutionaries whom Lenin in his speech at the Tauride Palace had offered a rallying point. That they would accept his offer became evident very fast. A full conference of the city's party members gave Lenin's policy an almost blanket endorsement—despite the fact that their committee had rejected it. It was obvious that the "old guard"—veterans of *Iskra* and 1905 though still mostly only in their thirties—had not realized the way their own rank and file were thinking.

Also, Lenin had found two stalwart supporters in the

Kshesinskaya Mansion who, though not among the party leaders, were very important. Vladimir Nevsky and Nicholas Podvoisky ran the newly created Military Organization They were in charge of the Red Guards, the units of armed workers—taking their lead from the factory units set up in 1905 to fight the Black Hundreds—which had been created in March when the soldiers had given them rifles. And they controlled the party contact with the regiments and were in overall charge of agitators.

Both had been Social Democrats since before the 1903 split and had played militant roles in the 1905 uprising. Podvoisky was thirty-seven, a tall, bearded, rather handsome man whose pictures always reveal him as unsmiling and hard. Nevsky was older, a short, stocky man who was a brilliant orator and a skilled agitator. They were a good team. Podvoisky was the organization man, operating usually from a central desk in the Kshesinskaya Mansion, sending out orders to the agitators on little pink slips or passing urgent messages to the field leaders by phone. Nevsky was the spellbinder. Whenever there was trouble, whenever the local agitators were having difficulty, Nevsky would speed there by car to deploy his remarkable powers as a speaker.

The two men were extremist militants. Under Lenin's brilliant direction, they would rally many of the masses behind him. They would also bring him disaster, for they resisted his control when he ordered caution. They were independent, romantic revolutionaries who believed that the people, when they became angry and united, was quite capable of grasping power.

In mid-April, Nevsky and Podvoisky commanded only a few hundred agitators, and their methods were crude. The Red Guards—who, with their belted jackets, peaked workers caps and red armbands were to be so prominent a feature of the strike for power in November—were at the earliest stages of training and formation. The Bolshevik contacts within the regiments of the garrison had only just been established when the revelations about the Sealed Train had virtually destroyed them.

During those few days after Lenin's arrival, with the Kadet

processions howling insults about the party through the streets of the city, with their agitators facing angry hostility, the two militants felt a little lost. Lenin realized that their morale needed stiffening. Sending for Podvoisky, he told him the daily Kadet processions should be answered.

"Nikolai Ilyich," he said, according to Podvoisky's memoirs, "we've got to show the bourgeoisie that we have armed forces behind us, too. . . . It's vital that you bring out onto the streets some troops marching under Bolshevik slogans—even if it's only one company."

The order was not easy for Podvoisky to carry out, but there was one regiment in which Bolshevik influence was still strong. During the revolution, the First Machine Gun Regiment had marched into the city from their barracks at Oranienbaum, some thirty miles away, and refused to leave. "Counterrevolutionists might attack the Soviet," they had insisted. The Bolsheviks had arranged quarters for them in a hall in the Vyborg and organized daily victualing at the Fortress of Peter and Paul. So the regiment was in the party's debt.

Podvoisky organized a demonstration. It was very small—a few companies of machine gunners, backed up by several squads of party workers—and it was not too provocative. But at least armed men were marching on the city's streets under party banners.

Lenin did not leave all the action to his military commanders—and this is a measure of the desperate situation he faced. For whenever he could, Lenin would avoid being in the foreground in any kind of conflict. His instinctive habitat was in the background at the controls. He rarely spoke in the Soviet, Kamenev being the party's main spokesman. He was virtually never present among the demonstrators in the street battles.

However, when absolutely necessary, Lenin would expose himself.

On April 24, six days after his arrival in Russia, Lenin was in the editorial room of the *Pravda* office when a comrade rushed in with the news that the men of the Izmailovsky Regiment were at that moment holding a meeting on their parade ground. Incited by agitators, they had voted a resolution against him and declared that if they had the chance, they would give him a hostile reception.

Lenin put down his pen. "I'll go to them at once," he announced—according to Praskovya Kudelli, secretary to the *Pravda* office.

The others in the editorial room were appalled. "They'll tear you to pieces," someone said.

"No, they won't," Lenin said, and taking Zinoviev with him, he went to the parade ground. And they did not. Although he started speaking to the sound of angry yells, at the end of his speech two soldiers hoisted him onto their shoulders and carried him triumphantly around the parade ground. He returned to the *Pravda* office with a broad smile on his face. "As far as I can see, the comrades were mistaken about the mood of the masses of soldiers," he remarked as he sat down as his desk.

A few days later, he had another chance to address troops in the city. A delegation arrived at the Kshesinskaya Mansion from several thousand soldiers assembled on the parade ground of the Mikhailovsky Artillery Regiment and asked if Lenin would explain his journey through Germany. Lenin was in a conference, and for all his success with the Izmailovsky, the party officials who received the delegation were nervous for his safety. They sent Nevsky instead.

As soon as Nevsky mounted the rostrum, he realized he was facing trouble. The mood of the thousands of men was angry. The soldiers began to sing the revolutionary song "Victim of the Cause." Then they began to yell, "Let's have Lenin here! Let's have the traitors here!"

Nevsky was well seasoned in handling mass meetings, and he could sense that this one was about to erupt in a very ugly manner. He jumped down from the rostrum, intent on disappearing before it did. He felt a touch on his back. To his horror, he found Lenin standing there.

"Tell them that Lenin wants to speak," ordered the veteran agitator.

Nevsky began to argue, pointing out that the situation was

very dangerous indeed, but Lenin just pushed him toward the platform.

"I'm waiting," he said.

Nevsky clambered back onto the rostrum and began to say what Lenin had ordered, but he was interrupted by one of the men on the platform. "Comrades," he yelled, "Lenin is here."

The announcement was greeted by an angry roar from the crowd. "Vladimir Ilyich," wrote Nevsky, "discarded his overcoat and appeared on the platform . . . before the eyes of an armed mob of 3,000. . . . 'I am Lenin,' he began and a graveyard hush descended upon the mass. . . . In a simple, lucid, understandable way he exposed . . . the Provisional Government's policy of . . . predatory war."

When Lenin finished, there was complete silence among "the crowd standing there, a mute subdued force. A mad thought flashed into my mind. But suddenly . . . there was . . . a unanimous yell . . . that filled the parade ground and the entire mass surged toward the rostrum." Lenin was seized by the soldiers, carried shoulder high out of the parade ground alongside his car, which moved slowly beside him. When eventually they allowed him to get into it, the troops ran after it, shouting and cheering as it gathered speed.

Toward the end of April, Milyukov's campaign against Lenin grew in intensity. Every day there were new demonstrations in the streets by students, civil servants, regiments—parades demanding support for the Provisional Government to pursue the war and, of course, to arrest Lenin, the German agent who was calling for peace. The yelling crowd outside the Kshesinskaya Mansion grew ever more threatening.

At last, on April 30, two weeks after Lenin's arrival in Russia, came the horrifying climax to the campaign against him—a vivid and macabre denunciation of his pacifist views on the war. Thousands of the wounded from the city's military hospitals paraded—legless men hobbling on crutches, men with stubs for arms, men in bandages with disfigured faces, men who were so immobile they had to travel in trucks—crawled slowly along the Nevsky Prospect, and curled left into the long, straight Liteiny toward the Tauride Palace. Their banners called for "war to the end," included the now-inevitable "Down with Lenin" and insisted that "Our wounds demand victory."

At the Tauride Palace, some of the marchers went inside to demand that Lenin be arrested and exiled "back to Germany." Others stood up and harangued the crowd of mutilated men with speeches in which Lenin was the prime target.

The Soviet leaders, however—especially the Mensheviks— were growing anxious about the persecution, realizing what could lie behind it. The Menshevik leaders M. I. Skobelov and Irakli Tseretelli, who disapproved of Lenin quite as much as the maimed soldiers, went out into the square in front of the palace to defend him on the ground that he was not being given a fair hearing. They were shouted down with yells of "Lenin is a spy and provocateur."

That morning *Izvestia*, the official journal of the Soviet, attacked the "dark forces" that were exploiting Lenin, "who has given his whole life to the service of the working class" as a way of discrediting socialists in general. This was a preliminary to an assault on the Soviet, the newspaper declared, "after which they hope to revert to the old system."

The Soviet leaders were not the only ones to be concerned. In Berlin, Arthur Zimmermann sent a wire to his minister in Stockholm: "According to the telegraph agency in Petersburg there has been a demonstration of the wounded and the maimed, supposedly attended by over 50,000 people, directed against Lenin. . . . Request further details as soon as possible."

The next day Milyukov took the gamble that he had been working toward since Lenin's return. He sent a note to the Allied ambassadors which was intended to settle all discussion of Russia's war aims. These, he said, had not been weakened by the revolution. Russia was still determined to fight with its Allies for "those guarantees and sanctions which are necessary for the prevention of new bloody conflicts in the future." He was promising to run an imperialist war, not the defensive war that the Soviet had agreed to back.

It was a direct challenge to the Soviet, which he regarded as ineffective—a chamber of debaters, not men of action. If his move was successful, the Soviet would soon cease to exist.

Lenin, of course, was delighted, for Milyukov's actions supported everything he had been saying. "The cards are on the table . . ." he heralded in *Pravda*. "Short and clear. War to a decisive victory. The alliance with the British and French bankers has been declared sacred. . . . Fight—because we want the spoils. Die, tens of thousands of you every day—because 'we' . . . have not yet received our share of the loot!"

As Milyukov intended, the masses rose, almost as they had in March in protest against the Foreign Minister's note. By three o'clock in the afternoon, five regiments were on the march toward the center of the city. So, too, were men and women from the factories—tens of thousands of angry people who were, what is more, entirely proletariat.

In fact, the Bolsheviks did not promote the crisis, although there were Bolsheviks among the crowds and they probably provided the banners emblazoned "Down with Milyukov!"

The Soviet acted with surprising firmness. Its leaders met the long processions as they streamed into the city center and urged them to return home and trust their representatives in the Soviet to force the government to amend its policy.

The main processions did turn back, but the city continued to seethe all evening. For Milyukov did not want the crisis ended; he sought confrontation. Throughout the center of Petersburg, orators harangued groups of people, attacking Lenin, "sent from Germany to overthrow the great patriot Milyukov." The Kadet Party held a big parade in Mariinsky Square, and Milyukov, speaking from a balcony of the dark palace that Tsar Nicholas I had given to his daughter Maria, assured them that the government would "preserve the dignity and freedom of Great Russia."

At a Cabinet meeting within the palace, General Lavr Kornilov, the belligerent commander of the Petersburg garrison, assured the ministers that he could quickly crush any disturbance. Armored cars and Cossacks were standing by. That night Milyukov told the British ambassador: "The troops are ready to arrest Lenin. . . . The Government is just waiting for the right psychological moment. . . ."

Meanwhile, in the Kshesinskaya Mansion, Lenin and the Central Committee were facing a problem that was to confront it repeatedly. To what extent should it associate itself with an uncontrollable mob demonstration that it had not organized? Should it attempt to lead it—and accept the blame for it? On the other hand, could it as a party of the workers stand back from it?

Late that night Lenin's hand was forced. *Rech* and the right-wing papers published a scream of abuse, blaming the Bolsheviks for inciting the people and threatening civil war. A threat of civil war, of course, would justify retaliatory action—which was why Lenin was being so cautious.

The next morning action was forced on him. In leaflets, distributed throughout the city and in a front-page appeal in *Rech*, "all who stand for Russia and her freedom" were summoned onto the streets by the Kadets to support the Provisional Government.

It was a challenge that Lenin had to accept, even though he knew its dangers. By that night the Cossacks could well be charging. But in the face of the planned Kadet parade, following the workers' retreat the night before, he could not stand back any longer. The party called the workers of the city to an *organized* demonstration. Under the direction of Nevsky and Podvoisky, agitators hurried to the factories.

Lenin, leaning on his military studies in 1905, gave strict orders on tactics in a planning meeting in the mansion. Inevitably, the Nevsky Prospect would be the focus of the clash. Thus, as one worker column marched straight along the avenue, others should be moving simultaneously in streets on either side, thus forming a "three-pronged claw." By this technique, they could block attempts to attack them in the Nevsky from side streets.

By three o'clock in the afternoon an enormous Kadet procession was moving through the Nevsky—and long columns of workers were approaching from the industrial suburbs on the edge of Petersburg.

Lenin. January, 1918.

Zurich, Spiegelgasse 14. The house where Lenin lived from February, 1916, until April, 1917.

Krupskaya.

Lenin and Krupskaya in Stockholm on their way from Switzerland to Russia, April, 1917.

Lenin addressing a crowd at Finland Station (painting with Stalin "faked" in behind Lenin).

Inessa Armand.

Trotsky.

Kamenev.

Zinoviev. October, 1921.

Podvoisky.

Bonch-Bruevich.

Stalin.

Sverdlov.

NOVOSTI PRESS AGENCY

Lenin and Krupskaya after attending the session of the First All-Russia Congress on Education in Moscow. August 28, 1918.

NOVOSTI PRESS AGEN

Lenin making a speech in Red Square, Moscow. May 1, 1919.

The hut in Razliv where Lenin stayed in August, 1917.

Alexander Kerensky (left) in 1917 when he was Minister of War in the Provisional Government.

NOVOSTI PRESS AGENCY

RADIO TIMES, HILTON PICTURE LIBRA

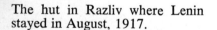

A breadline in Petrograd, 1917.

Soldiers of the Red Guard during the October days in Petrograd.

Russian Revolution, 1917.

Units of the Petrograd garrison march in support of the Revolution. May 4, 1917.

No troops were marching, for the Soviet had ordered them to remain within their barracks and to obey no orders—not even those of Kornilov, their commander—without its authority. In fact, at one moment news reached the Tauride Palace that Kornilov had ordered guns to be set up in Mariinsky Square, but the troops at the artillery barracks refused to comply.

As was inevitable, it was an afternoon of violent clashes—especially in the Nevsky, where the workers' column moved between pavements crowded with bourgeois. Near the intersection of the broad Sadovaya Prospect, there was shooting. All along the column there were sorties by Kadets.

Throughout the center of the city, trucks full of Kadets were stopping workers' columns, breaking them into small sections and ripping down their banners.

On Pushkinskaya, a side street off the Nevsky about a mile east of Sadovaya, one truck was even filled with girls. Here mounted men, who had been waiting, charged the halted column of 4,000 workers from the Rozhdestvensky District, heeling their horses into the marchers and grabbing their placards.

One procession which consisted entirely of women from a cotton mill was carrying a banner worded "Long live the international unity of workers." As they moved along the Nevsky, Kadets, lashing at the women marchers with sticks, fought their way through the column to rip down the offending slogan.

At one point on the Nevsky, students staged a mock trial of Lenin and the "German spies."

Late that afternoon the Soviet firmly stopped the crisis. Declaring that anyone "who called for armed demonstration" would be "a traitor to the revolution," it banned any street meetings or parades for two days. The Bolshevik Central Committee gave it full backing. The order, it decreed, "must be unconditionally obeyed by every member of our party."

The crisis was over, but in that mercurial city nothing was quite the same again. The Kadets claimed the day as their victory, but in fact Milyukov's gamble had failed. Within two weeks he was forced to resign—together with Alexander Guchkov, the hard-line war minister. General Kornilov, too, furious over the Soviet order to his troops, relinquished command of the garrison.

Prince Lvov reorganized his government, this time with six members of the Soviet among his ministers. In the new administration Alexander Kerensky, now elevated to the War Ministry, emerged as the rising star.

He had been popular with the masses ever since his spirited courtroom defense of the men accused of promoting the Lena Gold Fields strike in 1912. Now thirty-six years old, with close-cropped hair and handsome, youthful features, he was a dramatic orator, deploying techniques which included tears and even fits of fainting.

Everything about him was melodramatic. In public he wore a simple soldier's tunic and contrived an added effect by carrying his arm, which he had recently hurt, in a black sling from his neck. At home, he received visitors in a beautiful dressing gown.

Kerensky was neither so extreme nor so inflexible as Milyukov, but he, too, was a patriot. The vision of "Mother Russia" was present in all his speeches. He did not aspire to gain Constantinople, but he did want to reestablish the sense of national pride in his country that had been so frayed by the long conflict with Germany.

It was ironic that the May crisis should advance the fortunes of both the men from Simbirsk—for Lenin's position, too, was immensely strengthened. It is strange also that a single small Volga river town should have produced two men who saw themselves as selected by destiny to lead revolutionary Russia, yet were so different in ideology and personality. For there could hardly have been a greater contrast from Kerensky's high flamboyance and emotional oratory than Lenin's low-key intellectualism and hard, factual speaking style.

By May it had become clearly inevitable, as Lenin had known even when he was still in Zurich piecing together the situation in Russia from scraps of news in the press, that the final battle would be fought out between them.

During the crucial weeks that followed, they never met, but they were always highly conscious of each other. They recognized that they were the ultimate rivals, for Kerensky, in his new position, now commanded the army. He planned to achieve his ambitions for Russia through military victory, confident that his brilliance as an orator, his compelling personality could win over the troops and transform them into an efficient and successful army. He laid himself wide open to Lenin's charges in *Pravda* that he was a "Bonaparte."

Lenin, too, needed the army. Without its support he could never gain power, could never create a socialist society, could never ignite the world revolution. So while Kerensky embarked on a dazzling personal tour of the frontline troops, Lenin in *Pravda* urged them to fraternize and warned that their enemy at the rear was more of a danger than the enemy in front.

In May the conflict was muted and conducted at arm's length. Both leaders were engrossed with their immediate situations, but the positions were being established, the preparations made, for the first open clash.

For Lenin, the May Crisis crystallized the conflicts that had clouded events since his arrival in Russia three weeks before. Tens of thousands of workers had been organized and had marched as a class. The fact that few of those marchers had been Bolsheviks did not matter. Many of them had responded to the party's leadership, even though most were supporters of other Soviet parties. The sight of those long columns moving steadily through the streets had thrilled Lenin and, as he said later, "really opened my eyes for the first time to the true meaning and role of a popular uprising." Most important, though, was the fact that they had won the first clash with the counterrevolution—small in scale though it had been. Morale in the Kshesinskaya Mansion had soared.

The crisis had also ended Lenin's battle—at least this phase of the battle—with Kamenev and the party conservatives. An All-Russian Conference of the party—called to complete business that remained unfinished in April—endorsed Lenin's new policy and elected a new Central Committee on which he now had a majority who favored his policy. Apart from Zinoviev—always uncertain in his conflict, but voting so far for

Lenin—it was a majority of only one. Significantly, that "one" was Joseph Stalin, previously a staunch supporter of Kamenev on the right wing of the party. But Stalin had noted the change in the direction of the wind.

Sukhanov, in his role of observer and political commentator, could hardly believe that Lenin in only three weeks had succeeded in swinging the party behind him. "What the oldest Bolsheviks a month before had thought wild and absurd," he wrote, "had now become the official platform of the party that was hourly capturing more of the Russian proletariat."

Lenin now had his base of party unity. He could begin deploying the enormous resources he had behind him and exploiting his brilliant talent for promotion.

Chapter 11

FROM THE FRENCH WINDOWS of his office on the second floor of the Kshesinskaya Mansion, Lenin could see across the Neva the whole panorama of bourgeois Petersburg. It must have made him feel much like a military commander surveying a town he was besieging. For after that first week in May, Lenin was exactly in this position—and was so seen by his antagonists.[1]

He knew there was not much time. "Don't be complacent," he warned Nevsky and Podvoisky, who were justly proud of the events of May. "This was only a small swing to our side. . . . The bourgeoisie will now start preparing itself feverishly for the next clash. . . ."

Agitation and propaganda were Lenin's top priorities, and he drove his military leaders in an immense campaign to get the simple Bolshevik aims across to the ordinary Russian in the street. Even in April, before the May Crisis had made conditions easier, he had demanded an army of a thousand agitators who would gain access to the barracks and explain the party's policy to the troops. "They don't need long speeches," he said. "A long speech provokes many questions and in the end the soldier's attention wanders. . . . You do not need to say much. The soldier will understand in a very few words."

Then hostility against Lenin had been at its peak. Any Bolsheviks entering the barracks would have been beaten up. In any case, Podvoisky and Nevsky queried with wonder, where were all these agitators to come from?

"The sailors," Lenin had answered simply. "Bolshevik sailors. Send them to the barracks and tell them to say to the soldiers: 'You have a rifle and I have a rifle. You spill blood and I spill blood.' "

Lenin's plan was well conceived. Underlying it was the theory that if a man could be made to listen for a very few minutes, the sheer simple logic of the Bolshevik line would sway him. The whole concept of class war and class enemies—those who were smearing Lenin with the German accusation—must have great appeal to a soldier who until very recently had known the hard discipline of Tsar's officers.

The idea of using sailors was clever, too, for they had played a very prominent role in the March Revolution and were unlikely to be thrown out of the barracks without at least a hearing.

The navy, of course, was as angry about the revelations about the Sealed Train as the army, but the base at Kronstadt on the island of Kotlin, in the Gulf of Finland a few miles from the mouth of the Neva, was very radical, and young Theodor Raskolnikov had a substantial nucleus of loyal men he could rely on.

By the end of April several hundred sailors from Kronstadt were being given training in agitation in the Kshesinskaya Mansion by Podvoisky. These crude, illiterate men—peasants, most of them, who could barely write their names—were faced with the terrifying prospect of conducting intellectual argument.

"Can you talk about peace?" Podvoisky asked them when they voiced their doubts. Hesitantly they conceded that perhaps they could.

"Can you talk about land and who should own it? Can you talk about power and who should have the power and how the workers should take over control of production?"

By the time Podvoisky had finished their unaccustomed task seemed easy to them. If they were asked questions they could not answer, he instructed them, they were to tell the soldiers to choose a delegation and send it to the Kshesinskaya Mansion to talk to Comrade Lenin.

The sailors were sent off in groups, and before they left, Lenin spoke to them. "Until you reach a successful conclusion," he urged, "don't leave the barracks."

In May, as his sailors were promoting the party's message to the troops, Lenin mounted a big program to hammer the Bolshevik themes into the man in the city streets—by using groups of ordinary party workers, to set up discussions in public places.

"The party's peace policy," he urged, according to Podvoisky, "should be explained in every square, garden, avenue, street corner . . . from early morning until late at night." But agitators, he insisted, should never discuss more than three Bolshevik aims at any one time, for otherwise they would confuse their listeners.

At the Kshesinskaya Mansion itself a regimen of continuous propaganda was rigorously maintained. From the roof of a summer house at the bottom of the walled garden, where the Kronwerk Prospect joined the Bolshaya Dvoryanskaya Street, a Bolshevik orator was addressing a large crowd at all times. Each man spoke for half an hour and then would be replaced by another comrade. The party leaders, even Lenin, took their turn on the rota and became star attractions.

"You fools, babblers and idiots," Lenin would declare to the crowd from the summer house,[2] "do you believe that history is made in the salons, where highborn democrats fraternize with titled liberals. . . . History is made in the trenches where, under the foolish pressure of war madness, the soldier thrusts his bayonet into the officer's body and escapes to his home village to set fire to the manor house. . . ."

"I've been there twice . . ." the Countess Irina Skariatina wrote in her diary. "he is bald, terribly ugly, wears a crumpled old brown suit, speaks without any oratorical power, more like a college professor calmly delivering his daily lecture . . . yet what he says drives the people crazy . . . no, positively it is not the way this man speaks but what he says that electrifies his listeners more than any other orator I have ever heard—even more than Kerensky himself with all his splendid eloquence."

Soon Lenin was able to start using his new resources. A press bureau was set up under Vyacheslav Molotov, a militant who helped edit *Pravda*, and with "special funds" supplied by the

Central Committee, it set up ten new provincial papers. Within a few weeks, there were forty-one newspapers and journals being issued under the party's control throughout Russia. Twenty of them were published in minority languages. Many of them were given away free. In all, according to Professor Leonard Schapiro in his *Communist Party of the Soviet Union*, 1,500,000 copies of Bolshevik papers were distributed every week.

One of the most important of these new papers stemmed from an idea of Podvoisky's. Toward the end of April he had suggested to Lenin that the party start a special soldiers' newspaper that would be simpler than *Pravda*, which many of the troops found hard to understand.

Immediately Lenin saw its immense potential. Highly excited, he questioned Podvoisky. How had he got the idea? Had he discussed it with the troops? Did he know what they wanted in a newspaper?

"No other media of propaganda could have such impact," he said enthusiastically, "as a well-edited soldier's newspaper—but it must not be a paper for soldiers, or nothing will come of it. It must be a truly soldier's newspaper . . . with a focus on soldiers' special interests. . . . What they're talking about in the barracks. . . . If the soldiers themselves write in it, the paper will command readers."

In practice, *Soldatskaya Pravda* became the organ of the Bolshevik Military Organization. Both Nevsky and Podvoisky were on its editorial board, though most of the detail work was done by the two other board members, Zina Zinovieva and A. F. Ilyin-Genevsky, the soldier brother of Raskolnikov from Kronstadt. Although the formal office was the Kshesinskaya Mansion, Zina and Genevsky spent most of the time in a large office near the press. "Here we wrote articles," recalled Genevsky, "and prepared for publication the big batches of letters which arrived every day from the soldiers at the front and back home."

Part of the financing of the new paper came from the soldiers themselves—from collections in the barracks and at the front—but this was almost certainly more a promotional technique, designed to make the troops feel a sense of ownership, than a substantial source of finance. It was an integral part of Podvoisky's original proposal for the project as he outlined it in his meeting with Lenin.

Soon the idea of cementing close, if informal, links with the troops was developed. Part of the basement of the Kshesinskaya Mansion was converted into a soldiers' social club.

Meanwhile, the circulation of *Pravda* had soared to heights that made the old press on which it had been printed no longer adequate. At the end of May a jubilant Lenin proudly displayed the new press to the veteran Bolshevik Alexander Shotman. Since Shotman knew that the paper had been appealing for public funds, he wondered how the press had been financed, Lenin explained that the money had been contributed by the Finnish party, though the expense was certainly high for such a donor. Yet Shotman apparently did not question the source of the "special funds" that were financing the immense national propaganda effort that Molotov was directing.

Throughout May the Bolshevik campaign continued, with enormous impact at a whole range of levels. Lenin himself worked desperately hard. Even though he was editing *Pravda* and writing articles for it every day, he embarked on a strenuous speaking tour of the factories. He went to the giant Putilov works in the Narva, to the Nevsky shipyards, to the repair shops of the Nikolaevsky Railway and a whole range of engineering plants. Everywhere he was followed by trained agitators who, using skillful question-and-answer techniques, urged the workers to hold new elections for their delegates to the Soviet, which could be held at any time. Were their representatives in the Tauride Palace voting for peace, for worker control of factories, for power to the Soviet? If not, why not elect someone who would?

At the same time, Nevsky and Podvoisky were conducting a crash training program for Red Guards in the factories. Instructors, who had fought in 1905, were sent from the Kshesinskaya Mansion to train squads in riflery, formation fighting, drilling—and to recruit new men. The aim was to organize the guards into 400-man battalions of whom 360 carried arms. The eventual plan was for each battalion to have its own machine-gun section, communication corps, ambulance unit and armored car corps. These, though, were refinements of the future. In May there were not even enough rifles, and many guards had to drill with sticks.

At the front, too, Bolsheviks of the Military Organization exploited the gains of *Soldatskaya Pravda* which, with its soaring circulation, served as an outlet for the discontent of the troops in the trenches. Every week hundreds of letters arrived at the Kshesinskaya Mansion from the front. "Most of them," recorded Genevsky, were "written in a clumsy, often indecipherable hand writing by soldier correspondents [and] described the hardships that the soldiers had to undergo."

Every issue carried correspondence columns, but in addition, the staff tried to answer all the letters they did not publish.

As a result of this campaign, recorded Podvoisky, "the political education of the soldiers and worker masses . . . advanced in seven league boots!"

Meanwhile, as the party expanded under the dynamic leadership from the Kshesinskaya Mansion, Lenin had to settle many internal conflicts—especially among the local committees on which the party had been built. There was a struggle within the hierarchy of the Red Guards, the districts demanding autonomy for the units in their areas, and Lenin had to intervene to insist that control must be centralized in the Military Organization at party HQ, under the immediate orders of the Central Committee.

These were the early indications that Lenin faced a new dilemma: how to control an unwieldy, fast-growing party of people who had plenty of fervor but little intellect or understanding of practical revolution.

Lenin was alert to the dangers. When the Kronstadt Soviet suddenly voted to form an independent republic on the island under its own control—a kind of local grasping of control by the Soviet—a furious Lenin summoned Raskolnikov to Petersburg. "What have you done?" he demanded of the young midshipman. "How is it possible for you to do such a thing without consulting the Central Committee? This is a breaking of basic party discipline. For such things we're going to shoot people!"

When Raskolnikov explained that the proposal in the Kronstadt Soviet had not been made by the Bolsheviks but by delegates from other parties, Lenin snapped at him, "Then you should have laughed them out of it! You should have shown them that a declaration of Soviet power in Kronstadt alone, separate from the rest of Russia, was a Utopia, a clear absurdity! The Provisional Government will bring you to your knees!"

However, Lenin knew Raskolnikov's value to the party. Finishing his angry rebuke, he softened and held out his hand in almost friendly dismissal. "Instruct the Kronstadt comrades that never in future must they make so serious a decision without full consultation with the Central Committee."

At this stage in the party's development, the enthusiasm of keen militants like Raskolnikov was vital to Lenin's program, but he knew that the time would come very soon when his ability to control them would be crucial. To help him, he now had strong assistance at the center. Jacob Sverdlov, one of the party leaders, had taken over from Elena Stasova the ever-expanding post of secretary of the party. Elena was his principal assistant, and as before, Nadya seemed only to be tolerated in the secretariat.

Physically, Sverdlov appeared surprisingly frail and delicate. He was dark-haired and swarthy—"Black as tar," according to Trotsky—and wore steel-rimmed glasses over a thin, mournful face. He had a loud, booming voice that was strangely inconsistent with his slight body.

Sverdlov, who had been in exile in Siberia with Stalin when the revolution broke out, had only recently returned to Petersburg from a party assignment to the Urals.

He was a mere thirty-two, but like so many of the party leaders, he had been hardened by experience into a veteran since, while still a teen-ager, he had become a Bolshevik after the 1903 split.

Brisk and efficient, he was capable of working at such a pace that often his team of secretaries and assistants could not keep up with his output. He operated the party machine under tight control, insisting that all letters should be answered on the day of receipt and maintaining a record of all future party activities and the people assigned to them in a series of notebooks from which he tore the relevant page when each project was completed.

All day and through much of the night the corridors of the Kshesinskaya Mansion were crowded with workers waiting for instructions either from Sverdlov or one of his assistants in the Secretariat or from the Military Organization. Messengers constantly pushed their way through the thronged passageways either to bring information from the local committees or on their way to deliver instructions.

Lenin now had the support of an important new arrival in Petersburg. Leon Trotsky, his onetime protégé and later antagonist, had at last been released by the British in Halifax and welcomed at the Finland Station with a triumphant reception. The two men had lashed each other often enough in print and in speeches, but their destiny was now clearly together, for Lenin's new policy was close to the theory of continuous revolution that Trotsky had developed with Parvus. And the compromist attitude of the Mensheviks had killed Trotsky's dream of reuniting the Russian Social Democratic Party.

In a meeting in the *Pravda* office, organized by Kamenev, who was Trotsky's brother-in-law, Lenin invited the new arrival to join the party. Trotsky suggested he should not become a Bolshevik at once. He himself had a small party whose few members included several men of great quality such as Lenin's friend Anatol Lunacharsky, D. B. Ryazanov and Moses Uritsky—"a pleiade of brilliant generals without an army," as Trotsky's biographer Isaac Deutscher described them. To bring them all into the Bolshevik fold would take time. In the meanwhile, they would work closely with Lenin.

Another newcomer to the city was Julius Martov, Lenin's

erstwhile friend and bitter enemy in exile. Martov had long occupied roughly the same position among the Mensheviks as Lenin did among the Bolsheviks—a kind of undisputed intellectual architect—but he, too, was shocked by the party he found in Russia. He became isolated, surrounded only by a few faithful followers. Lenin invited him to join the Bolsheviks, but he declined. Perhaps he felt the rigidity of the party hierarchy would be too oppressive—which, after all, was what the quarrel in 1903 had been all about.

While Lenin's policy was being promoted with such effect through the regiments and the city streets and in ever-increasing number of newspapers throughout the nation, his main antagonist was also enjoying an enormous personal success. Since his appointment as Minister for War, Alexander Kerensky had been engaged on an elaborate speaking tour which was intended both to combat Lenin and to rally the nation. He visited troops at the front and toured the naval and military bases from Finland to the Black Sea. He attended mass meetings in Petersburg, Moscow and other cities.

"He spoke of freedom," recorded Sukhanov, "of the land, of the brotherhood of nations, and of the imminent glowing future of the country. He called upon the soldiers and citizens to . . . show themselves worthy of the great revolution."

The impression he created was dazzling. "Everywhere he was carried shoulder high and pelted with flowers. Everywhere scenes of unprecedented enthusiasm took place." Men tore their crosses of St. George from their breasts and flung them at his feet. Women stripped off their jewels and threw them onto the platforms from which he addressed them with such effect.

Even among the soldiers in the trenches, Kerensky was able to command an astonishing response. "Tens of thousands of fighting soldiers, at tremendous meetings, vowed to go into battle at the word of command and die for 'land and freedom,'" wrote Sukhanov.

In mid-May, while Kerensky was enjoying his triumph, the evidence that Lenin might have connections with the Germans seemed to develop dramatically. At headquarters at the front, he was shown a copy of the notes taken during the interrogation of a young Russian officer named Lieutenant Ermolenko, who had been taken prisoner by the Germans—and then released under strange circumstances.

Ermolenko claimed he had been freed on the condition he agree to become a spy for the Germans and agitate for a separate peace. The German intelligence officers had told him that Lenin was receiving German money and was working "to undermine the confidence of the Russian people in the government."

Ermolenko was a suspect character, and corroboration of his story was all but impossible. But one item in his statement conformed closely with the picture that the investigating committee of three ministers whom Lvov had appointed in April were already examining. The funds that Lenin was using, the young officer had been told, were being passed to Lenin by way of an official named Svendson in the German Legation in Stockholm.

Stockholm—where Jacob Fürstenberg, of course, lived and worked—was the focus of most of the conspiracy evidence relating to the German links to the Bolsheviks.

Even with Ermolenko, the evidence against Lenin was still not adequate to mount a prosecution, but the dossier was growing bigger. And there could be no doubt that the allegation by the German officers that Lenin was working to undermine popular support of the government was true. For there was no attempt to conceal this in the torrent of propaganda from the Kshesinskaya Mansion that urged the troops to fraternize with the enemy and exhorted workers in the factories to stop contributing to the fantastic profits that the capitalists were making out of their labor.

Under this barrage, it was not strange that anarchy and lawlessness increased. Marauding bands of troops roamed the countryside. Mutinies were frequent. Armed holdups became so regular in Petersburg that *Rech* compared the city with Texas and the Wild West. Factory after factory was closed down by frustrated managers as control broke down—for which they were accused by the Bolsheviks of using the "creeping lockout" as a weapon of counterrevolution.

And looming over the whole country—but particularly in the cities—was the threat of starvation. As the weeks went by, the breadlines grew longer. This was not Lenin's fault, but he exploited it. "Peace, bread, land" was the triple promise offered in the Bolshevik message that, the party insisted, would follow the transfer of power to the Soviet.

Kerensky's success on his tour astonished everyone who witnessed it, but—against a background of the continuous Bolshevik propaganda throughout a nation as large as Russia— its impact was geographically limited. He could not go everywhere—or remain to consolidate his personal victories.

Kerensky, of course, had his own government propaganda machine, and the Soviet was now working closely to support him in an effort to prevent the total collapse of the nation. Desperately they sought to establish order—which, of course, was what Lenin was working to prevent. For as long as there was growing chaos, he could continue to present "power to the Soviet" as a panacea. As long as people were discontented, they were more likely to obey the continuing calls of the party agitators to vote Bolsheviks into the Soviet. And the Bolshevik slogans had an obvious, simple appeal. Wake up! You are in a class war! You are being exploited in the factories and killed in the trenches to enrich the capitalists! Only when you, the working class, the people, take power through the Soviet will your miseries end.

To prevent a complete breakdown of army morale, Kerensky attempted to tighten discipline, restored the power to punish— including the death sentence, though it was not invoked—and warned the thousands of deserters to return to their units or face the consequences.

The Soviet supported him with a passionate appeal to the troops to ignore the insidious propaganda of the Bolsheviks. "Have we overthrown Nicholas to kneel before Wilhelm?"

demanded the manifesto. "Those who assure you that fraternization is the road to peace are leading you to your ruin. . . ."

Each move by the Soviet or the government was greeted by *Pravda* with a howl of mockery. Kerensky's "Declaration of Soldiers' Rights," which laid down the new rules of discipline, was pilloried as a "Declaration of Soldiers' Lack of Rights." On the Soviet appeal to the troops, Lenin taunted that the Mensheviks and the SR's had "sunk to the level of defending Russian Imperialism." When commissars were sent from Petersburg to give guidance to distant district Soviets that were trying to cope with local chaos, he warned that this was "a sure step toward the restoration of the monarchy."

The Bolsheviks were still very much a minority party, but they had a loud and beguiling voice. They were making steady progress.

In Berlin, Arthur Zimmermann was delighted with the results of his investment. "Secret reports," he noted on June 3, "show that the governments of the Entente countries continue to show great anxiety about Russia. . . . Lenin's peace propaganda is growing steadily stronger and his newspaper *Pravda* already prints 300,000 copies. Work in the armament factories is either at a standstill or has sunk to very low production figures . . . the supply of food to the towns and the army is suffering. There is therefore absolutely no possibility of the Entente receiving help from that quarter."

Already, the German High Command had grown confident enough to start transferring regiments from the Eastern line to the Western Front. For in the race with time that the war had now become, the crucial question was: Could Germany, with its all-out U-boat effort, cripple the Allies before America could deploy its massive aid of men and supplies?

The Allied governments understood the situation just as clearly as the men in Berlin. Their ambassadors were levering heavy pressure on Kerensky to mount an offensive to stiffen the German presence in the East—for their spring offensive in the West had failed—and demanded this as the price of a new war loan that Russia desperately needed. Kerensky was in favor of an offensive, for he believed that a military victory would provide the Russians with a boost to morale that was so lacking.

From every point of view, the army had to be persuaded to fight, and when Kerensky returned to Petersburg from his tour at the end of May, he believed he had achieved this aim—and he probably would have done so if it had not been for Lenin. The inevitable clash was growing closer every day, for while the Bolsheviks were winning gains among the workers, the middle classes were closing their ranks around Kerensky. By June the first battle was imminent. But before it occurred, as in the preliminary contests of ancient battles, the two men met personally in a public duel.

The occasion was the opening of the Congress of Soviets from all over Russia—convened primarily to take over the central role that until now had been carried by the Petersburg Soviet.* The 1,000 delegates who assembled in the Naval Cadet building on Vasilevsky Island formed a colorful polyglot gathering—"slant eyed tartars and fair haired cossacks," as reporter Albert Rhys Williams described them, "Russians big and little, Poles, Letts and Lithuanians—all tribes and tongues and costumes."

Lenin—"having left his underground cave for the light of day," Sukhanov commented sarcastically—made one of his rare appearances in public, sitting surrounded by his comrades at the back of the big auditorium.

*The Congress of Soviets was attended by delegates from district Soviets all over Russia, including, of course, the Petersburg Soviet. Until now, the Executive Committee of the Petersburg Soviet had been a kind of caretaker body that supervised the government. From June, a new permanent committee—the Central Executive Committee of the all-Russian Congress of Soviets—took over this responsibility, and the Petersburg Soviet became a district organization like the Moscow Soviet or the Kiev Soviet.

In fact, the most important members of the Executive Committee of the Petersburg Soviet were also members of the Central Executive Committee of the Congress of Soviets—so the same characters were usually involved with the future crises as had been in the past, even though the body they represented was sometimes different.

To avoid elaborate and confusing description of the two Soviet bodies, references to the "Soviet" on future pages refer to the Congress of Soviets unless I specifically state otherwise.

The tall elegant Irakli Tseretelli, who had returned to Petersburg from years in Siberia to become the outstanding personality among the Menshevik leaders, used the occasion to attack the Bolsheviks. Accusing them of gross irresponsibility, he asserted, "Only by pooling our efforts can we achieve democracy and victory. Today Russia has no political party which would say: 'Give us power, go yourselves and we will take your place.' "

At that moment, a voice rang out from the back of the big hall. "There *is* such a party!" To the astonishment of his comrades who knew his careful reticence in public, Lenin had stood up. "There *is* such a party," he repeated. "It is the Bolshevik Party!"

The shocked silence was broken by a wave of laughter from the big audience. To men from outside Petersburg, the idea that so small a party as the Bolsheviks—which only had 105 voting delegates among them—could form a government seemed absurd. By contrast, the other parties were represented by 822 delegates.

They laughed again when Lenin mounted the platform to demand that the Soviet should at once seize power from the Provisional Government.

"Laugh all you want," he challenged them. "Our program in relation to the economic crisis is this—to demand the publication of all those unheard-of profits, reaching from five hundred to eight hundred percent, which the capitalists make on war orders; to arrest fifty or one hundred of the more important capitalists and in this way to break all the threads of intrigue . . . to announce to all nations, separate from their governments, that we regard all capitalists—French, English, all—as robbers. . . ."

"You've lived through 1905 and 1917," he challenged. "You know that revolution is not made to order; that in other countries it was brought about through bloody uprisings, but in Russia there is no group or class that could oppose the power of the Soviets."

Deliberately, Kerensky—present not as War Minister, but as

a member of the Petersburg Soviet—took up the challenge. The two men had a background and a hometown in common, but they had not seen each other for years.

Early in 1914, Kerensky had met one of Lenin's sisters on a Volga steamboat. "Don't worry," he had told her, "you will soon see him again. There will be war, and it will open to him the road to Russia."

It is doubtful if, when he made that prediction on the riverboat, Kerensky could have foreseen that in only three years' time he would be engaged in a bitter struggle with Lenin for the leadership of Russia.

He stood before that big audience, stiffly upright, his arm in the black sling from his neck. "You've been told of 1792 and 1905," he said. "How did 1792 end in France? It ended in the fall of the republic and the rise of a dictator. How did 1905 end? With the triumph of reaction. . . .

"The problem for the Russian socialist parties is . . . to prevent such an end as was in France . . . to see to it that our comrades who have been let out of prison do not return there; that Comrade Lenin . . . may have the opportunity to speak here again and not be obliged to flee back to Switzerland. . . ."

Through the roar of applause, Kerensky began to mock his adversary. "We have been told," he asserted sarcastically, "that we should not fight with words . . . but show by deeds that we are fighting against capitalism. What means are recommended for this fight?" Kerensky paused carefully, his eyes scanning his audience, and then gave the scornful answer:"To arrest Russian capitalists." And again a great wave of laughter swept through the delegates.

"Comrades," Kerensky went on, "I'm not a Marxist, but I have the highest respect for Marx . . . but Marxism never taught such childlike and primitive means. . . . Socialism nowhere recommends the settling of questions . . . by arresting people, as is done by Asiatic despots. . . . You Bolsheviks recommend childish prescriptions—'arrest, kill, destroy!' What are you, socialists or the police of the old regime!"

Amid the uproar, Lenin was on his feet, flushed with anger.

"Call him to order!" he shouted at the chairman on the platform.

But Kerensky continued as soon as he could make himself heard. "You recommend that we follow the road of the French Revolution of 1789. You recommend the way to further disorganization of the country. . . . When you, in alliance with reaction, destroy our power, then you will have a real dictator. It is our duty, the duty of Russian democracy, to say: 'Don't repeat the historic mistakes.' "

Lenin did not wait to hear the end of the speech—so Kerensky recorded—but "picking up his briefcase, with his head bent, he stole out of the hall, almost unnoticed."

Kerensky believed he had won the contest. Lenin had retired from the field and the delegates to the Soviet did as Kerensky urged them and rejected all the important Bolshevik resolutions by large majorities.

No doubt he was pleased, too, by the progress in the secret investigation of his antagonist's links with the enemy. Only a few days before their clash in the Congress, Pereverzev, who was now Minister of Justice, had sent for Colonel Nikitin, the chief of counterintelligence who had tried to prevent Lenin and the Sealed Train party from being admitted to Russia.

"I have been informed by a member of the Bolshevik Central Committee," the minister told the colonel, "that Lenin is communicating with Parvus by means of letters carried by special couriers."

Nikitin acted promptly. His men searched anyone suspicious passing through the Finnish frontier post at Beloostrov. Within a week they had found a letter to Parvus concealed on a Bolshevik on his way through Finland. It asked for the delivery of as much "material" as possible—material being assumed by Nikitin to mean money. Handwriting experts examined it and declared it was written by Lenin.

Actually it is unlikely Lenin would ever have written directly to Parvus, so the experts were almost certainly wrong. But to the investigators at the time it seemed a highly valuable piece of evidence for the case they were preparing. Nikitin's men began shadowing all the Bolshevik leaders.

Meanwhile, despite Kerensky's satisfaction with the results in the Congress of Soviets, Lenin's campaign was constantly gaining ground among the workers. Gregory Zinoviev had recently organized a conference of representatives of all the Petersburg factories and trade unions. More than three-quarters of the delegates had voted the Bolshevik line and agreed to set up a permanent center in the city to coordinate action in the industrial plants. Steadily, too, the number of seats the Bolsheviks held in the Petersburg Soviet was increasing. Although, as Sukhanov wrote, "they still had no majority, it would come . . . there was no doubt of that."

It was against this setting that Lenin agreed to promote a clash between the forces at his disposal and those of the opposition. On Wednesday, June 19, two days after his duel with Kerensky, Lenin presided at a big meeting in the Kshesinskaya Mansion which was attended by the entire Bolshevik leadership: the Central Committee, the heads of the Military Organization, the Petersburg City District Committee and one or two others, such as Nadya, who, disillusioned at last by her treatment in the secretariat, was now a member of the district Duma—the local council—in the Vyborg.

Podvoisky and Nevsky had called the meeting because the Military Organization was under heavy pressure from some of the troops in the garrison—now in danger of being transferred to the front—to mount a mass demonstration against the offensive that Kerensky was preparing.

When the idea of a demonstration had been first mooted two weeks before, Lenin had vetoed it, holding it was far too soon. Now Podvoisky insisted that the party should reconsider. Several regiments were threatening to go out onto the streets on their own unless the party led them—and the anarchists were urging them to do so. The anarchists constituted two small parties that had their headquarters in the Vyborg and were as extreme and vocal as the Bolsheviks but differed from them on one important aspect. They wanted no state apparatus at all, no power in any real sense in government.

Podvoisky and his military comrades believed it vital the party should accept the leadership of the demonstration. For Lenin, since his clash with Kerensky, there were now arguments in favor of it. The sight of thousands of troops marching under Bolshevik banners would certainly show the provincial delegates to the congress how powerful the party was in the capital. Those who had mocked him should be taught some realities. Also, as Lenin admitted later, it was essential that Kerensky's offensive be sabotaged.

On the other hand, the danger of the demonstration's escalating into violence that the party could not control was clearly very great. Many of the militants in the MO and the Petersburg Committee wanted just this to happen, but Lenin knew that the party's support was not yet adequate for any real strike for power.

The Central Committee, which had to make the final decision, split into the two usual groups. Kamenev, like a friendly bear, wagged his head and insisted that the party's following was still too small. "To act now would be rash and premature." Zinoviev supported his friend, asserting in his strange high-pitched voice that the party would be "risking its life."

Sverdlov, who was now the key Lenin man on the Central Committee, was fully behind the military leaders. So was Stalin, displaying his new militant left-wing role.

Even Nadya joined in at one point when the issue of how the demonstration could be kept peaceful was being discussed. "It won't be peaceful," she said flatly, "so perhaps it shouldn't be staged."

At last Lenin took command—and did nothing, as he so often did when the risks were high and he was not certain of success. Probably he was wise, for while his military leaders were full of enthusiasm, their ideas as to how to organize a demonstration were limited. They never truly knew who was going to respond to their impassioned calls for action. When Lenin finally ordered

Nevsky to conduct a survey of the troops who would definitely march with them, the militant was irritated. "This seemed insignificant to me . . ." he admitted later. "We will start a demonstration, and that will be enough."

It was not enough for Lenin. They would meet again on Friday in two days' time, he said, and make the final decision when Nevsky had supplied the information on which to base it.

In fact, events overtook the time schedule—events that had nothing to do with the Bolsheviks. The government, provoked at last by militant acts by the anarchists, suddenly surrounded their headquarters—a villa in the Vyborg—and gave them twenty-four hours to vacate the premises. The anarchists appealed for help to the Vyborg workers, and by Thursday evening twenty-eight factories in the district were on strike.

It provided Lenin with the element that had been lacking in the proposals of his military leaders—emotion among the workers. Hurriedly, he advanced his scheduled meeting by twenty-four hours to that night—and invited representatives from the factories and the regiments to attend it.

That evening the Central Committee formally authorized a *peaceful* demonstration to start at 2 P.M. on Saturday—in less than two days' time. News of it was to be kept secret as long as possible. The Bolshevik press would not even mention it until Saturday morning, the day it was to be staged.

All that night, in the Kshesinskaya Mansion, the Military Organization was at work planning the demonstration—dispatching orders to its members in the barracks and in the Red Guard contingents in the factories. So, too, was the Petersburg Committee, operating through the party hierarchy in the districts.

The Central Committee orders were that the demonstration was to be peaceful—which politically was sound—but the planners in the Kshesinskaya Mansion that night were preparing for violence. The columns of workers were to be escorted by military units at the head and tail of the processions as well as at strategic intervals between. The massive march was to begin from three starting points, one of which was the Field of Mars.

183]

On Friday morning, agitators from the mansion fanned out through the regiments and the factories of the city. Leaflets, written by Stalin, were distributed. Mass appeals were set up in type for the next day's issues of *Pravda* and, especially, *Soldatskaya Pravda*, which laid down the directions for marching.

By Friday afternoon news of the plans had reached the Petersburg Soviet in the Tauride Palace—and caused acute alarm. Promptly, the Executive Committee banned the demonstration and appealed to the Congress of Soviets to add its authority to its own ruling.

The government issued an ominous warning that any use of force would be countered with all "the power at its disposal"—which, to the men who had been up all night in party headquarters, sounded as though Kerensky were hoping for an excuse for action.

On that light evening—when there would be no darkness for, in that northern latitude, it was the season of the "white nights"—Lenin waited in the Kshesinskaya Mansion as reports were brought in constantly from the districts by messengers on horses or motorcycles. He was far from the activity, giving no orders—waiting as the party executives carried out the duties they had been allocated. It was soon clear that the situation was developing well. The response to the party's appeal appeared to be strong. Tomorrow thousands would be marching under Bolshevik slogans—*and* they would be armed. Even the workers' units had rejected every suggestion that they should demonstrate without rifles.

Once a rumor came into the mansion that Kerensky had summoned troops to the city to stop the marchers. But as soon as the War Minister heard of it, he issued an immediate denial. He was relying on political pressure—and it was formidable.

At eight-thirty in the evening, a harassed Kamenev arrived in the mansion and demanded that Lenin call a meeting to consider cancellation. In the Congress of Soviets, he reported, feelings against the Bolsheviks were too strong to ignore. But at the meeting of sixteen party leaders which was hurriedly convened, Kamenev won no support, apart from Nogin, the conservative. Even Zinoviev deserted him. The demonstration was still on.

At the congress, as soon as Chkheidze learned that the Bolsheviks were going ahead with their plans, he interrupted the debate to demand the floor. Dramatically he warned the congress that unless it took decisive action, the next day "could be fatal."

Responding to this appeal, the congress barred all demonstrations in the city for three days and appealed to the masses to ignore the Bolshevik call to the streets. "Do not do what you are called upon to do. . . . Those who call you cannot but know that your peaceful demonstration could develop into bloody disorder. . . ." To back up their appeal, delegates agreed to split into small groups and tour the factories and regiments all night to urge them to obey the order of the congress.

At two o'clock in the morning Lenin was still at the crowded Kshesinskaya Mansion assessing the developments when once again Kamenev arrived, with Nogin and Zinoviev, to plead with him, even at this late hour, to prevent what he was convinced could only be a disastrous day for the party. The Bolsheviks were even in danger of expulsion from the Soviets. This would mean political isolation and make nonsense of the central element of Lenin's strategy.

The order from the congress *not* to demonstrate also put Lenin in a difficult position. How could he ignore an order from the Soviet when he was campaigning for it to be given power?

Wearily five members of the Central Committee—all who were then in the mansion—sat down for the second time in six hours to consider a decision to cancel. It was still light, of course—that strange endless evening light—and through the french windows they could see the trees of the park and the golden spire of the Fortress of Peter and Paul.

All of them knew that the repercussions of canceling at this late hour would be enormous. They might lose control, be discredited. Almost certainly, they would relinquish some of the recent gains they had made in the sympathies of the masses.

Lenin especially knew that the flame of revolutionary feeling he had been so carefully fanning would not just subside. There would be frustration, discontent, anger.

On the other hand, the dangers of continuing could be even greater.

Kamenev and Nogin, of course, had no doubts. They had not had doubts from the start. Firmly they voted to cancel. Zinoviev, changing his mind yet again, voted with them.

It now made no difference what Lenin and Sverdlov did, for the majority had spoken. But Lenin appeared, almost instinctively, to be avoiding the issue, as though he could not bring himself to vote formally for a backdown from an action to which he had tacitly agreed.

When it was his turn to speak, he hesitated, then grimly he said, "I abstain."

The four men looked at Sverdlov. He appeared even smaller, more mournful, than usual. He followed Lenin's example. "I abstain," he mumbled.

At the last minute, the party had bowed to the Congress of Soviets, but the crucial issue now was: Would the masses obey the party?

Comrades were dispatched to the barracks, to district party headquarters, to the factories. Telephone calls ordered *Pravda* and *Soldatskaya Pravda* to change their front-page calls to the streets to cancellation orders.

The order was greeted by impotent fury. In some factories, Bolsheviks tore up their party cards in disgust. Many of the touring delegates from the congress were angrily abused. The radical First Machine Gun Regiment insisted that they would go out anyway in a few days and "crush the bourgeoisie." At Kronstadt it required "inhuman measures" by the Bolshevik leaders to prevent thousands of furious sailors from invading the city—as indeed they were being urged to by the anarchists.

There were signs of mutiny within *Soldatskaya Pravda*, run as it was by the MO, for copies were still being distributed two hours after the cancellation order with the original summons unchanged. But the staff was at last brought to heel.

Lenin gained some solace from the fact that the order was obeyed, but the cancellation caused so traumatic a crisis within the party that he had to make a personal attempt to appease his angry critics. He appeared on Monday at a joint meeting of the Central and Petersburg Committees almost in the role of a delinquent. The atmosphere was icy.

"Your resentment," he told them simply in his guttural voice, "is completely justified, but, in the face of the order of the Congress of Soviets, the Central Committee had no alternative." He pleaded that news of an impending attack by the counterrevolution was one reason for the cancellation, though there is no evidence of this. "Even in simple warfare," he explained, "it happens that scheduled offensives must be cancelled."

His speech made little impact on his angry militants. Comrade after comrade stood up to attack the late-night decision to cancel, coldly reminding him that the Soviet veto and the threat of attack by the counterrevolution had been fully considered at the planning stage.

The decision was "hysterical," "hasty," "a political mistake," revealing "intolerable wavering."

In the sequence of events in which the Bolsheviks were now enmeshed, this was a crucial confrontation. The left-wingers believed that Lenin had been wrong and even weak. Their leader, who had so transformed the party and its prospects in only three months, had been exposed as fallible. As a result, he had lost some of his stature, a degree of their faith. Almost certainly this was the main reason why he was unable to control the party at the next crisis.

Just temporarily, he was able to divert some of their resentment into other channels. The Soviet leaders, badly frightened by the realization that the city had moved to the brink of conflict, had reacted in fury against the Bolsheviks. But they realized that a release was needed for the tensions of the city, and they decided to organize a demonstration of their own, open to all parties, to demonstrate the unity of the "revolutionary democracy."

Lenin saw this as a great opportunity. The Bolsheviks could now mount the canceled demonstration under the cover of official Soviet respectability. After his savaging, he did not face the militants himself but sent Zinoviev to deploy his skill "to bewitch," as Trotsky called it. They grumbled at him but at last agreed to obey the Soviet order to participate.

July 1—a brilliant day with a clear blue sky and the sun glistening off the golden cupulas and spires of the city—was a fantastic success for the party and, superficially at any rate, made up for the humiliations of a week before. Marchers from regiment after regiment, factory after factory, paraded past the saluting base on the tomb of the martyrs in the Field of Mars under red and gold Bolshevik banners: "All power to the Soviets! Down with the ten capitalist ministers! Down with the War?"

"Soldiers in drab and olive," recorded one eyewitness, "horsemen in blue and gold, white-bloused sailors from the fleet, black-bloused workmen from the mills, girls in varicolored waists surging through the main arteries of the city, on each marcher a streamer, a flower, a ribbon of red; scarlet kerchiefs around the women's heads, red rubashkas on the men. Above . . . tossed a thousand banners of red.

"As this human river flowed, it sang , . . the spontaneous outpouring of a people's soul. Someone would strike up a revolutionary hymn; the deep resonant voices of the soldiers would lift the refrain, joined by the plaintive voices of the working women; the hymn would rise, and fall, and die away; then down the line, it would burst forth again—the whole street singing in harmony."

"Here and there," recorded Sukhanov, "the chain of Bolshevik flags and columns was interrupted by specifically Social Revolutionary and official Soviet slogans. But they were submerged in the mass; they seemed to be exceptions. Again and again, like the unchanging summons of the very depths of the revolutionary capital, like fate itself . . . there advanced toward us: "All power to the Soviets! Down with the ten capitalist ministers![3]

As each contingent marched silently by the tomb, they lowered their fluttering banners in tribute to the dead and then raised them again as they continued toward Sadovaya Prospect.

One of the Menshevik leaders standing on the saluting base sneered: "The Bolsheviks distributed ready-made posters and they are carrying them without understanding anything."

Lenin, who was standing near him, winked one eye and asked with a smile, "Why aren't they marching along with your slogans? After all you have the power!" But his enjoyment in the day's achievement was marred by its dangers. Could he hold the people back until the moment was favorable?

That night, in the dining room of the Elizarov apartment on Shirokaya Street, the Central Committee and some of the MO leaders sat around the table on which Maria had placed a vase of red carnations that had been handed to Lenin as a bouquet during the demonstration. They reviewed the day's events, and Podvoisky, bearded, sallow, grim Podvoisky, warned them of what was imminent. "After this," he insisted, "the workers and soldiers will seek to stage an uprising."

Lenin knew his military leader was right but insisted that he must do what he could to curb them. "At this stage," he said, "a rebellion would be doomed to defeat because the workers in Petersburg would receive no support from the armies at the front or from the people in the provinces. . . .

"Nikolai Ilyich," he told Podvoisky. "This must be explained to the masses. . . . Forces must be alerted for a decisive assault but the party will indicate the time. . . ."

Chapter 12

THAT EVENING, AS LENIN was talking to the party leaders in the apartment in Shirokaya Street, Alexander Kerensky was at army headquarters at the front, considering the reports from the forward units of the Russian Army.[1]

At dawn that morning the offensive on which he was relying to rally Russia and check the Bolshevik threat had been launched.

The early reports were encouraging. The enemy line had broken at two points. Ten thousand German prisoners had been captured. Russian soldiers were attacking the German enemy in front of them and not—as urged repeatedly by Lenin's soldiers' press—"the class enemy at the rear."

For two days, the Seventh Army advanced, pushing the Germans back toward Berezhany. Then the momentum slowed; the forward movement ground to a halt. Morale slumped, even though special "shock battalions" had been carefully placed in the line, even though Kerensky had toured the regiments before the attack, performing his special magic.

Three days later, farther to the south, another Russian army attacked the Austrians, took the ancient town of Halicz and pushed on toward Kalush—and again, like their comrades to the north, failed to maintain the offensive.

In Petersburg, however, news of the early advances was greeted with rapture by the bourgeois classes. Once more Kadet processions marched in the Nevsky Prospect with banners calling the nation to rally to protect "Mother Russia." Orators renewed their attack on Lenin and his alliance with the Germans.

This time no confrontations with the Kadets were planned

from the Kshesinskaya Mansion, where Lenin faced trouble enough. The reality of the offensive had caused an angry upsurge of feelings in the barracks. A stream of demands arrived from regimental committees demanding action.

Soldiers of the 180th Reserve Regiment demanded of one Bolshevik agitator: "What are they doing there, fast asleep, in Kshesinskaya's palace? Come on, let's kick out Kerensky!"

The most serious challenge to Lenin came from the basement of the party headquarters where Military Organization men from all over Russia were in conference. Representing 30,000 Bolshevik soldiers—agitators in an already demoralized army— they were confident they could mount an immediate revolution.

So militant were they that Podvoisky sent an emergency call to Lenin to address them—and he lost no time answering the summons. "One wrong move on our part can wreck every- thing . . ." he told them. "If we were able to seize power, it is naïve to think that, having taken it, we would be able to hold it. . . . Events should not be anticipated. Time is on our side."

He prevented an immediate conflagration, but his listeners did not really want to listen to calls for delay. "It is necessary to look truth in the eye . . ." insisted one. "Believe me, the front will support us. At the front the mood is not Bolshevik; no, there the spirit is antiwar. And that tells all."

In another part of the mansion the Petersburg Committee was in session—and its impatient, critical mood was similar to that of the military men. A strike in the Putilov factory in the Narva had been checked with enormous difficulty to comply with party orders.

There were now signs of a disturbing new danger. In some areas, the apparent success of the offensive was causing a swing against the party. Patriotism—that seductive appeal to Russian nationalism against which, even in exile, Lenin had been forced to be so alert—had begun to emerge.

It provided an urgent reason to take action now before the movement spread and several disgruntled speakers, with whom the cancellation of the demonstration ten days before still rankled, attacked "the lack of leadership" at the top. One urged that the party should give the Soviet an ultimatum: Take power or else.

Agitators from the Vyborg grumbled about being "fire hoses," damping down the embers of rebellion which, under previous party orders, they had helped ignite.

Lenin did his utmost to dampen the emotional outpouring. In an article in *Pravda* that carried just a hint of desperation, he declared, "We understand your bitterness, we understand the excitement of the Petersburg workers, but we say to them: 'Comrades, an immediate attack would be inexpedient.' "

Kamenev—for once lined up with Lenin—made a similar appeal in *Pravda* the next day under the headline NOT SO SIMPLE COMRADES insisting that "sympathy" for the party was not enough.

By contrast, on the same day *Soldatskaya Pravda* ran an emotional article which reflected the erosion of Lenin's authority. "Comrades," it declared, "enough of sacrificing ourselves for the welfare of the bourgeoisie. . . . Wake up whoever is asleep. Be ready at any minute."

The mansion was burning with rebellion against Lenin. It was a rebellion that stemmed directly from the propaganda techniques by which his big German resources had enabled him to promote so effectively those simple themes that were reiterated day and night across Russia. It is interesting to consider whether Lenin, as he rethought his plans in the Sealed Train, possibly after meeting top German officials in Berlin, had considered the dangers that might lie in overpromotion.

Certainly, as he tried desperately to control the party from his corner room on the second floor of the mansion, he knew how delicate was the issue of timing. Too many of the masses were "wavering" but still supporting the two big parties in the Soviet. If Kerensky's offensive failed, the faith of these Russians would break, and there would be a massive swing to the Bolsheviks. That would be the moment for aggressive action by the party.

Meanwhile, the government prosecutors had made what they believed was enormous progress with their case against Lenin.

On July 4, the day that Lenin's appeal for restraint was published in *Pravda*, Colonel Nikitin received a visitor in his new offices on the Voskrenskaya Quay beside the Neva. Captain Pierre Laurent, military attaché to the French Embassy, handed the colonel what he regarded as final and convincing proof that Lenin and the Bolsheviks were using German money.

Both the French and the British clearly believed that the government was being far too careful in its approach to Lenin's arrest. Laurent, whose French agents had achieved more than Nikitin's, began applying pressure.

Laurent's evidence concerned a woman named Eugenia Sumenson who lived in the nearby suburb of Pavlovsk. Nikitin already had her under surveillance, and as a lead, she seemed enormously important. During the last few weeks, she had drawn 800,000 rubles from an account in the Siberian Bank—an astonishing figure for a "demimondaine," as Nikitin called her, living in a fairly modest way. There were still 180,000 rubles in her account. Bolsheviks had been noted among her friends— especially the Polish Bolshevik lawyer Mecheslav Kozlovsky, who was suspected of being the party's main channel to German funds.

Pierre Laurent now handed Nikitin a series of telegrams that he had intercepted between Eugenia Sumenson and Jacob Fürstenberg in Stockholm. Though coded, they seemed damning evidence. One, for example, from her read: "Nestle not sent flour. Agitate." Another from Fürstenberg to Petersburg was worded: "Cable what funds in your hands—Nestle."

Considering the large sums that Eugenia Sumenson was handling, these telegrams seemed to Nikitin certainly to justify prosecution. The fact that she worked for the firm that was Petersburg correspondent of the company part owned by Parvus and run by Fürstenberg—which could, of course, provide a legitimate commercial reason for the transfer of funds—only increased Nikitin's certainty that this was at least one way that Lenin was financing his campaign.

However, when Nikitin requested permission to prosecute, he was ordered not to take action for the time being. The reason was that Pereverzev had received an important tip, presumably from his high contact in the Kshesinskaya Mansion. Jacob Fürstenberg was coming to Petersburg. He would cross the border around July 18 and would be carrying documents that would provide conclusive proof for the case against Lenin.

In fact, it is highly unlikely that Fürstenberg, experienced as he was, would be so naïve as to carry incriminating evidence through a frontier post where a search of his person was probable. But since he was so central a figure in the network of evidence, it was clearly desirable that he be arrested and interrogated even if no documents were found on him. All action was therefore suspended until July 18. The frontier officers were warned to be on the alert.

Suddenly, on July 12, Lenin decided to take a vacation. It was a last-minute decision and, in light of the explosive situation within the city, quite astonishing. His control of the party had been weakened. Feelings among the troops were so intense that there was open talk of an imminent rising, yet it was vital that they be held back until the failure of Kerensky's offensive was an undeniable fact.

Still, Lenin chose this moment, when the situation was more critical than it had been at any moment since his return to Russia, to leave the city.

According to his letters, he was unwell. The pressure of the past three months had been immense. He was tormented by fierce headaches and severe stomach trouble. He could eat little. His nights were restless and marked by acute insomnia. His sisters, worried by the danger that he would have a nervous breakdown, had been begging him to take a few days of rest in the country.

Admittedly, his health offered a plausible reason for Lenin's leaving the city, but for him to do so was completely out of character. He had experienced long periods of crisis before, and each time his health had suffered. But he had survived them. Almost certainly other factors were involved, factors which must be considered in the light of subsequent events.

Nadya seems to have been with him little at this time. His

sisters, working as they did for *Pravda*, saw much more of him. It appears that Nadya had buried herself in her work at the Vyborg, perhaps giving up the unequal struggle in the Elizarov apartment over who should be the guardian of her husband's health. Elena Stasova recorded that at one point, when Lenin stayed with her for a few days, it was Maria, rather than Nadya, who gave her detailed instructions on his diet.

And it was with Maria, not Nadya, that Lenin traveled by train on July 12 to visit Vladimir Bonch-Bruevich's dacha in the village of Neyvola on Finland's Karelian Isthmus. They left the train at Mustiamiaki and cautiously, to mislead police agents, took a droshky to the home of Demyan Bedny, a celebrated poet who lived in Neyvola. From there, they walked.

The Bonch-Brueviches were not expecting them, though they had often invited Lenin to the dacha. They were surprised, therefore, when Demyan Bedny, a burly, jovial character with thick ginger hair, "clambered up the rickety stairs of the balcony," as Bonch recorded, "and said: 'Look who I've brought you.' "

Bonch and his wife, Vera, had been among the twenty-two people who had formed the nucleus of Lenin's Bolshevik faction in Geneva after the split of 1903. Ever since they had been staunch supporters, which was perhaps why he now chose their invitation from the many that had been proffered to him.

They sat on the balcony late in the fine, misty evenings and listened to the crickets. During the day Lenin rested on a rug underneath the shade of Bonch's lilac trees. Sometimes, he read books—nothing political, mainly novels in English. He went for walks with Maria beside the nearby lake. He bathed with Bonch and, though "a magnificent swimmer," caused his host concern by swimming "far far out."

The lake was deep, and Bonch warned him of the cold currents that created whirlpools, but Lenin laughed. "People drown, you say?" he called out.

"Yes, they drown," answered Bonch, "and not long ago."

"Well, I'm not going to drown," answered Lenin, disappearing under the water "like a dolphin." He swam inshore, stood up in shallow water waist high, shook his head and smoothed back his hair with his hands. "It's wonderful here," he shouted. "Wonderful." This exuberant activity also suggests that his ill health can hardly have been serious enough for him to leave the city in crisis.

Some of the local fishermen, who knew about the currents, asked Bonch about his bold friend. "He's a sailor from the Baltic fleet," Bonch told them. "A relative of mine."

At Neyvola, Lenin slept well, helped by a green sedative liquid that Vera Mikhailovna insisted he drink every night. Sometimes his friend Demyan Bedny, who was a skillful chessplayer, came over, and they would sit in the Bonch-Bruevich yard hunched over a board laid out on a stool.

The vacation lasted four days. At 6 A.M. on July 17, Bonch was awakened by a hammering on the windowpane of his bedroom. It was a comrade from Petersburg. There had been an uprising in the city.

According to Bonch, after Lenin had been roused, he sat staring gloomily into a glass of milk. "It's absolutely the wrong time," he said.

There was no question that it was the wrong time, but Lenin's comment must be seen in context. The rising can have come as no great surprise, for the danger of it was only too evident before he left the city. Strangely, too, the Central Committee allowed the crisis—the most serious crisis since March—to escalate for some twelve hours before even informing Lenin.

Why did they delay? Part of the answer was that a contingency plan had been drawn up before Lenin left the city. It is inconceivable that he would have gone to Finland at such a time without considering what action the party should take in the event of trouble. The crucial question is: What was the nature of this plan?

The July Days, as the crisis is known, are marked with controversy. The official Soviet version is that the rising was started by one regiment and spread through the city. The party tried to stop it and, when it failed to do so, assumed leadership in an attempt to control it. This may be true, but when considered along with Lenin's strange departure and the Central Committee's delay in sending for him, the explanation seems a little oversimplified.

Some eminent Western historians have asserted that the rising was a Bolshevik bid for power. Yet this does not agree with Lenin's clearly recorded efforts to damp down passions within the party and outside it or with his interests. For the rising was bound to fail unless it had major backing among the workers and the troops—especially the soldiers at the front. It did not, at that stage, have such support on any large scale. For Lenin to initiate an uprising without this support would have been out of character and in direct contravention of all Marxist teachings on revolutionary tactics. And the vacillation of the party leaders during the crisis makes such an explanation untenable.

Consider, however, what *would* have been in the party's interest during that first week in July when Lenin was forced to exert all his efforts to curb his militants. What was needed to swing the masses to the Bolsheviks was the unequivocal realization that Kerensky's offensive had failed. But this would take a few weeks until the offensive petered out and it became obvious that no further progress was going to be made. If, however, the Germans counterattacked *in response to Kerensky's offensive*—a limited counterattack that took relatively little territory but subjected the Russian Army to yet another humiliating defeat—then the conditions that Lenin needed to increase his support among the masses would be created much more quickly. Kerensky and his policy would be discredited. Lenin could then remove the curbs from his militants, whom he was finding so hard to restrain, and order an uprising with an overwhelming chance of success.

If this was Lenin's plan, it meant he was timing his party's operation in coordination with the movements of the German Army—collusion that went far beyond the acceptance of funds for the pursuit of a common aim. This would mean that a live communication system existed between Lenin and Berlin, and unlike the matter of German money, there is absolutely no evidence for this—at least no prime evidence. It can also be argued that even allowing for the German policy of taking no provocative military action that might inspire Russian patriotism, a counterattack was a reasonable response to Kerensky's offensive.

However, the fact is that the communication channels between Lenin and Berlin did exist and their use would be a logical development of the financial links, since this would facilitate the target of seizing power. There is clear proof in the German documents that Parvus was in regular contact with the Foreign Office and even with Zimmermann himself. It is a matter of record that Parvus was closely connected with Jacob Fürstenberg, who, again without question, was in communication with Lenin and Kozlovsky.

Even more significant is the admission by the German socialist historian Gustav Mayer in his book *Erinnerungen* that in Sweden Mayer acted as a link between Fürstenberg and Karl Radek—whom he used to meet in their seaside villa at Neglinge—and the German authorities. Furthermore, he reported direct to Berlin—personally to Diego von Bergen, the senior official in charge of political subversion in Russia.[2]

If Lenin had known that a German counterattack was scheduled for July 16, it would explain his strange departure from the city on July 12 for the rest he so desperately needed. For with a Bolshevik bid for power timed for the reaction to this offensive, he knew he had time for relaxation before he would need to return to Petersburg to direct the rising. The other party leaders, he probably believed, could keep the party under control without his assistance for the few days before the plan went into operation—and he had reason to believe this. Had not the canceled demonstration on June 10 proved that although the militants might fight against the party's orders, they would in the ultimate obey them?

The Bolshevik plan to hold back the uprising until the humiliation of Kerensky's failed offensive was truly established is well recorded—notably by Stalin in his account of the July Days at the Sixth Party Congress in August—though not, of course, that Lenin had any prior knowledge from Berlin.

Kerensky, however, also concluded in his memoirs—and in

an attacking speech in November in the Mariinsky Palace—that the German counterattack was planned in collusion with Lenin. As a theory it had some logic, for although the main German counterattack did not take place until July 19, General Ludendorff has confirmed that it was scheduled for July 16—when the rising in Petersburg started—but postponed owing to bad weather.

Kerensky saw the plan as a simultaneous attack on two fronts—from within and from without—and although it can be argued that as a participant he was a prime source, it still does not conform with Lenin's plan to exploit the humiliation of the failure of the Russian Army, since for this he needed to wait. Also, the desperate efforts of the party leaders to stop the rising—which are clearly recorded—and the sheer muddle in which they found themselves make Kerensky's theory untenable.

However, what could explain these efforts and confusion of the Central Committee was the simple fact that the impatient militants, unaware of secret plans with the Germans, if there were any, set off the uprising too soon—and thereby created disaster. Lenin's belief that they would ultimately obey party orders was wrong. He had lost control. So when he insisted in the Bonch-Bruevich dacha that early morning that the timing was "absolutely wrong," he meant that his whole strategy had been ruined.

As they traveled by droshky to Mustiamiaki Station on their way back to Petersburg, Lenin was in the position of a field general who knew that his troops had been committed to the wrong battle plan, but who had no way of withdrawing the orders to attack.

The crisis, as Lenin was now aware, had begun to emerge three days before, on July 14—ironically within the one regiment in which the Bolsheviks had their greatest support, the First Machine Gunners. A section of the regiment had been ordered to the front. The men refused to go and were demanding an uprising to overthrow the government.

When the situation was reported to the party leaders in the

Kshesinskaya Mansion, they ordered the MO to stifle the movement. At that stage it seemed easily controllable, seemed no more than an example of the militancy that the party was having to restrain all the time in the restless city.

The leader of this mutiny, however, was a Bolshevik—a hothead named Lieutenant A. Semashko—and he had a lot of sympathizers among the MO leaders. "This time there is no stopping them," Semashko assured Nevsky, who, as the party's ace troubleshooter, had been sent to talk the soldiers out of their plan. But Semashko was certainly not trying to stop them. Nor did Nevsky. When he addressed the machine gunners, he paid lip service to the party line, but, as he admitted later, he spoke in such a way that "only a fool could come to the conclusion that he should not demonstrate."

The crisis came on July 16. Throughout the morning and early afternoon, under Semashko's urging, machine gunners toured the factories and the barracks of the other regiments throughout the city asking for their support. One group took a boat out to Kronstadt to urge the sailors to join them. Trucks with guns mounted were on the move throughout Petersburg. The regiment took possession of the Finland Station, set up roadblocks on the Troitsky and Liteiny bridges, the main arteries from the industrial areas on the north side of the city, and patrolled the Nevsky Prospect. Men in one truck, bearing a flag lettered THE FIRST BULLET FOR KERENSKY, went in search of the War Minister. But he had just left the Mariinsky Palace on his way to the front, where danger of a German counterattack was imminent.[3] Only minutes after his departure, his pursuers roared into the forecourt of the Baltic Station to discover that they were too late.

At two thirty in the afternoon, most of the Central Committee were in the Bolshevik rooms in the Tauride Palace when news of the rising reached them. Immediately, they took action to stop the crisis. Formally, the Central Committee issued an order to the soldiers not to demonstrate. Hurriedly, Kamenev and Zinoviev drafted an appeal for that night's *Pravda* urging the masses to reject the machine gunners' summons. Stalin hurried to a meeting of the Soviet Central Executive Committee and insisted that the party's declared policy to curb the uprising should be read into the record. But the delegates mocked the grim mustached Georgian. Often enough, they had read *Pravda* and *Soldatskaya Pravda* in which an uprising had been openly discussed. To them the Bolsheviks were just being devious as usual.

Nothing the party leaders did had any effect. Raskolnikov telephoned from Kronstadt to ask for orders. When Kamenev told him firmly that he was to stop the sailors from coming into the city, he said he would do his best but he doubted if he would be successful.

At eight o'clock that night, the machine gunners—led despite party orders by Lieutenant Semashko—started marching toward the city center.

On the way the procession massed in front of the Kshesinskaya Mansion, where an action committee was trying to decide what to do as reports came in from all over the city. Sverdlov addressed the troops from the balcony and urged them to stay on the north side of the river. He was followed by Podvoisky and Nevsky, who went through the motions of appealing to them to stop the demonstration. "That's enough talking," cried out one soldier. "Now it's time for action." And they marched off, their band playing the "Internationale," toward the Troitsky Bridge.

In the Tauride Palace, Kamenev knew that there was no way to stop the processions now reported to be approaching from several directions, so he attempted a skillful ploy to give respectability to the crisis and protect the party from the violent backlash that would come if it was forced to assume the leadership of the movement. He made a desperate plea to the Soviet to take over the demonstration and guide it into proper channels. But the Menshevik and SR leaders declined to help Kamenev out of the predicament they believed to have been created by the militancy of Bolshevik propaganda.

With thousands of troops and workers swarming into the city center, there was bound to be serious trouble. A battle began in the Nevsky Prospect. Marksmen in the doorways and attics fired into the crowds of marchers. The troops and Red Guards retaliated. "Fighting in the streets is panicky business," wrote reporter Albert Rhys Williams. "At night, with bullets spitting from hidden loopholes, from roofs above and cellars below . . . the crowd stampeded back and forth, fleeing from a hail of bullets in one street only to plunge into leaden gusts sweeping through the next. Three times that night our feet slipped in blood on the pavement. Down the Nevsky was blazed a train of shattered windows and looted shops. . . ."

By midnight the streets surrounding the Tauride Palace were packed with excited soldiers and workers. Several Soviet leaders made speeches in an attempt to calm the crowd. Trotsky and Zinoviev addressed them, too. But they did not go home. They stayed—a great mass of faces in the darkness lit by flaming torches and the lights of the palace.

After midnight, in the Bolshevik rooms on the first floor, the Central Committee was still trying to find a way out of the impasse. Trotsky was there, too, together with two of the leaders of his small party, Uritsky and Lunacharsky. Kamenev argued that it would be fatal for the party to assume the leadership—but eventually there was no alternative.

Raskolnikov phoned again from Kronstadt to say that he had failed to stop the sailors. Ten thousand of them would be arriving in the city the next morning. Almost at the same moment that Zinoviev was speaking to him on the phone, news reached them that a procession of 30,000 men, women and children from the vast Putilov works in the Narva District were approaching the palace. They, too, had been fired on. They swarmed into the gardens at the rear of the palace. Many lay down on the ground, vowing not to leave until the Soviet assumed power.

Reluctantly, the Central Committee decided that the party had to take over the leadership of the movement and organize a peaceful demonstration for the next day.

The new decision, reached at 2 A.M., required a quick change of plans. It was too late to reset the appeal *not* to demonstrate that Kamenev and Zinoviev had written for *Pravda*, for the presses were due to start running. So the printers just broke out the matrix, leaving a large blank white space on the paper's front page that testified to the party's indecision.[4]

At last, now that the decision was taken, the Central Committee decided to send for Lenin. They had not done so earlier no doubt because their major problem in dealing with the leaders of the Soviet Bolsheviks had been one of credibility. No one believed the Bolsheviks had not inspired the crisis. The fact that Lenin was out of the city was the one factor that supported the Bolshevik leaders' plea of innocence. For would they mount an uprising without Lenin's being present to direct it?

Chapter 13

LENIN, TOGETHER WITH THE OTHERS in the Bonch-Bruevich dacha, caught the six forty-five train from Mustiamiaki. As they studied the morning papers in the train, they heard the other passengers angrily blaming the Bolsheviks for the riots.[1]

The Finland Station bore all the signs of crisis. The trams had stopped running. On the far side of the square, a big procession of workers was moving toward the Liteiny Bridge.

There was a lone waiting droshky which Lenin and Maria took to the Kshesinskaya Mansion, leaving Bonch to walk to his apartment on Khersonskaya. They had agreed to meet later at the Tauride Palace. Gloomily, Lenin peered out of the droshky. It was a heavy, overcast day, dampened by drizzle. The streets were crowded with marching groups of both troops and workers. From the sidewalks, groups of people eyed the marchers with hostility.

At the mansion the military leaders of the party were directing the final stages of a massive military operation. Podvoisky and Nevsky had anticipated the Central Committee's decision to back the demonstration and had sent preparatory orders the previous day to the party cells at all the barracks. Bolshevik committees were to be appointed to lead each battalion. A party leader was to be selected for each company.

By nine o'clock in the morning seven regiments were already on the march under Bolshevik control. Armored cars, their noisy engines throbbing, waited at all the main street intersections to be on hand in the event of attacks by counterrevolutionaries.

The operations room was a master bedroom on the third floor. As Lenin joined the party leaders there, the 10,000 sailors from Kronstadt were disembarking at the quays on Vasilevsky Island a mile downriver. As their fleet of boats had approached the mouth of the Neva from Kotlin Island, a Soviet delegate had gone out by tug in an effort to persuade them to turn back. But the vessels from Kronstadt had not even eased speed. Soon the first of the black columns of seamen were crossing the Malaya Neva, one of the strands of the river that divided Vasilevsky Island from Old Petersburg, on their way to the Kshesinskaya Mansion.

As always, Lenin stayed out of the mainstream of the action, leaving the implementing of his strategy to others. He was only too conscious that although the MO leaders had established some control over the marching units, they were all being swept along by events.

"Do you think the movement can be the beginning of the seizure of power, Vladimir Ilyich?" asked Michael Kalinin, a Petersburg Committee member, according to his account of the scene.

"We shall see," answered Lenin. "At present it is impossible to say."

Lenin was doing his best to keep his options open, hoping that a situation would emerge that he could exploit to Bolshevik advantage. But in truth nothing could alter the fact that the timing was tragically premature. If the party took over Petersburg, which it probably could do since even those regiments that were not marching with the party were staying neutral, it could never hold it.

On the other hand, if Lenin declined to use the troops and the masses that were now responding to the orders of his military commanders, there would be a severe reaction against the party leadership.

Either way, much of the national opinion that would have swung to the Bolsheviks in the aftermath of Kerensky's failure would now be lost. The party might even be declared illegal.

His only hope, and it was a very slim one, was that the

massive pressure that would be generated that day would persuade the Soviet to assume power.

According to Sukhanov, quoting Lunacharsky who was present in the mansion, a plan to take power was agreed on at that morning meeting. Later Lunacharsky formally denied this, but Sukhanov insisted that he had not misquoted him.

There can be no doubt that such a course of action was considered. For the German counterattack was discrediting Kerensky's claims of military triumph. But it was too soon for a reaction to a new national humiliation to have set in. All the evidence and subsequent events indicate that no decision was made—no decision, that is, other than to lead the demonstration demanding that all power be given to the Soviet.[2]

The thousands of Kronstadt sailors massed in the Alexandrovsky Park beside the mansion. Sverdlov had gone out onto the balcony to greet them, and as the discussion progressed in the master bedroom, Lenin heard the party secretary's booming voice. "Comrade Raskolnikov," Sverdlov shouted, "would you invite the front ranks to move closer to the mansion?"

After a few minutes, Raskolnikov entered the room and shook hands with Lenin. He asked his leader if he would address the sailors.

But Lenin's thoughts were concentrated on his defense when the day was over. He shook his head. "Fedor Fedorovich," he said, "I am opposed to this demonstration. If I refuse to make a speech to the comrades, this will be clear."

Podvoisky urged him to change his mind. "I'm not well, Nikolai Ilyich," Lenin insisted, changing the tack of his argument. But outside the mansion, thousands of sailors were chanting, "Lenin! Lenin! We want Lenin!"

At last, he stepped out onto the little balcony with the black wrought-iron railing and looked out across the sea of seamen's hats that stretched far back among the trees—a small figure in his shapeless suit.

"An irresistible wave of ecstasy," recorded Trotsky, "a genuine Kronstadt wave, greeted the leader's appearance on the balcony. Impatiently—and as always with some embarrassment—awaiting the end of the greeting, Lenin began speaking before the voices died down."

"Comrades," he declared hoarsely, "you must excuse me if I limit myself to a few words. I have been ill. I greet you in the name of the workers of Petersburg. . . . In spite of temporary difficulties I am certain that our slogan 'All power to the Soviets' will be finally victorious though this demands from us restraint, determination and constant alertness."

It was not the fiery speech the sailors expected, and one of them recorded later that some of the sailors "could not see how a column of armed men, craving to rush into battle, could limit itself to an armed demonstration."

But Lenin was certainly not trying to rouse them, and in this his instincts were sound for even though his speech was innocuous in the extreme, it was exploited later as a strident call to revolution.

Then Sverdlov took over once more, his big voice as always seeming strangely out of keeping with his dark, narrow face and his frail figure. He gave the sailors firm instructions. They were to demand that the capitalist ministers should resign. "If the Soviets refuse power, the situation will become clear. . . . In this event you should wait for further instructions."

The sailors formed. The bands struck up, and once more the column began marching—this time toward the Troitsky Bridge and the city center. With them went a big column of workers who had crossed the Malaya Neva from the factories on Vasilevsky Island to join them. Armored cars positioned at strategic intervals moved with the long column. In one of the vehicles traveled Nevsky and Podvoisky, Lenin's field commanders.

The military leaders had designed a strategy to seize power, deploying their forces into battle positions. All they lacked was the order to attack. It was a rough strategy, not thought through, planned only in the broadest terms.

At its core were the sailors—the center of the line. But there were two powerful wings. As the stream of seamen was crossing the Neva by the Troitsky Bridge, the machine gunners, backed by workers from the Vyborg, were moving over the Liteiny Bridge, three-quarters of a mile upriver. At the same time the thousands of Putilov workers were approaching from the Narva District on the far side of the city along Sadovaya Prospect.

All three columns and many smaller ones from other districts were heading for the Tauride Palace. All bore banners demanding ALL POWER TO THE SOVIET! and DOWN WITH THE CAPITALIST MINISTERS!

To oppose them in the Tauride Palace were fourteen soldiers of the Pavlovsky Regiment and eighteen men of the Armored Car Division—thirty-two men against the tens of thousands that were converging from all sides of the city. Their commander, strangely enough, was Colonel B. V. Nikitin of counterintelligence, the man who had worked so assiduously to help gather the dossier of evidence against Lenin. He had been given the command by chance. He had just happened to be in Military Staff Headquarters the previous day. No one else could be spared for the task of defending the Soviet—which was more than a little ironical since no one in Petersburg could have disapproved of the Soviet and all it stood for more than the reactionary colonel.

In addition to Nikitin's little band of defenders at the palace, four squadrons of Cossacks were available as a reserve in their barracks, but even they could not be expected to make much impact against thousands of armed troops.

Cautiously, the government ministers had forsaken the Mariinsky Palace for the greater security of the Military District Headquarters in the square in front of the Winter Palace—within the triumphal arch that Nicholas I had erected to celebrate the defeat of Napoleon. But, with even the most reactionary regiments, such as the Preobrazhensky, staying neutral in their barracks, the situation for the government was clearly critical. They *could* call in troops from the front, but so far the Soviet had not approved this extreme course—which, although it might reestablish control, could have overwhelming repercussions and produce far more bloodshed, *and* martyrs, than the March Revolution.

Like Lenin, the ministers in the triumphal arch were waiting to see how the crisis developed before making any final decisions.

Lenin, of course, had not accompanied the column of sailors with Nevsky and Podvoisky since spectacular leadership was not his style. He had traveled quietly by car to the Tauride Palace. As he passed the continuous columns of marchers, he must have recalled his journey in the Sealed Train. For this is precisely what he had planned in the swaying rail coach—thousands demanding that the Soviet should take power.

It was strange that on this damp, cloudy day, if he could have stopped them, he would surely have done so.

Through most of the afternoon, Lenin stayed within the party rooms in the Tauride Palace. When necessary, he gave orders and even made decisions, but he was not seen by anyone except the Bolshevik leaders. Always it was others—usually Zinoviev—who made contact with other parties, delivered speeches in the Soviet, addressed the masses outside the palace. Indeed, seen from outside the party room, Zinoviev was the Bolshevik star of these crucial hours.

The crisis had brought Lenin and Zinoviev closer together— almost in the same team relationship that they had enjoyed in exile. Now there were none of the conflicts over policy with Kamenev which always tore at Zinoviev. The three men were working as one, trying to extricate the party from the morass into which the left wing had thrust it.

When Lenin arrived in the Tauride Palace, he had a quick private meeting with Zinoviev and Trotsky in the gallery of the main hall near the buffet—almost certainly drinking tea in lieu of lunch. He was still undecided exactly what to do, but clearly the sight of the marching thousands had been tempting. "Shall we try now?" he mused, according to Zinoviev; then added quickly the fact that they all knew so well: "No, we can't take power because the troops at the front are not with us yet."

He returned to the party room on the second floor to hear reports of the up-to-date situation regarding the approaching processions. No major trouble had yet been reported—only incidents. There would be, though, as he well knew. There was certain to be the same kind of provocation that had occurred the previous night and even in May—the same sniping from attics and doorways designed to spark off a major bloody conflagration for which the party could be blamed.

Lenin walked up and down the room deep in thought. To Bonch-Bruevich, watching him, he seemed at that moment a lonely figure. The situation he faced was truly impossible. If he could not lead an uprising, all he could do was to wait for the crisis to peak and then hope the participants would all go home. Had Lenin known of the plans that were being discussed at that very moment in Military Staff Headquarters he would have been far more anxious even than he was.

It was just after 3 P.M. in the Sadovaya Prospect. The truck leading the enormous column of Putilov workers, was just passing the intersection of Apraxin Street when the bell of the Church of the Assumption, two blocks back, began to toll. It was the signal for the shooting to start. The demonstrators ran for cover as bullets struck into the column. Women screamed. People fell in the road, some killed, some wounded.

The Red Guards swarmed into the houses where the gunmen were hidden and shot them to death.

The long column of sailors now stretched most of the way along the Nevsky from the Liteiny Prospect. Raskolnikov and the other leaders at the head of the marching men were not far from the Tauride Palace.

"The sound of the band could barely be heard," recorded one of the Kronstadt leaders. "The sun peeked out from behind the clouds . . . and suddenly there was the sound of gunfire behind us."

At points all the way back along the Liteiny and the Nevsky, machine guns and rifles were firing. The sailors panicked, for they could not see their assailants, who were shooting from rooftops and high windows. They broke ranks and began firing at random. Some lay down in the road. Others scattered to seek cover in the doorways. Many of the seamen were shot down in the road.

As the buildings where the shooting was coming from were pinpointed, Bolshevik armored cars lumbered along the big avenues spraying the windows with machine-gun fire.

At last, after more than an hour, the shooting stopped, and Raskolnikov and the other leaders persuaded the men to re-form and continue the march. But they were angry men—thousands of angry men—when they arrived at last at the Tauride Palace, to be greeted with cheers by the Machine Gun Regiment.

Raskolnikov left his furious sailors and went into the palace to report to the Bolshevik leaders. In the hall he met Trotsky, but they had hardly exchanged greetings when someone ran up excitedly. "The sailors have arrested Chernov."

Victor Chernov, a leader of the Social Revolutionary Party which had many members among the sailors, was Minister of Agriculture and concerned with the delicate question of land. When he had stood up to speak to the angry sailors, he had been howled down. One of them had shaken his fist in his face. Then the seamen had grabbed the minister and manhandled him into a car.

Trotsky was well known to the sailors, for he often traveled down to Kronstadt to address them and defended them frequently in the Soviet. He was confident he could rescue Chernov without trouble. But he had never seen the seamen in this mood. One man, to whom he offered his hand, refused to take it. When Trotsky clambered onto the hood of the car in which Chernov was imprisoned to address the mob of yelling men, he could not make himself heard.

At last, with the help of a naval bugler who was nearby, Trotsky managed to curb the noise of the yelling enough to appeal to them. "Comrades . . ." he pleaded. "Why hurt your cause by petty acts of violence. . . . Whoever is for violence, let him raise his hand."

Evidently, no one among those thousands of furious men

packed in front of the palace was for violence—even though moments before they had been howling for it—for no one raised his hand. The badly shaken Chernov was released from the car and hustled into the palace—watched by a pale and anxious Colonel Nikitin.

The Bolsheviks had now taken over a room on the ground floor as an operations center, and it was here that Raskolnikov now reported for further orders. On the way he met Lenin, who smiled at him pleasantly, but it was Zinoviev who took command. When the midshipman asked for instructions, Zinoviev said, "We must discuss it immediately," and convened a meeting.

Since Lenin and the leaders were not prepared to make an actual bid for power, the thousands of armed and angry sailors in the small square in front of the palace were an embarrassment. At last, it was proposed that the demonstration should be formally declared to be over. Simon Roshal was ordered to march them to quarters which had been allocated them for the night—some were to sleep in the basement of the Kshesinskaya Mansion, others in Peter and Paul and various halls on the north of the river.

Lenin was still keeping his forces at hand. The sailors would be available to him should the situation change.

Slowly, reluctantly, the sailors consented to march from the palace, but their place was taken by the thousands of Putilov workers, also angry from the mauling they had encountered on Sadovaya.

They were even more aggressive than the sailors. A group of some forty workers forced their way into the palace, and one man strode into the hall where the Central Executive Committee of the Soviet was in session. He leaped onto the platform. He was "a classical sans-culotte," recorded Sukhanov, "in a cap and a short blue blouse without a belt, with a rifle in his hand. . . . He was quivering with excitement and rage. . . .

" 'Comrades, how long must we put up with treachery?

You're all here debating and making deals with the bourgeoisie and the landlords. . . . You're busy betraying the working class. Well, just understand that the working class won't put up with it. . . . We have a firm grip on our rifles."

Chkheidze, always adept at handling angry workers, thrust into his hand a copy of the Soviet manifesto. "Here, please take this, Comrade," he said. "It says what you and your Putilov comrades should do."

Outside, though, the crowd was chanting ominously for Tseretelli. "Tseretelli," they yelled. "We want Tseretelli." More workers broke the doors. One man in the crowd yelled, "If he won't come out, bring him out!"

In the ground-floor operations room, Lenin told Zinoviev to go out and calm them. Zinoviev went almost jauntily, confident in his capacity, as Trotsky put it, "to infect himself with the mood of the masses. . . ." He stood in front of the palace between the tall white pillars and surveyed the "sea of heads such as I have never seen before. Tens of thousands of men were solidly packed together, shouting, "'Tseretelli! Tseretelli!'"

Tseretelli was tall and elegant. Zinoviev was short and fat. So when Zinoviev held up his arms for quiet, grinned and said, "In the place of Tseretelli, it is I who have come out to you," the contrast caused a ripple of laughter through the listening mass of people. It broke the tension and enabled him to manipulate the mood of the crowd—which he proceeded to do brilliantly.

Zinoviev's purpose, of course, was to persuade them to leave. But Colonel Nikitin did not have the same faith in the Bolshevik leader with the high tenor voice as Lenin and the party leaders—or in his motives. The colonel was alarmed. The thin line of sentries he had posted to keep the crowds from the immediate approaches to the palace had long since been forced to retire within the building so that "we were," as he wrote, "literally surrounded by an impenetrable wall of humanity."

The urgent cries for "Tseretelli" and the break-in of the Putilov workers had decided him that the situation demanded extreme measures. He made an emergency call to Military District Headquarters, and two squadrons of Cossacks, together with a couple of field guns, set off from Palace Square.

The mounted troops clashed with the sailors in Suvorovskaya Place by the Troitsky Bridge as the seamen were on their way across the river and broke the column. From every point of view, it was an unhappy day for the sailors.

Then the Cossacks encountered the First Reserve Regiment by a barricade at the Liteiny Bridge. The confrontation developed into a battle in which the Cossacks were badly savaged.

The gunfire could be heard clearly in the Tauride Palace, and the delegates were alarmed. Was this the expected Bolshevik attack? It broke the remaining resistance in the Central Executive Committee to the proposal to summon troops from the front.

On telephoned approval from the Soviet, the officers in the Military District HQ wired a call for help to the northern front. Kerensky, too, had been informed by wire. He telegraphed back orders to suppress the revolt with the severest measures and to arrest the Bolshevik leaders.

The crowd milling outside the palace suddenly heard the sound of galloping horses. In fact, they were riderless horses fearfully escaping down the Liteiny Prospect from the battle by the bridge. The mob, however, believed the Cossacks were charging them. Shooting broke out in front of the palace, though no one was quite sure what he was shooting at. Panic swept the tight-packed mass as those at the front tried to claw their way to safety through the dense ranks behind them. Others shattered the ground-floor windows of the building and clambered inside for cover.

It was the climax of the demonstration. At last, as everyone realized that there were no Cossacks, the tension eased. Then heavy rain began to fall, and the downpour cleared the crowd, which had begun in any case to disperse. Soon the anxious Soviet delegates could look through the broken windows of the

[214

ground floor onto an almost empty square. For the Soviet the crisis was almost over, but for Lenin it was just beginning.

Bonch-Bruevich had left the palace and gone home to Khersonskaya. He was in the apartment when the telephone rang. A male voice greeted him by name. "Who is it?" asked Bonch.

The caller would not say. "Don't you recognize my voice?" he asked.

For a moment, Bonch was puzzled, and then he realized who was speaking—*and* why he was being so cautious. Nicholas Kransky was a radical lawyer he knew who was assistant to Pereverzev, the Minister of Justice.

"I'm ringing you to warn you," said Kransky urgently, so Bonch recorded with his usual elaborate use of dialogue. "A mass of documents are being assembled against Lenin. . . . It's serious."

"What's it all about?" queried Bonch.

"They're accusing him of espionage for the Germans . . .they're going to prosecute him—and all his friends. . . . I can't tell you any more . . . take action." And he hung up.

Immediately, Bonch phoned the Bolshevik room in the Tauride Palace. Quickly, he told Lenin what he had just heard, insisting that he could not give the name of his caller on the phone.

"Is your source really reliable?" asked Lenin.

"He holds a high official post."

"Was he informing you of a rumor or on the basis of documents?"

"He told me he himself had read the documents. . . . You'll leave the palace at once, won't you, Vladimir Ilyich?"

"*Nichevo*—don't worry," answered Lenin lightly.

"It's impossible not to be worried."

"*Nichevo. Nichevo.* I'll be leaving here soon."

In fact, the rumor of prosecution had already been reported to Lenin, for by then it was an open secret within the Tauride Palace. Lenin was slow to take the action that Bonch had urged—possibly because at this stage it would make him look as though he were guilty or possibly because he did not believe that all his options had been exhausted.

It soon emerged that the government was not just mounting prosecution. They were exploiting the evidence in the dossier on Lenin as a political weapon. On the orders of Pereverzev, the Minister of Justice, a letter had been handed to the press listing the facts in the case against Lenin: the huge funds handled by Eugenia Sumenson; her links with the Bolshevik lawyer Mecheslav Kozlovsky; her coded communications with Jacob Fürstenberg and his association with Parvus; the letters seized from the searched Bolshevik couriers at Beloostrov; and the evidence of Lieutenant Ermolenko.

Lenin was appalled, for promoted in this way without a trial, the evidence was clear persecution. And the news was not made any less painful by the fact that the damaging official letter was signed by a man who had once been nearly as close to Lenin as Zinoviev—Gregory Alexinsky, the leader of the Bolshevik faction in the Duma. The two men had clashed over Lenin's war policy, and their relationship had since deteriorated into bitter enmity. Now Alexinsky was scoring—and scoring well.

Lenin acted immediately. He dispatched the Georgian Stalin to see Chkheidze, also a Georgian, who was at a meeting of the Central Executive Committee. Stalin demanded that the Soviet should intervene to prevent publication of the letter by newspapers until there had at least been an investigation in which Lenin could answer the charges against him.

Chkheidze, who was no friend of the Bolsheviks, was outraged by the government action. The entire Soviet leadership responded with a speed that Lenin could not fault. They telephoned editors throughout the city with a formal request from the Soviet not to publish the story. "It goes without saying," wrote Sukhanov, "that not one of the people really connected with the revolution doubted for a moment the absurdity of these rumors."

The Soviet leaders were violently opposed to Lenin's theories, even frightened by his tactics, but years later—when the proof of the German Foreign Office papers was published—

they still refused to believe that he could have acted in collusion with the Kaiser. They still did not realize or would not accept that for Lenin it was the end that counted—not the means. He was working to create the world socialist revolution. With an aim of such global and historical importance, the source of the funds was barely relevant.

This support by the Soviet was one reason why Lenin was in no hurry to go into hiding—even temporarily while the party considered what policy they should adopt in the new conditions. But Pereverzev had been more skillful than Lenin realized. He had also summoned representatives of the Preobrazhensky—the most reactionary of the "neutral" regiments in the city—and shown them his proof. The soldiers were appalled. All the resentment that had followed the Sealed Train revelations in April was revived, but now the emotional shock was far more intense. The news spread quickly to other "neutral" barracks, where it drew the same response of violent anger.

The Soviet was still in session when "suddenly a noise was heard in the distance," Sukhanov wrote. "It came nearer and nearer. The measured tramping of thousands of feet. . . ." It was a key moment of history. The Izmailovsky, which had arrested the leaders of the Soviet in 1905, had come to protect them in 1917. They were a bit late, of course, for the thousands who had been surging around the palace for most of the day had long dispersed. But the arrival of the famous regiment was symbolic of the end of the crisis. The government was once more in control. The delegates in the Soviet began to sing the "Marseillaise." "A classic sign of the counterrevolution," snapped Julius Martov to Sukhanov.

As soon as the news spread throughout the city, the bourgeoisie went on the offensive. Everywhere Bolsheviks were attacked and even killed. Groups of Junkers, the officer cadet corps, militant Kadet Party members and patrolling Cossacks, incensed by the casualties among their comrades in the battle at the Liteiny Bridge, began to take their vengeance.

"Now is their moment," Lenin confided to Trotsky. "They can overthrow us."

No order, however, had yet been issued for his arrest, and

even after the Izmailovsky had arrived at the Tauride Palace, Lenin presided at a meeting in the Bolshevik operations room. Astonishingly, its ostensible purpose was to consider the possibility of a militant call to arms by the Military Organization. Podvoisky and Nevsky were not there, but K. Mekhonoshin, one of their senior comrades, urged action before it was too late. They still had large forces available—some regiments, many of the workers, the sailors.

Lenin went through the motions of listening to Mekhonoshin, who, like many of his colleagues, had no idea of the political realities of the situation. Most of these passionate revolutionaries thought in terms of dying on the barricades for the cause instead, like Lenin, of winning.

Coldly, Lenin rapped out a string of questions at the man who was urging him to fight on. "Give me an account of your strength. Name the units that will definitely follow us. Who is against us? Where are the armories of weapons . . .? Where are the food supplies concentrated . . .? Has the security of the Neva bridges [drawbridges] been provided for? Has the rear been prepared for retreat in the event of failure?"

Mekhonoshin was crushed. Like Nevsky, he believed that to succeed they had only to get the people onto the streets—as they had in March. As Lenin's acid questions made evident, they had got the people onto the streets again now in July—and what had this achieved?

Lenin and Zinoviev drove to the Pravda office on Moika Street. A bodyguard of armed sailors rode on the fenders and running boards of the car.

On Liteiny a long line of carriages moved slowly through the congestion toward the bridge over the Neva that led to the Finland Station. As they passed, the sailor bodyguards yelled mocking insults at the passengers within them. "The bourgeois are running to Finland," remarked Lenin wryly. For they did not know, as Lenin knew, that there was no need for them to flee—not yet anyway.

At the Pravda office Lenin approved the final makeup of the paper. A short statement on the back page declared that the demonstrations had been ended "because their goal of presenting the slogans of the leading elements of the working class and the army had been achieved."

Then Lenin and Zinoviev left the office for their homes. As Lenin crossed the Neva on his way to Shirokaya, the sun was glistening on the golden spire of Peter and Paul. The day was going to be fine.

Lenin had not been asleep long when Jacob Sverdlov arrived in the apartment and awoke him. Government troops had raided *Pravda*, broken the press and searched the offices for documents. More serious still, one small right-wing newspaper *Zhivoe Slovo* ("The Living Word") had ignored the request from the Soviet, which even Miliukov's *Rech* had observed, not to publish the German agent allegations until they had been investigated. The headline was unequivocal: LENIN, GANETSKY AND KOZLOVSKY GERMAN SPIES! "Ganetsky," of course, was Jacob Fürstenberg. *Zhivoe Slovo* had only a tiny circulation, but it was enough. The story had been broken. Now the other newspapers would surely publish it.

Clearly there was imminent danger of a police raid on the apartment, and Sverdlov insisted that Lenin should leave immediately. The two men hurried through the streets to the Kshesinskaya Mansion.

At the mansion the debate with the militants was still continuing—even though the party now knew for certain that the crisis in the city had won little sympathy in the provinces and that the troops summoned on the previous day were on their way to the capital. There was angry talk of a mass march and a strike, but Lenin knew this would be pointless. It was time to cut their losses, to ride out the storm that was now inevitable and to concentrate on organizing for the future.

All the party leaders were in danger of arrest, though Lenin himself was clearly the prize. A show trial for treason could be of great propaganda value to Kerensky. There were arguments in favor of Lenin's standing trial, but in those early hours of crisis it seemed wise for him to remain out of sight for the time being. It was agreed that Lenin should stay in the apartment of the secretary of the Military Organization, Sulimov, in the Vyborg. He was not, therefore, in the Elizarov flat when Colonel Nikitin personally led a raid on it.

Early the next morning government troops deployed to attack the Kshesinskaya Mansion. Reluctantly, since it would be hard to hold, the party military leaders withdrew their force of some 500 troops and sailors and fell back on the Fortress of Peter and Paul, whose garrison was still friendly to the Bolsheviks.

When Zinoviev reported the latest events to Lenin before breakfast in the Sulimov apartment in the Vyborg, Lenin sighed. His militants still had not learned their lesson. "They're going to have to surrender in the end," he said. "To delay matters only means increasing the defeat. Go and explain to them, Gregory."

Lenin knew he could not stay where he was, for his host's signature was on many documents, and now that the Kshesinskaya Mansion had been taken, these would be found. The apartment was sure to be raided.

It was hard to find premises that would not draw police attention, and all that day Lenin, in disguise, moved from place to place in the Vyborg.

All day, too, troops from the Northern Front were arriving in Petersburg and forming in the vast square in front of the Winter Palace.

That evening Kerensky himself reached the city. Furious that his telegraphed orders to arrest the Bolshevik leaders had not been obeyed, he dismissed the commander of the Petersburg garrison who came to meet his train at Tsarskoe Selo Station. He was even angrier to learn of Pereverzev's release of the Lenin dossier, for this action—which Kerensky attributed to panic—had lost them the big fish they had been waiting to catch. Jacob Fürstenberg, Kerensky learned, had indeed been on his way to Russia when he had been alerted by the news of the scandal. He had turned back and returned to Stockholm. Later Kerensky would insist in the Cabinet that Pereverzev also be dismissed from his post.

On the way by car to the Military District HQ in Palace Square, the garrison commander explained why it had not been possible to arrest the Bolshevik leaders. Even now there was delegation from the Soviet at headquarters insisting that it would be "premature to arrest the Bolshevik leaders, pending an investigation of the facts. . . ."

Kerensky received the delegation as soon as he arrived. He had only begun to discuss the issue with them when an aide brought a telegram from the front. The Germans had attacked and achieved a major breakthrough near Tarnopol. Dramatically, the War Minister read it aloud to the Soviet delegates. "I trust," he said coolly, "that now you will no longer object to the arrests."

Even though they had received no more "facts" about the Bolshevik ties with the Germans, the Soviet delegates no longer objected. Warrants were issued for the arrest of Lenin, Zinoviev and Kamenev.

That night the party leaders met Lenin in the apartment of Marguerite Fofanova, a friend of Nadya's, in an old red-brick tenement in the Vyborg. They now knew of the arrest orders. They had also been able to test the mood in the Soviet, for, at Lenin's request, Zinoviev had courageously appeared before the Central Executive Committee to demand that it refute the "monstrous slander" staged by the Black Hundreds. His reception had been frigid. So it seemed wise for Lenin and the other two under indictment to remain in hiding—at least until the picture was clearer.

After the meeting, Lenin and Zinoviev, both in disguise, crossed the Neva to the Rozhdestvensky District and moved into the apartment of Sergei Alliluyev, a friend and later father-in-law of Stalin. It was chosen because there were several exits from the building—vital for a quick getaway—and for the fact that the Alliluyevs were newcomers to the area and were not yet known to the police.

By the next morning, Lenin had decided to stand trial—as he

told Maria and Nadya when they visited him. "Gregory and I have decided to appear," he told his wife. "Go and tell Kamenev."

Maria tried to argue with him, but Nadya had been with him in too many crises. She got up without a word to carry out her orders. " 'Let's say good-bye,' Ilyich checked me," Nadya recorded. " 'We may not see each other again.' We embraced. I went to Kamenev and gave him Ilyich's message."

That night, however, at yet another meeting of some of the party leaders in the Alliluyev apartment, the decision was changed. Sverdlov, in particular, was violently opposed to Lenin's standing trial.

This decision struck many of Lenin's contemporaries as strange—as indeed did his total reaction to the charges against him. Sukhanov described it as incomprehensible given the situation at the time. "Any other mortal," he wrote, "would have demanded an investigation and trial even in the most unfavorable conditions. Any other mortal would personally and publicly have done everything possible to rehabilitate himself."

The official Soviet line is that Lenin believed his life was in danger. When he learned that the Kshesinskaya Mansion had been raided, he told Sulimova, "At worst, they'll arrest you, but *I'll* swing." Every action he took over the next few weeks supported this contention that he would face a death sentence if he were found guilty, that a fair trial was impossible. "There are no guarantees of justice in Russia at present," he wrote.

Like so many aspects of Lenin's relations with the Germans, this appears reasonable in theory but does not stand up to scrutiny. Treason was a serious charge, but the evidence at hand was clearly inadequate. More significant was the political background. The idea, set forth by Trotsky and other Bolsheviks, that Lenin was in real danger was mocked by Sukhanov. "In the summer of 1917, there could be no question of lynch law, of the death penalty, or of hard labor . . ." he wrote. "Lenin risked absolutely nothing but imprisonment. The example of his comrades completely confirms all this. Many of them were arrested and put on trial for the same crimes. They safely sat out six weeks or two months in prison. . . . Then . . .they returned to their posts.''

The point, however, was whether Lenin could afford a thorough investigation into the German association. When Sukhanov asserted that anyone else would have welcomed a full inquiry, he was assuming that Lenin was innocent. But the fact that Lenin did receive funds from the Germans, which cannot seriously be challenged in view of the German evidence, unless the Secretary of State lied to the Kaiser, placed him in a very different position. Further inquiry would almost certainly lead to the uncovering of more facts which could only be more damaging. If Lenin did not stand trial, on the other hand, the Bolsheviks could accuse the government of employing smear tactics, of political persecution.

The fact that Sverdlov was the leader who most adamantly opposed a trial could be highly relevant. For even if other party leaders were in doubt about Lenin's deal with the Germans, Sverdlov could not have been. As secretary he ran the party. He organized the distribution of all party funds. He was completely and utterly behind Lenin in every action he took—the only man Lenin could rely on without question in the most crucial Central Committee meetings and his partner in whatever tactics were necessary to persuade the others to a certain decision. Sverdlov knew the situation exactly and was fully aware what evidence a full investigation could reveal.

So the issue was decided. Lenin and Zinoviev would stay in hiding.

For a couple of days, the fugitives remained in the Alliluyev apartment. Lenin worked hard, writing passionate articles asserting his innocence and attacking the government. These appeared mainly in the *Pravda Bulletin*, a rough illegal two-page sheet that replaced its banned parent newspaper, or in Maxim Gorky's *Novaya Zhizn*, of which Sukhanov was now an editor. Under emotive headlines such as CALUMNY AND FACTS! and DREYFUSADE!—in which he compared his own persecution with that of the famous Dreyfus Case—Lenin attacked the evidence.

Lieutenant Ermolenko had lied, he asserted. There had been

no contact whatsoever with Parvus, whom he had condemned two years before as "a renegade" and had refused even to speak to in Stockholm. "No money" had "ever been received by the Bolsheviks from either Hanecki [Fürstenberg] or Kozlovsky." Further, neither was a member of the party. Naturally, Lenin made no reference to the Bolshevik Foreign Bureau that Fürstenberg ran with Karl Radek's help in Stockholm.

In fact, among the papers that had been seized by Nikitin in the raids of the past few days were several copies of letters that indicated clearly that the party had received money from both Fürstenberg and Kozlovsky. Later both Fürstenberg and Radek confirmed that the Foreign Bureau had channeled funds into Russia. And, Lenin's assertion that the two key figures were not members of the party was only narrowly true. They were Polish Bolsheviks, not Russian Bolsheviks.

No prosecutor, however, ever brought the case to trial. Under interrogation Eugenia Sumenson admitted to Nikitin that she had been instructed by Jacob Fürstenberg to hand over to Kozlovsky any sums he requested *without requiring a receipt*. But the case was still not solid. A prosecutor could show that the party received money, but he could not prove it came from the Germans.

Eventually , as Trotsky wrote, all that was left in the way of hard incriminating evidence was Lenin's "trip through Germany . . . the very fact, advanced most often before inexperienced audiences as proof of Lenin's friendship with the German Government. . . ." And the trouble with this, for a prosecutor's purpose, was that the Sealed Train journey had never been a secret.

In Berlin the news of the July crisis caused deep concern and drew denials that Lenin was a German agent or linked in any way to Parvus. Even before the crisis, a drop in the surge of public support for Lenin had been noted—and exaggerated. "The waning of the Bolshevik influence," reported the counselor to the German Legation in Stockholm, "must be seen as the result partly of the offensive and partly of the inordinate demands made by Lenin's group."

Parvus thought it politic to soothe the anxieties in the Wilhelmstrasse. On July 17, the day when the crisis in Petersburg reached its climax, he called on Arthur Zimmermann and assured him that Lenin's influence "was continuing to grow, in spite of all claims to the contrary made in the press of the Entente countries. . . . Disappointment had already set in [among the soldiers] and would result in a further softening up of the army."

Meanwhile, in Petersburg, a massive hunt was launched within the city for Lenin and Zinoviev. Militia, troops, dogs—including one celebrated animal named Tref—were aided by hundreds of civilian volunteers. Fifty officers of one of Kerensky's "Shock Battalions" vowed to track down Lenin or die. Already Kamenev had been arrested.

"There were signs," according to Zinoviev, "that the apartment was being watched." Clearly it was becoming too dangerous to stay in the city. At night on July 22, Lenin and Zinoviev left the apartment with Sergei Alliluyev and Stalin. Their new hiding place was to be in heavily wooded country near the Finnish border—not far from the Sestroretsk plant, from which the workers had crowded on the Beloostrov Station to give him his first welcome on his return to Russia.

Because the Finland Station was heavily policed, it had been planned that they should go on foot to the suburb of Novaya Derevnya and board a train there. Walking was considered safer than traveling by car or cab, for vehicles were constantly being stopped by the patrols.

Lenin shaved off his beard and donned a brown coat and cap of the sort worn by the Finnish peasants who traveled into the city every day from the border.

The four men did not depart from the building until eleven o'clock, leaving as late as possible to take advantage of the very short period of mid-July darkness in Petersburg, but they encountered no trouble. Near Novaya Derevnya, a veteran Bolshevik named Nicholas Emelyanov was waiting by the Stroganov Bridge over one of the tributaries of the Neva.

While Alliluyev and Stalin returned to the center of the city,

225]

Emelyanov led Lenin and Zinoviev to the station on the outskirts. To avoid having to stand on the platform, they crossed the tracks, crawling under a line of waiting freight cars, and clambered onto the last coach of their train as it moved out of the station.

Lenin, recorded Emelyanov, insisted on sitting on the footplate of the coach so that, if necessary, he could jump off.

"It's dangerous," the escort warned.

"Never mind," answered Lenin, smiling. "I'm good at holding on."

At one of the stations where the train stopped, a group of boisterous officers emerged from the buffet where they had obviously been drinking and got into the next coach. They sang obscene army songs, talked politics and abused Lenin.

After the train was in motion, one of them left the compartment and moved along the corridor to the end of the coach, where the three men, sprawled across the steps and platform, were pretending to be drunk. The officer became interested, wondering who they were, and peered closely at Lenin, who was sitting on the step, his shoulders hunched and his head dropping forward. "In time with the train wheels," Emelyanov wrote later, "he swayed from side to side bending his head lower and lower. When the officer tried to catch a glimpse from the right, Ilyich swayed left and vice versa."

At last, the officer tired of the investigation and went back to his boisterous companions in the next coach. And Lenin, in disguise, feigning drunkenness, clinging to the footplate of the train, went furtively back up the same stretch of track along which three months before he had traveled to his triumphal welcome.

At a small station a few miles from Beloostrov, Lenin and his companions slipped from the train and made their way to a new hiding place—at first in the loft of a shed near Emelyanov's cottage and then in a shack deep in the woods.

Meanwhile, the status of the other political leader from Simbirsk had risen sharply. Prince Lvov resigned, and Alexander Kerensky replaced him as Premier, determined to give the nation the strong leadership necessary to raise it from the chaos in which it was floundering. His offensive, of course, had been transformed into a disaster as the Germans thrust deep behind Russian lines, taking thousands of prisoners and provoking mass desertions of entire units—but this was blamed on Lenin and his German agents.

The new Premier took firm steps to stamp out "the revolt"—with the full support of the Soviet. The sailors were sent back to Kronstadt in disgrace without their arms. All regiments which took part in the rising were disbanded, their men divided among other more reliable corps. The volatile machine gunners were forced to pile their weapons in Palace Square.

Many of the party leaders were arrested—as well as militants such as Raskolnikov at Kronstadt. Unofficial repercussions were savage. Bolsheviks, even sympathizers of the party, were beaten up. Groups of right-wing officers toured the city seeking victims.

It was symbolic of the changed conditions that the Cossacks who died in the battle on Liteiny were buried with all the ritual of the March martyrs, but the dead workers were interred quietly with only private ceremonies.

The Bolsheviks had no legal headquarters, and their press was once more forced underground. Ironically, in view of its antireligious bias, the Central Committee met in the premises of the St. Sergius Brotherhood on Furshtadtskaya Street. For all practical purposes, the party was in ruins. If its hopes of achieving power had been absurdly small in March, they had been greater then than most people would rate them now—most people, that is, other than Lenin.

Chapter 14

"A COOL NIGHT marked with stars; the smell of the cut hay," wrote Zinoviev of their stay in the woods near Razliv. "Smoke from a small fire where venison simmered in a small pot. . . . We go to bed in the little shack. It is cold. We cover ourselves with an old blanket that Emelyanov found. It is narrow and each of us tries to leave the larger part of it to the other. Ilyich says he has a *fufaika* [an anorak type of padded coat] and does not need the blanket.[1]

"Sometimes I cannot sleep for a long time, lying there in absolute silence. I can hear the beating of Ilyich's heart. We are sleeping closely, pressed against each other. . . ."[2]

The arrival of a company of Cossacks, scouring the area for the two fugitives, had forced them to leave their first hiding place in the loft of the Emelyanov's shed. For the troops were searching the homes of all known Bolsheviks.

So Emelyanov leased some land in the remote swampy fields beyond Lake Razliv, and Lenin and Zinoviev played the roles of Finnish peasants who were helping him cut the long grass. He told his friends at the factory that he was planning to keep a cow there in the autumn.

It was an isolated spot, most easily approached by boat, and Emelyanov made a shack for them out of thatch. Food and sometimes comrades from Petersburg were brought out daily by dinghy.

"During the first few days," recorded Zinoviev, "Vladimir Ilyich hardly read at all." He rested—continuing the badly needed vacation that had been interrupted so sharply by the crisis. Gregory himself scoured the newspapers, brought across the lake by Emelyanov or his sons, and was appalled by the extent of the press campaign against Lenin and party. One report even quoted Lenin's query to him and Trotsky while they had a quiet cup of tea in the Tauride Palace on July 18—"Shall we try now?"—although it had not really been posed seriously. Clearly, they had been overheard, and even though the comment hardly fitted the general pattern of the charge that they were acting on specific German instructions, it had a conspiratorial color to it that added a sinister note to the other accusations.

Lenin shrugged off the attacks. "Don't let yourself get upset," he said. "You shouldn't read these newspapers. . . . Let's go and bathe."

Typically, Lenin was waiting for the reaction to the present storm. For the pendulum always swung. He knew that, despite the July failure, the crisis had displayed one thing that in time would become obvious: The Bolsheviks were the only party on which the workers could rely to promote their interests. The other two parties of the lower classes—the Mensheviks and the Socialist Revolutionaries—had joined Kerensky and the counterrevolution, placing power in "the hands of a military clique that shoots down the insubordinate soldiers at the front while it raids the Bolsheviks in Petersburg."[3] At the heart of this new power was the sinister figure of Paul Milyukov and his Kadets. "Now the blind shall see," Lenin wrote from his lakeside retreat at the beginning of August, "and stones shall speak. . . . The despicable slandering of political opponents will help the proletariat to understand sooner where the counterrevolution is and to sweep it away. . . ."

During those first few days of relaxing, Lenin worried a little about whether he should have seized power when he had the chance, "dozens of times weighing the pros and cons," reported Zinoviev. But each time he reassured himself that the decision he had made was right.

After a short while, Lenin began to work. Four comrades alternated in traveling out to see him from Petersburg—being ferried across the lake by one of the Emelyanovs—to keep him up to date with events in the city and to carry back his letters and instructions.

A new all-Russian party congress had been called in

Petersburg, and Lenin, even though he could not attend it, wrote all the resolutions and laid down its direction. The delegates, now representing 177,000 party members, met in secrecy, first in the Vyborg and then in the Narva District, under strong guards of workers. They appointed Lenin as honorary chairman *in absentia*, endorsed his new decision that an armed uprising must now precede Soviet rule, and formally welcomed Trotsky and his colleagues into the party.

By the lake at Razliv, Lenin continued writing *State and Revolution*, one of his most famous works, which he had begun in exile in Switzerland, and in which he predicted a two-stage transition from preliminary socialism to full communism. "Lying on his stomach or squatting" at a table formed by a tree stump, he worked in a blue notebook and surprised Zinoviev by reading passages to him. "I don't recall a previous occasion when he had read a manuscript aloud," Zinoviev observed, "but here there was a unique situation. . . . There was a lot of spare time and . . . a special mood. . . ."

Meanwhile, as government troops searched for Lenin, Alexander Kerensky was attempting to rule Russia from his large office overlooking the Neva in the Winter Palace. The Bolshevik Party had not been made illegal, though its press had been banned, its headquarters taken over and its leaders indicted, but Lenin's continuous propaganda, which had so damaged everything that Kerensky attempted, had been curbed. Now that Lenin was no longer a major force in the country, Kerensky believed he could make headway with the task of uniting the nation to overcome the colossal problems that Russia faced. However, having dealt so firmly with the left wing, he was soon to encounter an even greater threat from the right.

In August at Razliv the nights began to grow bitter, and the first of the autumn rains fell. The roof leaked, despite Emelyanov's airy assurances to Zinoviev when he had expressed anxiety. The rains brought danger, too. For hunters on shooting expeditions in the woods sometimes took shelter in the shack, thinking it was a barn. One of the Emelyanovs had always been present to deal tactfully with these unwelcome visitors until one night, when the two men were alone, a stranger stepped into the hut. Zinoviev pushed the books they had been working on under some hay and gave brief, cool answers to the questions the hunter asked by way of making conversation. Lenin pretended to be asleep. When the rain eased and the visitor left them, it was obvious that it was dangerous for them to stay there much longer.

By then the Central Committee was already alarmed by the persistent rumors in the city that Lenin was hiding in Sestroretsk, and as a result, troops were making repeated searches of the district. The right-wing papers also maintained their attack. "It is not a secret to anyone," declared *Zhivoe Slovo*, which had broken the German agent story during the crisis, "that the July shooting of citizens was organized by Mr. Lenin and the 'sealed' Bolsheviks who arrived with him . . . a significant majority of these traitors remain at liberty and continue their agitation. . . ."

The paper's credibility was, however, damaged by the fact that it gave a picture of Lenin's private life so lurid and out of character that it could only be fiction. Under the name of Comrade Chaplinsky, it charged, he had been a regular visitor to one of Petersburg's fashionable café-theaters, had dined often in a private room with Swedish actress Erna Aimusta, and paid 110 rubles a bottle for champagne. He had undertipped the waiters and even cursed them as "lackeys."

"No one doubts," *Zhivoe Slovo* predicted darkly on September 2, "that Lenin will soon go to Berlin."

By that date, Lenin had been in Finland for more than a week. The crossing of the border, closely guarded as it was by militiamen, had required detailed planning. Alexander Shotman, one of the liaison comrades, had joined an amateur theatrical group in the Vyborg so that he could buy a couple of wigs from a barber without arousing suspicion. A Bolshevik photographer had visited the shack at Razliv to take pictures so that Lenin and Zinoviev could be issued false worker passes to the Sestroretsk plant. Lenin now had a new identity. He was Constantine

Petrovich Ivanov, whose home was in the local district of Razliv.

On the night of August 21 Lenin and Zinoviev left their lakeside retreat. The plan was that they should travel by train to Udelnaya Station in the Petersburg suburb of Novaya Derevnya, where they had met Emelyanov on the July evening they had left the city, and spend the next day in the apartment of a party comrade. The following night Lenin would cross the Finnish border in the guise of a stoker on a locomotive driven by a trusted Bolshevik railwayman. Clearly, this plan could accommodate only one man, and Zinoviev, it was decided, should stay in hiding in the city.

From the start, the escape plan went badly. While it was still daylight, Lenin emerged from the hut to find to his alarm that Emelyanov was talking to a stranger—his neighbor, as it turned out, who was taking a stroll. When the Bolshevik explained that Lenin was a Finnish worker who could speak no Russian, the other man asked if he could employ the fellow to do some work for him.

"No . . ." explained Emelyanov. "He wants to get back home. Something's wrong there."

At last, the neighbor left them to continue his walk. "Thanks, Nikolai Alexandrovich," Lenin murmured, "for not hiring me out as a farmhand."

After dark, when they left the hut, they encountered more serious difficulty. Emelyanov led them, together with two of the liaison comrades, Alexander Shotman and Eino Rahja, on a roundabout route through the woods—presumably to avoid the village. He lost his way—much to Lenin's fury. Eventually, the five men succeeded in finding Duibun Station, but only after having to ford a deep stream.

Then, as Emelyanov went ahead to survey the station, he was stopped and arrested by the militiamen on duty. But he served a purpose, for by diverting the attention of the officers, he enabled the others to slip onto a train as it moved out of the station.

The next night, Lenin—wearing a blond wig and the overalls and cap of a stoker—waited outside Udelnaya Station until the

Helsinki train, drawn by Locomotive No. 293, steamed alongside the platform. Then he walked briskly up to the engine. From the cab, driver Hugo Yalava cautiously scanned the station area for the Bolshevik lookouts. "As had been agreed upon," he wrote, "one of Lenin's companions stood at the crossing smoking a cigarette, the other stood beneath the lamppost pretending to be reading a newspaper."

Lenin clambered into the cab and began to throw logs into the boiler fire. The genuine stoker moved into a carriage as a passenger. Yalava sounded his whistle, and the train moved off toward the Finnish border. Rahja and Shotman were on the train as passengers. At every station they got out onto the platform to watch for any signs of danger.

Shortly before 2 A.M. the train arrived at Beloostrov, the frontier station. Since July, all identity papers were being rigorously checked here. Even at that early hour in the morning, several officials stood waiting on the platform.

Carefully, Yalava uncoupled his engine and drove it to a water tower. While the militiamen went down the train examining the passports of the passengers, Lenin in the cab watched Yalava top up his engine.

At the last possible moment, as the guard summoned him by whistle, the driver reversed to the engine, coupled up, and drove the train into Finland.

At Terijoki, horses were waiting and Lenin left the engine and traveled the ten miles to Jalkala, where he stayed with Rahja's parents-in-law. But Jalkala was too far from the rail line to permit easy communication with Petersburg, and after a few days, he moved to Helsinki, traveling disguised as a Finnish pastor. There he stayed in the apartment of a Bolshevik, Kustaa Rovio, who of all things was the Helsinki police chief. After a couple of weeks, he moved to a new hiding place, since Rovio's neighbors had begun to take an interest in the police chief's friend who so rarely went out. Before leaving the city, he had to move to a third refuge.

Correspondence with the party was now simple, for a friend of Rovio's worked in the mail car of a train that ran regularly between Helsinki and Petersburg. Yalava, too, took letters from time to time.

Living molelike in his hiding place, Lenin worked hard. He finished the first and, as it turned out, the last part of *State and Revolution*. Every day he scoured all the newspapers and analyzed developments in letters to the Central Committee. At first, when he was living in Rovio's apartment, he refused to go out at all, existing on eggs and tea that Rovio brought him.

As the weeks went by, Lenin grew increasingly optimistic. In an article about the "Bonapartism" of Kerensky he assured the Party that "all the signs seem to indicate that the march of events continues at an accelerated pace and that the country is approaching the next epoch, when . . . the revolutionary proletariat will take power. . ." He ordered the Central Committee to overhaul the leadership in Moscow, "this tremendous proletarian center, which is larger than Petersburg."

Certainly, by the end of August, the reaction to Kerensky's iron-fisted rule was evident in a strong upsurge of support for the still only semilegal party. On September 2, in the Petersburg city council elections, no less than one-third of all delegates elected were Bolsheviks—representing virtually the city's entire working class.

However, although Lenin had long known that plans for a military dictatorship were afoot in army and right-wing circles, even he was surprised by the dramatic new events that now took place in Petersburg.

The Germans were under assault again in France, and there was a need to reinforce the Western Front with regiments from the east. Because of this, General Ludendorff needed to reorganize his line to permit it to be held by reduced forces. On September 1 his troops attacked the Russian 12th Army, which was holding the Northern Front. Two days later, the Russians fell back from the important Baltic port of Riga. With the Kaiser's soldiers now barely 300 miles from Petersburg, Russia's continuing internal crisis boiled to a new peak. This time the controversy centered not on Lenin, but on General

Lavr Kornilov, the man who had been the garrison commander of the capital until the May Crisis.

In July, Kerensky had appointed Kornilov commander in chief of the Russian armies, and it was in this capacity that he became the central figure in a military coup—supported by most of the officer hierarchy, Milyukov and his Kadets and, probably, the Allied governments.

The rightists planned to set up a dictatorship that would liquidate the Soviets, restore order to the country and establish discipline in the army. Almost certainly, the general allowed Riga to fall to the Germans in order to create the ideal crisis climate for his bid for power. On September 7 he ordered Kerensky by wire to declare Petersburg in a state of siege and transfer all power to him as supreme commander.

When Kerensky responded furiously instead by dismissing his rebel general, Kornilov ordered his troops to advance on the capital.

With the army so involved in the conspiracy, Kerensky had no alternative but to ask the Soviet to help fight off this new threat. And the Soviet in turn had no alternative but to accept the Bolshevik offer of assistance, for it was the only party with any kind of formal military organization, badly damaged though it had been after July.

As soon as news reached the party of Kornilov's advance, the Bolshevik Central Committee had summoned the people to defend the city. Once more, the Red Guards, disarmed in July, were issued rifles. So, too, were other workers.

Podvoisky and Nevsky, suddenly thrust once more into the forefront of events, organized the defense of Petersburg, though there was in fact no confrontation. The railwaymen took up the tracks in front of the advancing troop trains. Kornilov's communications were broken by the telegraph operators. Agitators were dispatched to his soldiers in the name of the Soviet to persuade them that they were being exploited by the counterrevolution.

The advance faltered and stopped. On September 12 Kornilov was arrested. The reaction was violent. In the army, it produced a savage antagonism to the entire officer class. Throughout Russia, officers were murdered. In the Vyborg, generals, colonels and captains were flung into the river and either shot in the water or beaten to death with heavy sticks as they made their way to shore.

Inevitably, in the basic underlying conflict of revolution and counterrevolution, Kornilov gave a gigantic boost to the movement that had already been swinging toward the Bolsheviks.

Within a week, the party had gained voting control in the Petersburg Soviet, and a few days later Trotsky replaced Chkheidze as its president—the post he had held in 1905! By the third week in September the Bolsheviks had also won the important Moscow Soviet.

For Lenin, the Kornilov revolt and the party's majority in the two most important Soviets in Russia dramatically transformed the entire political situation. As he saw it, conditions were now ideal for the party to stage an uprising, but they might not remain favorable for long. The pendulum could swing again to reaction. Speed was essential, and in an urgent letter to the Central Committee, he demanded immediate action. "History will not forgive us if we do not assume power now. . . . We will win absolutely and unquestionably."

There is little doubt that the internal situation in Russia dictated Lenin's sudden decision that the party should move for an immediate uprising, but it is interesting that General Ludendorff simultaneously reached the same conclusion as Lenin that there was danger of another right-wing coup that might not fail a second time. He asked the Wilhelmstrasse to step up subversion within Russia—and a few days later gave orders that his troops should be encouraged to fraternize with the enemy soldiers across the front lines. Ludendorff wrote to Berlin on September 24, and Lenin wrote to Petersburg, according to the editors of his works, between September 25 and 27.

The closeness of the dates makes it tempting to infer collusion. It is more likely, however, that both Lenin and the

German commander in chief analyzed the situation in the same way.

On the other hand, there is some indication that Lenin initiated an approach to the Germans soon after learning of Kornilov's revolt. On September 8—some two weeks before he demanded that the party strike for power—he wrote Jacob Fürstenberg in Stockholm a long, meandering letter that he said he had been preparing for some time.

The letter is intriguing. In it, Lenin speaks of the difficulty of dispatch—which is strange since underground communication routes between Finland and Sweden had long existed and even the efficient Okhrana had not succeeded in permanently breaking them. Why should it be so difficult now? The letter also appears to anticipate discovery and contains demands for proof of his innocence against the slander of German financing, which centered on Eugenia Sumenson. "Who is this lady?" he asks. "It's the first time I have heard of her." He urges that Fürstenberg have his accounts with her independently audited and published.

This seems convincing until Lenin turns to asking questions about a German agent named Karl Moor. "What kind of man is Moor?" he asks. The fact that he knew Moor well makes it clear that the letter cannot be taken at face value. There is also the question of why he had delayed so long before instructing Fürstenberg to take action to counter the slander. This should have been done in July. Certainly, the audited accounts were not published.

There are also interesting questions about money in the letter. "How are the financial affairs of the bureau abroad which was appointed by our Central Committee?" he writes. "It is clear that our Central Committee cannot help. . . ." This could be translated as saying: They are short of money in Russia. Can you get some from the Germans?

On September 29, three weeks later, Richard von Kühlmann, who had now replaced Zimmermann as Foreign Secretary in Berlin, wrote to the High Command about the Wilhelmstrasse's support of the "Bolshevik movement." "There is every indication," he asserted, "that the movement will continue to grow."

For Lenin, the period following his call for an uprising was one of extreme frustration. In July he had been unable to hold the party back when he knew the timing was wrong. Now his problem was to galvanize it into action when he was convinced the moment was ideal. For after the traumas of the past months, the Petersburg Bolsheviks had become extremely cautious. Kamenev and the conservatives were dominating the leadership once more—and were virtually unchallenged, for even the left wingers were not demanding militancy after their savaging in July.

There was talk of ties with the Mensheviks, of coalition. It was the same sort of compromise thinking that had bedeviled Lenin repeatedly in one way or another ever since 1903.

More important still, most of the Central Committee did not agree with Lenin that the time was ripe for uprising. Halfheartedly they discussed a proposal for a strike for power which would coincide with the next all-Russian Congress of Soviets although, owing to the rise of Bolshevik influence, the plans to call this congress were being opposed by the other socialist parties. In Finland, Lenin was adamant that they would be too late if they waited for the congress, whose future was so uncertain.

For Alexander Kerensky was now striving to organize behind him all who were opposed to the looming threat of the Bolsheviks. And Lenin believed the Premier had a very good chance of succeeding unless the party acted quickly. Since the Bolsheviks now controlled the two main Soviets in the country, Kerensky was focusing his strategy on the Constituent Assembly—but the organizing of national elections in a vast country that had never had them before was complex and controversial.[4] As a stopgap, he planned a Pre-Parliament, a kind of temporary assembly, in which all sections of the community would be represented, which would sit until the elections were held.

Lenin saw the Pre-Parliament as a tactic by Kerensky to

broaden his base and consolidate his forces. Without question it must be sabotaged. When he learned that his party leaders were planning to cooperate, he flew into one of his *rages*. "You will be traitors and scoundrels," he wrote to the Central Committee if it did not act immediately to check Kerensky's plans and "arrest all the scum!" If it did not take militant action, he threatened, it—the Central Committee—would "face dire punishment."

It was an astonishing attack, fully conforming with Valentinov's vivid description of his *rages*, for the Central Committee ruled the party. It could not be threatened by one man, not even Lenin.

Agreeing among themselves that Lenin had become temporarily unstable, the Central Committee formally ordered the letter burned.

To Lenin, raging in Finland, it was obvious that the party leaders had no understanding of the critical situation that now existed—especially of the narrow limits of time within which they had to strike before Kerensky became too strong.

Moving in disguise to the Finnish town of Vyborg (not the Petersburg suburb) so as to be nearer the border, Lenin began to make his own plans for an uprising. He wrote to Ivan Smilga, a Kronstadt militant who had been on the Central Committee in July, and urged him to start organizing the fleet and troops within Finland for the "overthrow of Kerensky."

He bombarded Nadya with letters instructing her to use her influence in the capital's important Vyborg industrial area to press the Central Committee to organize an uprising. He sent an urgent demand to the just-assembling Petersburg city conference to pass a resolution calling for immediate action and wrote a passionate appeal to the Moscow Committee insisting that it throw its weight behind his campaign for immediate insurrection.

In a long and angry communication to the leaders of the party, he charged them with leaving his letters unanswered, of altering the militant nature of his articles and of "gagging" him. Defiantly, he tendered his resignation from the Central

Committee, leaving himself free to appeal directly to the lower ranks of the party. "For it is my deepest conviction that if we await the Congress of Soviets and let the present moment pass, we will ruin the revolution."

He also asked their permission to return to the capital and was incensed when he heard that it had been refused. When Alexander Shotman, his main liaison comrade, went to see him in Vyborg, Lenin snapped at him, "Is it true that the Central Committee has forbidden me to go to Petersburg?"

Shotman conceded that this was so, adding it was only in his own interest since police control at Beloostrov was very rigorous. Lenin began to stride up and down the room, repeating angrily, "I'm not going to tolerate this! I'm not going to tolerate this!"

And he did not. Secretly, he summoned to Vyborg Eino Rahja, who had organized his escape to Finland, and asked him to arrange a return journey without informing the Central Committee. He had already written to Nadya to find a good hiding place for him within the city.

Rahja planned the journey carefully. And on October 21,[5] Lenin traveled by train in his old disguise as a Lutheran pastor to Raivola, a station near the border. Then, to cross the frontier, he adopted his previous role of a locomotive stoker, passing through Beloostrov in Engine No. 293 with driver Hugo Yalava, while a watchful Rahja traveled in a carriage. At the familiar station of Udelnaya, he left the train and made his way to Marguerite Fofanova's Vyborg apartment, where one of the meetings of the party leaders had been held in the traumatic days after the July fiasco.

Lenin had returned to Petersburg to force his reluctant party to immediate revolt. In many ways, his situation was similar to that in March when news of the first uprising had reached him in Zurich. Then he had known it was vital for him to reach Russia without delay so that he could prepare and build his party against the inevitable erosion of compromise and counterrevolution.

Now, in October, seven months later, the critical time that he had foreseen had come, the moment when the working class could, provided it rose at once before Kerensky was completely ready, seize power and set in motion the world revolution that Karl Marx had predicted.

And once again, Lenin knew that he was the only man who could make it do this.

Chapter 15

IN OCTOBER THE CAPITAL was dark by three in the afternoon, and the wind blew chill and damp from the north west across the Gulf of Finland. It penetrated the heavy coats and fur hats of twelve persons who, on the evening of the twenty-third, made their way singly through slushy, ill-lit streets to a secret meeting in an apartment block overlooking the Karpovka River which enclosed the central island of Old Petersburg from the north.[1]

For the first time since he had fled from the city in July, Lenin was attending a meeting of the Central Committee, confronting those comrades whom he had threatened and accused of treachery.

From a security viewpoint, the meeting place was ideal. It had the two entrances that were obligatory for all secret rendezvous. More important, the apartment belonged to a prominent Menshevik—the last place that Kerensky's militiamen would search for Lenin.

Sukhanov, the journalist-politician who wrote the fullest day-to-day record of the whole revolutionary period, learned later that one of the most important meetings in the history of Russia had been held in his own home. "Oh, the novel jokes of the merry muse of history!" he cried out in his memoirs.

Galina, his wife, was a fervent Bolshevik. She had suggested to her husband with affectionate concern that since he would be working late, he should sleep near the office, as he sometimes did, instead of making the six-mile journey home late at night.

The participants arrived one by one: Zinoviev, now bearded and with his black hair cut short to change his appearance, pleased to see his leader but apprehensive of the meeting; Kamenev, who greeted Lenin warmly but was firm in his own conviction that an immediate uprising would destroy the party and the revolution; the emaciated Sverdlov, party secretary and completely reliable; Stalin, still editor of the party journal (now called *Rabochy Put* since *Pravda* had been banned in July) and a man whose loyalties shifted, a conservative in March, a militant in July and now hovering again on the right of the party spectrum; Trotsky, a man of power in his new role as president of the Petersburg Soviet, but an independent whom Lenin could not completely trust to accept every aspect of his leadership.

Others arrived who, like Trotsky, had been elected to the Central Committee during the party congress in August—men such as Sokolnikov, co-editor with Stalin of the party journal and one of the thirty-two comrades who had traveled on the Sealed Train—Lenin knew him from Switzerland to be another man of independence; Uritsky, one of Trotsky's "brilliant generals"; Felix Dzerzhinsky, still barely recovered from the illness he had developed in the Lubyanka, Moscow's grim prison, a dedicated and ruthless revolutionary soon to be feared more than any chief of the Okhrana; George Lomov, who had traveled to Petersburg from Moscow before Lenin's return to urge the rest of the Central Committee to accept its leader's line.

In all, there were twelve sitting at the round table in Sukhanov's living room beneath a single hanging lamp—plus Varvara Yakovleva, who was taking the minutes. Outside, Yuri Flakserman, Galina's brother, kept watch for any sign of danger.

Lenin studied the others intently. With Sverdlov, he had planned the strategy of the meeting with great care. He wanted an unequivocal resolution authorizing an immediate uprising to be led by the party, and he expected strong resistance before he got it.

The meeting began quietly enough.[2] As was customary, Sverdlov, as party secretary, reported on the general situation. But, as Trotsky commented later, Sverdlov was preparing the ground for Lenin by concentrating on the reports from the party committees at the front. For it was the attitude of the front-line troops that had made Lenin sure, in his postmortems of the July Days, that it would have been fatal for the party to have attempted to seize power then.

Now, Sverdlov indicated, the situation was different. "At the front . . ." he told them, "they [the troops] will follow us against Kerensky."

Ominous signs of counterrevolution had been reported. On one section of the front a Kornilov type of conspiracy was being prepared with the help of the Cossacks. On the Northern Front there were rumors of a plan to order a retreat that would open Petersburg, the heart of the revolution, to the Germans. As everyone around that table knew, many of the bourgeois now saw the Bolsheviks as a greater threat than the enemy.

As soon as Sverdlov had finished, Lenin took over the meeting. "Since the beginning of September," he rasped, "there has been a certain indifference to the question of insurrection."

Patiently at first, Lenin explained why the time was now ideal for revolt—why, as he had written from Finland, "to delay means death." There had been a mutiny in several German ships in the Baltic which indicated the international spread of lower-class unrest. A recent spate of insurrection in the villages throughout Russia—featuring a massive increase in the burning of big houses—showed that the peasants, that enormous but uncertain section of the Russian population, were tired of promises of land and were ready to support an organized revolt.

"Since July," Lenin insisted, "our upsurge has been making gigantic strides. . . . The majority are now with us. Politically, the situation has become entirely ripe for the transfer of power. . . ."

So far the mood at that secret meeting had been relatively, if somewhat artificially, calm. Lenin, said Trotsky, "was obviously restraining himself: He had too much feeling piling up in him."

Now, characteristically, Lenin moved to the attack. He "began to storm" at Trotsky, who was as enthusiastic for an uprising as Lenin himself, but believed that it should be organized by the Petersburg Soviet. There was no risk in this, since by now, in Lenin's absence, Trotsky personally controlled the soviet with Bolsheviks in command of every section.

Trotsky's plan was to give the operation legality by timing the uprising to coincide with the new All-Russian Congress of Soviets that had been summoned amid violent controversy to meet on November 2—in only ten days.

Fiercely, Lenin fought this whole idea. Despite his statements of the past months, he had personally never trusted Soviets, not even in 1905.[3] He preferred the disciplined control of a single party, even if this had broken down in July.

Also, the Soviet, with its delegates and motions, was a cumbersome machine to use. Trotsky's plan would involve delay.

Passionately, Lenin demanded "decisive action" within five days. October 28 was the latest date he would consider for the revolt since the operation must be completed before November 2, and it might well take a few days to complete. "We must not wait," he insisted. "We must not postpone. At the front, as we have heard from Comrade Sverdlov, they [the counter-revolution] are preparing an overturn. Will the Congress of Soviets ever be held? We do not know. We must seize power immediately and not wait for any congresses."

Lenin's main conflict, though, was with his once close comrades of the Troika, the men who had shared his exile, who had been his principal aides, who had joined those long discussions in the cafés of the Avenue d'Orléans in Paris.

Ironically, now at this crucial moment in history, there was no common ground, no room for negotiation, between Lenin and his two closest comrades. Even Zinoviev, who for months had wavered in his loyalties between his friend and his leader, was now firmly and immovably behind Kamenev.

Their disagreement was simple: To them there was nothing to be gained and everything to be lost by an armed uprising. If they waited a few weeks for the Constituent Assembly, their chances of legally winning a big majority in the elections "were excellent." There was no demand among the people for an uprising. If the party mounted a revolt, they would push the petty bourgeoisie, "the huge third camp" of shopkeepers, lower-echelon civil servants, better-off peasants into the arms of the counterrevolution. The support of the troops could not be relied on. Even more critical, the government forces—with their Cossacks and Junker military cadets in the Petersburg environs—were far stronger than they seemed.

"Comrade Lenin's proposal," insisted Kamenev,[4] "means to stake on one card not only the fate of our party, but also the fate of the Russian and International Revolution. . . . We have no right to stake the whole future on the card of an armed uprising."

Angrily, Lenin fought his two old friends on the issue. The party could command far larger forces than the government, he argued. The people would rise if they were called. Their apparent lack of enthusiasm was because they were tired of words and resolutions. The troops would fight in support of the party.

Most vital of all, Lenin could not persuade his stubborn opponents of the danger Kerensky's plans presented. This would not be just another abortive Kornilov putsch. Kerensky and his ally Milyukov would have learned the lessons of September just as the Bolsheviks had learned from July. This time, the move would be well organized.

Again and again, he repeated, "The success of the Russian and world revolution depends on two or three days struggle."

Insistently, his voice rising as he pounded the table, he tried to ram into their heads the basic fact that unless they acted now, it would be too late. There would be no second chance. Their conception of gaining power by constitutional means was naïve. Kerensky would never let them. Once he gained control of the country he would liquidate the Soviet. This was the party's last opportunity for a socialist revolution, for the world revolution— at least for many years. At the same time, conditions were such during this short period that an uprising could not fail.

[246

But Kamenev, with his red beard and spectacles, just sat at the other side of the table shaking his head.

For ten hours they argued, pausing at intervals as Galina Sukhanova served them tea with bread and sausage. At midnight the electricity was cut off, as it always was at this time in the city, for the current was only on for six out of every twenty-four hours. They continued the argument by the light of candles and at last, near three o'clock in the morning, Lenin forced the issue.

Leaning forward over a table that by then was littered with crumbs and dirty teacups, he wrote a resolution "with a gnawed pencil" on a page in a child's schoolbook of graph paper. "Recognizing . . . that an armed rising is inevitable and the time perfectly ripe," he scrawled in his small, tight writing, "the Central Committee proposes to all the organizations of the party to act accordingly and to discuss and decide from this point of view all the practical questions. . . ."

Then, formally, in the light of flickering candles, Sverdlov put it to to the vote. For Lenin it was a tense moment. Obviously, Trotsky might demur. So, too, might Uritsky, his comrade from his previous organization who had argued that neither the party nor the Soviet was prepared. Stalin had been very quiet all evening, but he was likely to support Kamenev as he had in March. Sokolnikov was clearly closer to Kamenev than he was to Lenin. Between them Sokolnikov and Stalin had altered Lenin's articles from Finland, editing out some of the militancy.

Despite Lenin's fears, ten of the twelve voted with him—all except for Kamenev and Zinoviev. But if Lenin won a majority of ten votes to two, this very fact leaves unanswered questions. Why did Uritsky support the uprising when he was so dubious about it? Why did Stalin desert Kamenev in the crucial vote? What convinced Sokolnikov?

One possible clue is that within two weeks the Austrian Foreign Minister would inform Kerensky that he was prepared to make a separate peace with Russia. The vital question is therefore whether, by the evening he met his comrades in Sukhanov's apartment, Lenin had been warned from Berlin about the possibility of such an approach. If he had, and this can only be speculation, it puts his demands for urgency in a different light. For if Kerensky could offer the Russian people an end to the fighting on the large section of the front held by troops of the Austro-Hungarian Emperor, he would "trump" Lenin, as he put it in his memoirs. The Bolshevik program for peace was, he believed, the key reason for the party's new surge of support. For Lenin, it was essential, therefore, that the rising should be staged before Kerensky could act in liaison with Vienna. Otherwise, it would be too late.

If this hypothesis is correct, there can be little doubt that Lenin was also under great pressure from Berlin—had there been any contact. For a separate peace with Austria would mark the disintegration of the Central Powers alliance and leave Germany isolated at a time when America had just entered the war.

Was the knowledge of an impending Austrian peace the crucial factor that convinced Uritsky and Stalin? Did it fail to convince Kamenev and Zinoviev only because they believed that, despite a peace with Austria, the party could still gain its objective through the Constituent Assembly?

The minutes of the meeting are sketchy and provide no support for this contention. Trotsky, who is the main informant on the events of that night, does not refer to it, but he could hardly have done so without revealing Lenin's links with Berlin—which he always fiercely refuted, though he must have known of the facts revealed by the German Foreign Office papers.

From Finland, Lenin had made the point in late September that "to offer peace to the people means to win," but then he had feared that the party would be "trumped" by a separate peace between Germany and Britain—which again would have ended in securing Kerensky's position. He did not mention Austria in his letters—strange in itself, since Austria's attitude was certain to be relevant.

Peace, organized by whatever means, clearly presented a major danger and was one reason why the Central Committee

[248

committed the party to an immediate uprising that night. In theory, at least, for in practice it was not quite so simple.

It was raining when Lenin left Sukhanov's apartment, clad in a raincoat borrowed from Dzerzhinsky, and made his way to Rahja's flat, where he planned to grab a few hours' sleep, since it was nearer than Marguerite Fofanova's home in the Vyborg. Most of the others spent the rest of the night on the floor of the room where they had made their critical decision before leaving the next morning for Smolny.

Since July, when the Tauride Palace had been vacated to make room for the still nonexistent Constitutent Assembly, the Smolny Institute had been the home of the Soviet. A massive gray domed and pillared mansion, some two hundred yards long, it stood in a U bend of the Neva at the edge of the city center where the tram lines ended. It lay in a small park beside the Smolny Cathedral which was painted blue and white, like many Russian churches, and dominated by three immense dull-gold cupolas.

Until the past spring it had been a school for the daughters of the Tsarist aristocracy, and there was a certain irony in the fact that the Petersburg Soviet met in the ballroom where the girls had learned the dance steps of a world that was now extinct.

It was at Smolny that Trotsky—Lenin's onetime protégé, his antagonist for years and now once more his firm ally even if Lenin did not entirely trust him—was to perform the star role in the party's bid for power. For as always, Lenin remained in the background. This time he had to do so, for he was still under indictment and Kerensky's police were scouring the city following rumors he had returned.

In Trotsky, history had given Lenin a perfect chief executive—a complement to himself. For Trotsky excelled in those facets of character and personality in which Lenin was weak. He was a natural public performer—which Lenin was not—and his oratory and style were coupled with a rare depth of intellect and a great talent for organization and command.

By that crucial night meeting of the twenty-third Trotsky had begun to prepare his base. The previous evening the Petersburg Soviet had agreed to set up a Military Revolutionary Committee to defend the revolution and, in particular, Petersburg.

The Germans were close. There was constant talk of moving the capital to Moscow—talk which acquired a new impetus when the Germans badly mauled part of the Russian fleet in a naval battle off Riga on the very day Lenin was engaged in his bitter dispute with his party leaders. The commander in chief seized the opportunity provided by this critical news to order a third of the regiments of the city to leave for the front.

This gave Trotsky his chance to start developing the theme for the uprising, cloaking a strike for power in the guise of defense. The commander's order, he alleged, was the first move in a counterrevolutionary plot to evacuate the capital. Under Trotsky's direction, plans were made for the Military Revolutionary Committee to oppose the order and defend the city, the heartland of the revolution.

Technically, the MRC did not yet exist, for, as Lenin had argued, it took time for the Soviet to act, but in practice it now became the hub of plans for the rising.

Trotsky was never officially a member of the MRC, though he directed it. Its titular head was an eighteen-year-old member of the Socialist Revolutionary Party. "We made use of him," wrote Trotsky. "Whether or not he perceived this . . . I don't know."

Ostensibly, the MRC was an instrument of the Petersburg Soviet, formed to defend the city against counterrevolution. In practice, it was the old Bolshevik Military Organization. One of its chiefs of staff was Nicholas Podvoisky. Another was Vladimir Antonov-Ovseenko, who had known Lenin in Paris. He was a slim young man who looked more like a poet than a militant revolutionary, but he was to play a central role in the events ahead. Nevsky, too, was prominent, but since July, he seemed to have lost some of his previous status.

Smolny was also the home of the Central Executive Committee of the All-Russian Congress of Soviets which was still dominated by SR's and Mensheviks. It was, therefore, under the eyes of the Bolsheviks' enemies that the MRC quickly developed as the headquarters of a revolutionary force. The party cadres in the army were alerted for revolt. The Red Guards in the factories were fast shaped into fighting units under rigorous instruction. Almost every night, meetings were held at Smolny to establish the lines of command and the network of liaison between workers and soldiers.

To counter the efforts of the opposition parties to sabotage the Congress of Soviets, Trotsky made a dramatic national appeal by radio, summoning all the Soviets of Russia and the army to send delegates to Petersburg.

Meanwhile, as Trotsky was setting up his command structure, Lenin was facing yet another mutiny—by far the most critical since the party had been established. Refusing to accept the Central Committee decision of the twenty-third, Kamenev and Zinoviev had appealed over Lenin's head to the party—where many of the upper-echelon comrades agreed with their views. Even Nevsky, the overzealous militant of July, was highly dubious that the country would support an uprising. Although some peasants were in revolt, others had warned that they would cut off bread supplies in the event of an insurrection. Nevsky was even doubtful about Moscow.

Most of his comrades believed the Central Committee's decision was premature, that they needed time to prepare the masses.

Watching events from the seclusion of Fofanova's apartment, Lenin realized that he would again have to intervene personally to force the party to act. On October 29, six days after the night meeting in Sukhanov's apartment, he trudged through the rain with Rahja to attend a large conference of the entire Bolshevik leadership—including the party chiefs in the factories, the railways, the Military Organization and the Petersburg districts—in the building of the Vyborg Duma.

It was a mortifying experience. The men who had been his two aides for years in exile had grown confident in their opposition to him. "Apparently," Zinoviev mocked him, "the resolution [by the Central Committee for the uprising] is not considered ordered. Otherwise, why are we discussing it?"

"A week has passed," challenged Kamenev—"shamelessly

shouted," as Lenin put it. "The Central Committee has been defeated, for it has done nothing for a *whole* week."

Lenin sat fuming as his former friends tried to tear his policy to ribbons—and, even more heinous, to sabotage what he knew must be done. "I could not refute" Kamenev's argument, he explained later, "because I could not tell what really was done." For Trotsky was not present to inform him. Lenin, therefore, could do nothing but listen helplessly as Kamenev insisted, "We have no machinery for an uprising. Our enemies have a much stronger machinery and it has probably increased further this week."

Just a little triumphantly, Zinoviev rose and "with an innocent air," as Lenin described it bitterly, put a resolution to the meeting that the decision on the uprising should be postponed until it could be considered by the Bolshevik delegates to the All-Russian Congress, now scheduled for November 2, four days away.

But Kamenev and Zinoviev were too optimistic. Many of the party agreed with them, but in the black or white decision Lenin demanded, they were reluctant to vote down their leader on so crucial an issue.

For Lenin was adamant. "There are only two alternatives—a dictatorship by Kornilov [the Kornilov forces now were ranged behind Kerensky] or a dictatorship of the proletariat."

To the surprise of Kamenev and Zinoviev, Lenin won the vote by an overwhelming majority. The rising was to proceed as ordered. His objective was achieved. He could return to the seclusion of Fofanova's apartment.

During these few weeks, Lenin took enormous pains as to his security. He was convinced that Kerensky would execute him if he could find him and that police were scouring the city for him, for he was now a serious threat.

Lenin rarely left the small room that Fofanova had given him, and on the occasions that he ventured into other parts of the flat he always wore his wig—presumably in fear of sudden visitors. It caused him trouble. "He kept trying to straighten it," Fofanova wrote, "and he was always asking people if he had put it on properly."

[252

There were not many people to ask. To avoid attracting the attention of the police, he held no meetings there at the apartment, always going elsewhere instead. Apart from Fofanova herself, Nadya, Maria and Rahja were the only visitors.

He even rejected Fofanova's suggestion that he should take some air sometimes on the balcony of the fifth-floor apartment. He went out onto it only once, and that was to check the drainpipes in case he had to use them as an emergency exit.

Fofanova was a married woman of thirty-four who had been a Bolshevik delegate to the Petersburg Soviet and to the Vyborg District Duma where Nadya had met her. She also had a job with a publishing house on Vasilevsky Island. On party orders, she had in August sent her two children and their nurse to live with her parents in the country. Her husband did not live with her.

As always, Lenin spent a lot of time reading the newspapers, and since they were not all on sale locally in the Vyborg, Fofanova had to take a streetcar into the center of the city to get them for him every morning before setting off to work. He would sit hunched over them, marking passages he was interested in with blue pencil.

Two evenings after the party conference in the Vyborg Duma, Lenin was working in his room when Fofanova called him to the phone. At first, so he said later, he could not believe what the comrade told him at the other end of the line. It was only after he had heard, read out aloud to him over the phone, what Kamenev had written in *Novaya Zhizn*, the newspaper owned by Maxim Gorky and edited by Sukhanov, that he realized there could be no doubt. Incredibly, Kamenev and Zinoviev had still refused to accept defeat. They had now published a public appeal to the party and to the people of Petersburg warning that the plans for "an armed insurrection . . . a few days before the Congress of Soviets would be . . . fatal to both the Proletariat and the Revolution."

From any standpoint, it was a fantastic betrayal by men trained in the rigors of party discipline throughout their long hard illegal years as revolutionaries. They had revealed the plan for the uprising, indicated the timing and, almost worse, exposed the deep division within the party.

It took Lenin a strangely long time to absorb the enormity of what his friends had done. He waited twenty-four hours before writing a bitter reply to his "former comrades" in *Rabochy Put.* "I do not consider them comrades any longer . . ." he declared. "I will fight with all my power in the Central Committee and at the [Bolshevik] Congress to expel them from the party."

But the Central Committee stubbornly refused to comply with his expulsion demand—possibly because he was not himself present at the session, relying on Sverdlov to argue the case.

Kamenev stepped down tactfully from the Central Committee, but apart from this, the two men were barely disciplined.

Alone, impotent and frustrated in Fofanova's apartment, Lenin fumed at the Central Committee's attitude and grew even more suspicious than he had been before. He was consumed by dark fears that the leaders would suddenly and openly side with Kamenev and Zinoviev and call off the uprising.

Even Trotsky, who had been too busy preparing the revolt to take part in any way in the party quarrel, was the object of Lenin's morose uncertainty—with some reason, for Trotsky had given his leader little information about the insurrection he was planning. And he was of course preparing it under the name of the Petersburg Soviet instead of that of the party as Lenin had demanded.

In fact, he was making enormous progress. On October 29—the day that Kamenev mocked Lenin that the party had no machinery—Trotsky produced his first results. The regiments of the garrison declared their refusal to accept the transfer directive to the front. Within hours, to test the authority of the Soviet in its new militant stance, Trotsky signed an order in its name to the arsenals to release 5,000 rifles to the Red Guards.

The action opened him up to inevitable attack in the Soviet from the Mensheviks. But even as a young man of twenty-three in the 1905 Soviet Trotsky had been a skilled debator. Questioned on the Bolsheviks' plans for a coup, he demanded, "In whose name?" the question was asked. "In the name of Kerensky, the counterintelligence, the secret police or some other body?"

When challenged on his order to the arsenals, he declared "on behalf of the Soviet that we have not decided on any armed action," which, of course, was technically true. The Soviet had not made any decisions, though the party had. Justifying the arming of the workers, he warned, "We must be ready. . . . We must be constantly prepared for the counterrevolution."

His denial was enough to alarm the already-suspicious Lenin in his refuge in the Vyborg—especially since the opening date of the Congress of Soviets had been put back five days to November 7, though this was not Trotsky's fault.

Lenin summoned Trotsky to his apartment and his anxiety was soothed to some extent by his field commander's explanations. Grudgingly, he conceded that Trotsky's tactics in the Soviet had been adroit.

Even so, he was still afraid that Kerensky might act before they were ready to strike. "Are you sure they won't steal a march on us?" he asked Trotsky anxiously. "Are you sure they won't surprise us?"

Trotsky was reassuring. "Now everything will follow automatically," he said.

The mood in the city was strange, for a Bolshevik uprising was discussed daily in the newspapers—as was the possibility of a right-wing coup. The city grew tenser with each passing day.

"On the streets," wrote John Reed in *Ten Days That Shook the World*, "the crowds thickened toward gloomy evening, pouring in slow voluble tides up and down the Nevsky, fighting for the newspapers. . . . Hold-ups increased to such an extent that it was dangerous to walk down side streets. . . . On the Sadovaya one afternoon I saw a crowd of several hundred people beat and trample to death a soldier caught stealing. . . . Mysterious individuals circulated around the shivering women who waited in queues long cold hours for bread and milk, whispering that the Jews had cornered the food supply—and that while the people starved, the Soviet members lived luxuriously. . . ."

All day and most of the night, Smolny was alive with activity. Men and women worked continuously in the committee rooms. Upstairs in the great hall, beneath crystal chandeliers, the hundreds of delegates to the Petersburg Soviet shouted, argued, objected and demanded the floor. At night, the long passages were thick with the sleeping figures of soldiers and workers. From outside with the lights blazing all night at three levels in the long façade, Smolny resembled an ocean liner.

The mood of the city was strangely unreal. The cafés of the Nevsky were crowded until the early hours of the morning as fur-clad prostitutes paraded on the pavements as they had under the Tsar. Patrons in the gambling clubs played for enormous stakes with a lemminglike intensity.

"And in the rain, the bitter chill," wrote Reed, "the great throbbing city under gray skies, rushing faster and faster towards . . . what?"

On the evening of November 1, at one of the nightly meetings at Smolny, Podvoisky outlined the progress of the plans for the uprising. In the big industrial areas of Vyborg and Narva, the Red Guards and the troops from the local barracks were working closely together. Through the party cells in the Armored Car Division the party controlled most of the military vehicles in the city. The Artillery regiments and the Guards regiments were prepared for the uprising. So, too, were the sailors. Troops had already been assigned to hold the roads leading from the city against any movement from Cossacks or other troops loyal to the government.

As the conference ended, Sverdlov, who had been presiding, told Podvoisky that Ilyich wanted to see him together with Antonov-Ovseenko and Nevsky. For security, they were to travel to the Vyborg by different routes and meet in the apartment of Dmitri Pavlov, where, in the old illegal days before March, the Bureau of the Central Committee used to hold its secret meetings. It was in Serdobolskaya Street, close to the block where Lenin was living.

Lenin was waiting for them in the apartment in his elaborate bewigged disguise. He demanded a report of the detailed military plans for the uprising. Then he led Podvoisky to a sofa and sat down beside him. "Tell me, Nikolai Ilyich," he said, "have you checked everything?"

"Certainly, Vladimir Ilyich," Podvoisky assured him. "The commanders of the Military Organization, including myself, visit all Red Guard units and the military divisions every day."

Because the party organization had been so poor in July, Lenin grilled the three men on detail—especially about the Red Guards, who were vitally important politically since they were workers in a working-class revolt, but who were inexperienced as fighting instruments. In particular, he questioned Podvoisky about the Red Guard commanders. "Is he a good shot?" he asked about one man Podvoisky described as a "wonderful fellow." "Can he fire a big gun . . .? Will he be able to drive a vehicle if necessary? Does he know anything about the tactics of street fighting?"

Embarrassed, Podvoisky admitted he did not know. "I haven't looked at the Red Guard commanders from that angle, Vladimir Ilyich," he said.

"Ai, ai, ai!" Lenin exclaimed. "What a fine chairman of the Military Organization! How are you going to direct a rising if you do not know what sort of men your commanders are? It's not enough that they are good agitators . . . that they give good speeches. An uprising is not a meeting to listen to speeches. . . ."

He demanded that all Red Guard commanders who had not been trained in street fighting should be immediately replaced, no matter how reliable they were politically. "And are you convinced that the commanders of the regular troops will not give way?" he asked. "After all, they are Tsarist officers."

Podvoisky was on surer ground here. "Only those commanders who accept the control of the soldiers' committees are still in their posts," he said.

Lenin strode about the room, looking like a little old man in his wig, lying down points of strategy he believed they should adopt.

At one moment Podvoisky suggested that he should order the

printing of the decrees that the new government would enact on assuming power. Lenin burst out laughing. "What are you thinking of, Nikolai Ilyich?" he asked. "The first thing we must do is to achieve victory and afterwards we can print decrees. . . ."

In the early hours of the morning the three men returned through the damp darkness of the city to Room 17 on the third floor of Smolny and immediately began a review of the whole organization, studying it carefully for the weaknesses that Lenin's grilling had revealed, tightening it, dispatching commissars to issue new orders. In particular, the party organization in Finland—a vital area since it was a Cossack base, the home of much of the Navy and close to Petersburg—needed more attention. By dawn Nevsky was on his way to Helsinki.

This meeting with the planning staff appears to have been a sop to Lenin—probably instigated by Sverdlov, who understood his frustration. For Lenin was in an unhappy position. The revolution he had planned all his life, that would not be taking place if he had not returned to Petersburg to insist on it, was now happening despite him. In the Vyborg he was on the sidelines, almost ignored. The leaders were working so hard they barely had time to sleep, let alone travel out to the far end of Bolshoy Sampsonievsky Prospect to discuss events with their leader.

Trotsky, in fact, had the operation well under control, building up his power base surely and methodically. He had the pledged support of most of the regiments in the city and of all the barracks in a large ring around Petersburg which reached almost as far as Moscow. He had the Red Guards poised for action. The sailors of the fleet awaited the order to act.

Reassuring news had come in from the front: New elections to the regimental committees showed a surge to the Bolsheviks.

Systematically, Trotsky set the machine of insurrection in motion under careful control. On November 3 he instructed all regiments in the garrison to obey no orders that were not approved by the MRC—and a meeting of delegates of the regiments the next day declared their acceptance of the committee's authority. In one move, the garrison commander had been stripped of all power.

Only four days now remained before the convening of the controversial Congress of Soviets—four days during which power must be seized. Already delegates from all over Russia had begun to arrive in the city. They reported somewhat apprehensively to Smolny, whose approaches were crowded with Red Guards demanding passes that were changed every few hours.

Although time seemed short, Trotsky and Sverdlov were preparing the strike with deliberate care. Sverdlov was the heart, the basic channel of incoming information and outgoing instruction. Trotsky was the dynamic force. The MRC leaders in Room 17 with their big map of the city were the planning staff.

Sunday, November 4, was to be the final day of preparation—a kind of last review of the forces at the MRC's disposal, a search for undetected signs of weakness. "The Day of the Petersburg Soviet," as it was rather grandiosely named, was not to be marked by the provocative street demonstrations that had featured similar days in the past but by meetings everywhere—in factories, barracks, public halls, theaters.

Trotsky drove out to a large hall near the Peter and Paul Fortress. "All around me," wrote Sukhanov of the thousands at the meeting, "was a mood bordering on ecstasy. It seemed as though the crowd, spontaneously and of its own accord, would break into some religious hymn."

"The Soviet government," Trotsky told his audience of thousands, "will give everything the country contains to the poor and the men in the trenches."

He demanded a mass expression of support, a unanimous vote for the revolution. The crowd of thousands raised their hands.

"Let this vote of yours be your vow—with all your strength and at any sacrifice to support the Soviet that has taken upon itself the glorious burden of bringing to a conclusion the victory of the revolution and of giving land, bread and peace."

The vast crowd voted and vowed—like other crowds of

thousands throughout Petersburg. "This actually was already an insurrection . . ." wrote Sukhanov.

More precisely, it was a demand, an enthusiasm for an insurrection that only days before Kamenev and Zinoviev had insisted did not exist.

Lenin had been right. He had sent out the call, and the people had responded. As he hid in Fofanova's flat in his wig, the news of that Sunday must have given him pleasure and reassurance, though he does not refer to it. He was still ravaged by agonies that his Central Committee which had refused to expel Kamenev and Zinoviev would back down, still haunted by the suspicion that it would compromise with Kerensky, who was sure to offer a deal—as, indeed, he did. But Lenin need not have worried, for by now Kerensky had little enough to offer.

Chapter 16

FROM THE START OF TROTSKY'S planning, information had streamed into Kerensky's big room overlooking the Neva, but supported as he thought he was by the entire right wing and the two big socialist parties, he was not too anxious. "All I want them to do is act," he told Sir George Buchanan. "Then I will crush them."

The reason for Kerensky's confidence was the Pre-Parliament, which in its sessions every day in the Mariinsky Palace had assumed much of the role formerly carried out by the Soviet, as well as performed the function of an assembly. Although the Bolsheviks had boycotted it, the other socialist leaders played a prominent part—as indeed did the heads of the bourgeois parties. Kerensky felt that because he had the support of the Pre-Parliament, he led the nation.

As soon as Trotsky had started to make overt moves to control the garrison through the MRC, Kerensky had acted to counter him. The Petersburg commander had warned all regiments that anyone provoking the masses to civil war must be "a conscious tool of the Emperor Wilhelm." At the same time, Kerensky had called in the Junker military cadets from the nearby towns to strengthen the defense of the Winter Palace. Six field guns had been brought from the Mikhailovsky Artillery Academy. Outposts had been set up in Millionnaya Street to the east of Palace Square and in the Alexandrovsky Gardens to the west.

The "Day of the Soviet," when Bolshevik orators gained such ecstatic receptions throughout the city, made it obvious that a Bolshevik revolt was imminent. The next morning, Monday,

Kerensky summoned troops from the front—including Cossacks—and called in a "shock" division stationed at Pavlovsk.

The government staging area was the Winter Palace with its complex of buildings around the big square on the south of the river and, on the north of the Neva, the Fortress of Peter and Paul. The garrison of the fortress was still loyal. Palace Bridge linked the two bastions.

That Monday morning, at a meeting of the Cabinet in the palace, the ministers agreed with Kerensky's proposal that the government should at last act against the Bolsheviks. That day the party newspapers would be closed down and the leaders of the MRC arrested.

As a precaution, the cruiser *Aurora*, the only big ship on the Neva that had been undergoing a refit in the docks, was ordered to sea for trials. Her crew, like so many of the sailors, were unreliable.

Meanwhile, in Smolny, the men whose arrest was being planned in the palace were completing their own arrangements to seize power—making the last-minute appointment of commissars to all units. The committee from the *Aurora*, whose sailing orders were even then being phoned to the ship's captain, was being instructed in person by Sverdlov. The warship would not be going to sea, for the MRC had plans for her.

Smolny was being fortified. Machine guns were placed at strategic points on the ground and on the balconies. Barricades were made out of piles of firewood. Fifteen hundred Red Guards as well as some professional machine gunners had been detailed to man its defenses. Near the entrance, guards warmed their hands at braziers.

In a public announcement, the MRC informed the people of the city that commissars had been appointed to all military units and key points in the capital. "The commissars as representatives of the Soviet are inviolable," the committee warned. "Opposition to the commissars is opposition to the Soviet. . . ."

That Monday, near lunchtime, in crowded Room 17 on

Smolny's top floor, the MRC leaders studied the map of the city as reports flowed in: the lean, bearded Podvoisky, his eyes red with lack of sleep; Antonov-Ovseenko, unshaven, his long hair disheveled, his collar filthy. All the others in the room were haggard with fatigue. They had not been home for days, grabbing sleep when they could on the floor or on sofas.

"They knew the temperature of each regiment," recorded Trotsky, "and followed every shift in the sympathies and views of each barracks. . . . There remained, however, some dark shadows on the map."

One shadow was crucial: the Fortress of Peter and Paul. That day the commander had felt so confident of the garrison troops that he had threatened to arrest the commissar the MRC had appointed.

The problem could be postponed no longer. They could not leave the fortress in Kerensky's hands. Trotsky was called into Room 17 for a final discussion on tactics. Antonov urged aggressive action. "Why don't we march into the fortress with a reliable battalion of Pavlovskys and disarm the hostile units?" he said.

Trotsky shook his head. That would be too drastic, and it could be exploited by the officers. "The troops cannot be unsympathetic," he mused.

That afternoon he traveled to Peter and Paul to address the men and expose them to his fantastic personal magnetism. Happily, he phoned Smolny from the fortress that the garrison had agreed to take orders only from the MRC.

By that night everything was ready for the rising. All that was lacking was some provocative action by Kerensky, so that Trotsky could present the uprising as a defense of the revolution rather than a grab for power.

Before dawn, a restless Trotsky was roaming the long vaulted corridors of Smolny with Podvoisky. Two people, a man and woman, ran up to him, panting. Government Junkers had closed down *Rabochy Put* and *Soldat*, the party journals, and fixed seals on the doors.

Immediately, Trotsky sent an order to the troops stationed

near the press to break the seals and to protect the printers. Production of the papers was soon resumed.

Meanwhile, Trotsky had the excuse he needed, the instrument with which he could present an aggressive strike for power as a defensive maneuver against the "conspirators" of the counter-revolution, as he branded the government. "The Petersburg Soviet is in danger . . ." the MRC wired all regiments in the garrison, ordering them "to be in complete readiness for action. . . ."

"The enemy of the people took the offensive during the night," a seaman operator on board *Aurora* radioed a warning to the barracks outside the city. "The Military Revolutionary Committee is leading the resistance to the assault of the conspirators." They were to hold up all "counterrevolutionary echelons" moving toward the city, by which the MRC meant government relief forces.

"Citizens!" the MRC appealed to the people of the city. "Counterrevolution is raising its head. The Kornilovists are mobilizing their forces to crush the All-Russian Congress of Soviets. . . . The Petersburg Soviet of Workers' and Soldiers' Deputies assumes the defense of the revolutionary order. . . . Citizens, we call upon you to maintain complete calm and self-control. . . ."

That morning, in the Mariinsky Palace, Kerensky mounted the rostrum to address the Pre-Parliament. "The capital . . ." he declared, "is in a state of revolt. We are faced with an attempt to incite the mob against the existing order . . . to lay open the front lines to the armies of Kaiser Wilhelm. . . . Let everyone remember that Kalush and Tarnopol [where the German counterattack broke through the line] coincided with the July revolt. . . ."

Kerensky was convinced that Lenin had set the timing of the uprising in agreement with Berlin. For only three days before, the premier had received the information from Count Ottokar Czernin in Vienna intimating that Austria was ready to make a separate peace. Its significance had been enormous. It was to have been his means of solving his massive problems, of consolidating his position, of curbing the Bolsheviks.

Unhappily for Kerensky, it had come too late. For as he was addressing the Pre-Parliament in the Mariinsky Palace, the Bolshevik Central Committee was making final plans in Smolny. Lenin, of course, was not there. In fact, the impression given by contemporary documents suggests that he had been forgotten in his hideout in Bolshoy Sampsonievsky Prospect. He had served his historical purpose. He had assessed the situation and forced the party to revolt. He was not needed for the actual uprising—or at least he was not used.

Zinoviev, too, was absent. So was Stalin, engrossed in his role as editor of the party journal. However, Kamenev was present, even though technically he was not a member of the Central Committee. He had now dropped his opposition and was giving all the help he could.

Sverdlov, as usual, was in the chair. Calmly, the committee made the decision to grasp power that night. Special duties were allocated. One comrade was placed in charge of radio and telegraph communications; another was assigned to maintain contact with the railwaymen; a third was responsible for food supplies. Two men were appointed liaison officers with the party committee in Moscow. Sverdlov himself was to keep a special watch on the government ministers and stay in constant touch with the Fortress of Peter and Paul that was to be a reserve HQ if Smolny should be attacked and taken. Kamenev was ordered to open negotiations with the two opposition socialist parties whose leaders preferred him to the other Bolsheviks. According to Kerensky, Kamenev's assignment was to lull them off their guard. This may have been a part of the tactic but certainly the cooperation of the left-wing SR's, the party of the peasants, could be useful to the revolutionary government after the rising.

Soon after midday, John Reed was at Smolny. "A steady stream of commissars came and went," he reported of the smoke-filled MRC's operations room. . . . "In the hall I ran into some of the minor Bolshevik leaders. One showed me a revolver. 'The game is on,' he said and his face was pale."

In fact, it was Kerensky who took the initiative. Early in the afternoon detachments of Junkers occupied the railway stations. Government troops set up command posts at the main street intersections and began to commandeer all private vehicles. The main bridges over the Neva and its branches were raised— except for Palace Bridge, which was left down, under heavy guard.

The MRC had not planned to start its operation until darkness fell, but as reports of what was happening began to filter in to Room 17 at Smolny, it became clear that some action was needed. For movement over the bridges was crucial to the whole strategy.

Podvoisky began phoning the commissars on duty at the points nearest to the bridges to discover the true situation. Some bridges had been raised, though most commissars had taken action to lower them. Podvoisky placed each bridge in the custody of the nearest barracks. "The bridges are to be kept down at all costs," he ordered.

For twelve hours, through the afternoon and evening, the city was in confusion. The bridges were the focus of the fighting. Some were raised and lowered several times. The Nikolaevsky, which linked Vasilevsky Island with the city center, was not brought under firm MRC control until long after midnight.

Meanwhile, rival patrols roamed the streets. Only Smolny and the Winter Palace complex—both fortified with artillery, machine guns and barricades—were firmly under the control of one side or the other.

Despite Kerensky's moves, the MRC did not change the early-morning schedule already laid down for the rising—almost certainly because, with the great numbers involved, an alteration to the plan could cause confusion.

Suddenly, on government orders, the operators in the

telephone exchange, most of whom were Kadet Party members, refused to connect any more calls from Smolny—and the commissar from the Keksgolmsky Regiment was dispatched to persuade them to change their minds.

There was more trouble at Peter and Paul—from the bicycle regiment that had not attended yesterday's meeting to hear Trotsky's address. Again Trotsky had to rush across the Neva, with a strong escort, to persuade the hostile troops—the same troops who had stormed the Kshesinskaya Mansion in July—to support the Soviet. And again his personality and his near-magical gift of persuasion broke down the opposition.

During the evening, the MRC conducted a couple of small preliminary operations. They sent out units to seize the central telegraph office—retaken later by Kerensky's troops—and the government news agency. Then, as heavy rain washed the streets of the city, they waited.

Lenin was waiting too in the Vyborg apartment, uninformed even of the Central Committee's decision to stage the rising, unaware that already there was fighting in the city center— presumably because a phone call would have been dangerous at this critical time.

Fofanova was still in her office at the publishing house on Vasilevsky Island when at four o'clock in the afternoon she heard that the bridges had been raised and that troops were on the march.

The people of the city, accustomed to conflict, were taking what were now routine preparations for crisis in their stride. Everyone was leaving his office for home. The shopkeepers were putting up shutters.

Hurriedly, Fofanova caught a streetcar home and reported to Lenin.

He was acutely alarmed—for the fact that some of the bridges were raised meant that the government had taken the initiative. "It's impossible to postpone things any longer!" he exclaimed angrily. "It's vital that we start the armed uprising immediately."

He sent Fofanova to the Vyborg District Committee with orders to find out definitely whether or not the bridges had been lowered—and with a brief note to Nadya, who was at the committee office, telling her to press for action and demand party permission for him to leave for Smolny.

Fofanova left Lenin in agony. He still believed that Trotsky and the Central Committee were holding back, were even now at the last minute hoping to seek power by constitutional means as Kamenev and Zinoviev had demanded. Newspaper reports had even referred to negotiations between the MRC and Kerensky's Military Headquarters.

Sitting down at the table in his room, he wrote an impassioned appeal to the party for action: "Comrades, I am writing these lines on the evening of the 6th. The situation is extremely critical. . . . With all my power I wish to persuade the comrades that now everything hangs on a hair, that on the order of the day are questions that are not solved by conferences, by congresses (not even congresses of soviets), but only by the people . . . by the struggle of armed masses. . . .

"We must not wait! We may lose everything! . . . The government is tottering. We must deal it the deathblow at any cost. To delay action is the same as death."

It was a release for Lenin, a bloodletting, for the letter could not possibly reach any but a very few party members that night.

By the time Fofanova returned about nine o'clock Rahja had joined Lenin in the apartment. The bridges had now all been lowered, Fofanova told him—although this was not accurate—but the Vyborg Committee had insisted that he did not go to Smolny. With Junker patrols out in force, it would be far too dangerous.

Angrily, Lenin insisted she return to the committee. "Ask them . . . what they're afraid of. Aren't there a hundred Bolshevik soldiers . . . with rifles, who would defend me?" Quickly he wrote yet another note to Nadya for Fofanova to take with her. And if she had not returned by eleven o'clock, he told her, he would take whatever action he considered necessary.

[268

* * *

The Petersburg Soviet had been in almost continuous session in Smolny's second-floor ballroom. That night, as the Junkers were clashing with troops directed by the MRC, Trotsky mounted the rostrum—"borne on a wave of roaring applause," as one eyewitness described it, "his thin pointed face was positively Mephistophelian. . . ."

"We are asked," he declared, "if we intend to have an uprising. I can give a clear answer to that question. The Petersburg Soviet feels that at last the moment has arrived when the power must fall into the hands of the soviets. . . . We feel that our government, entrusted to the personnel of the Provisional Cabinet, is a pitiful and helpless government, which only awaits the sweep of the broom of history. . . .

"Tomorrow, the Congress of Soviets opens. It is the task of the garrison and of the proletariat to put at its disposal the power they have gathered. . . ."

It was a delicate and specious strategy that Trotsky was conducting. He was still not admitting that the MRC was planning to mount an offensive operation. He put everything in terms of defense.

Around midnight, orders went out from Smolny for two preliminary moves. Sverdlov wired Helsinki: "Send Regulations"—the code order for the immediate dispatch of 1,500 sailors. The *Aurora* was ordered to proceed upriver to the Nikolaevsky Bridge, which was still raised and under the control of the Junkers. "Restore traffic by all means at your disposal," the MRC commissar on board the cruiser was instructed.

All of the *Aurora*'s officers were under arrest because they had refused to obey the orders of the commissar, but at the last moment the captain could not bear the thought of a naval rating trying to navigate his big ship upriver in the relatively shallow water. He sent a message up to the commissar that he was willing to take the ship up to the bridge.

Tugs towed the cruiser into the river from the wharf at which she had been lying. Slowly, she steamed upstream.

269]

Fofanova had returned to her apartment before the eleven o'clock deadline that Lenin had given in his note to Nadya. But she had found the flat in darkness. On a clean plate on the dining-room table beside the unfinished remnants of Lenin's supper was a note: "I have gone there, where you did not want me to go. Good-bye—Ilyich."

By then, with Rahja, Lenin was trudging south through the rain on the way to Smolny. He was disguised in the inevitable wig, with a scarf wrapped around his chin and cheeks to give the impression that he was suffering from a toothache. Huddled in an overcoat with the collar up as he was, not much of him was visible.

A streetcar drew up at a stop as they were passing it, and they clambered aboard. "Where are you going?" Lenin asked the conductor.

The conductor looked at him strangely. "Don't you know there's going to be a revolution?" he asked the man who had been pleading for one for weeks and was still unconvinced it was going to happen. "We're off to beat the bourgeoisie!"[2] The streetcar was on its way back to its depot. This meant that it would not cross the Neva, but would turn off by the Finland Station.

Lenin and Rahja got off while the train was still in Sampsonievsky Prospect, walked past the Finland Station carefully, as stations were obvious points for government patrols, and approached the Liteiny Bridge.

The bridge was down and the northern side was controlled by a unit of Red Guards. But as the two men were allowed onto the bridge after their MRC passes had been examined, the guards warned that the other end was in the hands of government troops who would demand government permits.

However, when they reached the other end of the long bridge—the Neva was wide at this point—the Junker sentries were arguing with a large group of workers whom they had stopped, and Lenin and Rahja were able to slip past unnoticed.

They walked on down Liteiny Prospect, turned into Shpalernaya and passed the Tauride Palace. A patrol of mounted

Junkers stopped them. Rahja pretended to be drunk and began to argue with them—diverting their attention so that Lenin could move on down the street in the darkness.

When at last they arrived at Smolny, blazing with lights on every floor, there was a large crowd at the entrance. For security reasons, passes were being changed every few hours and many were out of date, as indeed were those of Lenin and Rahja. Lenin and Rahja presented their passes, and the Red Guards on duty promptly refused them admission. But the guards were no longer being very strict in enforcing a badly organized pass system. The crowd was turbulent and jostling. The two men slipped past the guards into the building.

As Lenin entered Smolny, the hour for the uprising was imminent. "Are you agreeing to a compromise?" were the first words he snapped at Trotsky.

Trotsky realized that Lenin had referred to the newspaper stories that the MRC was negotiating with the government. He smiled and shook his head. "We issued that soothing news to the press deliberately," he said. "It was only a stratagem to cover the moment of the attack."

"Well, that is good," answered Lenin, drawling his words appreciatively. He rubbed his hands in excitement—so Trotsky recorded—and began to pace up and down the room. "That is very good." Then anxiety welled up in him again. "Why are the streets so quiet?" he demanded.

Trotsky explained that everything was under control. Throughout the city the party was poised to seize power. By daylight the operation would be completed.

The scene on the third floor—where the executives of the revolution, red-eyed with weariness, were giving orders over the phone—partly calmed Lenin's concern at last. He was not witnessing delay or even compromise. Even so, he remained cautious. He did not share Trotsky's supreme confidence. "Nothing is yet attained," he said and bombarded Trotsky with questions on the details of the planning.

Soon after he had arrived at Smolny, he had taken off his cap

271]

and removed the scarf from his face. He continued to wear his wig. It was not until later that Bonch-Bruevich suggested he should take it off. "I'll keep it for you," his friend said, adding with a wink, "After all, we might still need it. . . ."

At two o'clock in the morning the operation started. Units of soldiers and workers led by MRC commissars moved through the dark wet streets to take control of the targets to which they had been assigned: the rail stations, the electricity plants, the waterworks, the state bank, the food warehouses. Control of the telephone exchange and the telegraph office—which had been the object of countermoves by government troops during the evening—was now established firmly. The phones at the Winter Palace and Military District Headquarters were disconnected.

One by one, the bridges that were not already under full MRC control were taken. There was little fighting now. In most cases, the government troops just surrendered the posts.

At three thirty the *Aurora* dropped anchor in the middle of the river, her searchlights probing the Nikolaevsky Bridge, one side of which was raised. As at most other points, the Junkers did not resist. Sailors landed from the cruiser and lowered the bridge—and a mass of Red Guards and troops who had been waiting on Vasilevsky Island swarmed across.

In the Winter Palace, Kerensky was meeting with several members of the Cabinet on the crisis when an aide interrupted with the news that Red Guards had seized the telephone exchange and key government buildings, and rebel detachments were approaching Palace Square. Soon Kerensky was to learn that several ships of the Baltic fleet had entered the Neva in battle readiness and that the *Aurora* was at the Nikolaevsky Bridge—within easy gunshot of the palace.

The garrison commander proposed a dramatic plan. Why did they not storm Smolny! They had enough loyal troops. But Kerensky did not believe that this was practical. Furthermore, he had begun to suspect his military staff of treachery. Certainly the uprising had met with little resistance so far. And suddenly Kerensky believed he knew why. His right-wing officers—men who had secretly supported Kornilov—wanted Kerensky deposed, for they regarded him as too weak. They did not believe that Lenin would be able to head a government for long. With the entire officer corps behind them, they would then sweep him from power and establish the kind of iron-fisted government for which so many of them hankered.

Kerensky hurried across the square to Staff Headquarters and took over personal control of the government forces. There was little he could do, however. The Cossacks, who were in their barracks, were uncertain. Some of them had voted to stay neutral. Others had pledged their support. Now, however, as Kerensky phoned the barracks repeatedly, he met continual procrastination. "We are saddling our horses," he was told several times. But in the event they never mounted them.

By dawn Kerensky's position was serious. Even the Palace Bridge was in the hands of Bolshevik sailors. His telephones had been disconnected, although he still had a direct wire to headquarters at the front that was intact. The Junker military cadets within the Winter Palace had been threatened with dire punishment by the Bolsheviks if they stayed at their posts.

Kerensky's only hope now lay with the troops and Cossacks approaching from the front in response to his emergency call. Soon after daylight he drove out of the city to meet them at Pskov, ordering his driver to proceed at normal speed until they were out of the center of Petersburg—so that they would not unduly alert the pickets. The strategy was successful, and though Kerensky was recognized, he was not stopped. Reacting instinctively, some of the Bolshevik troops even snapped to attention.

The situations of the two antagonists from Simbirsk had been dramatically reversed. Now it was Kerensky who was fleeing the city. Soon Lenin would be assuming the role of head of state.

As the information coming into Smolny showed that the city was being brought under control with such ease, Lenin went with Kamenev and a few other comrades to a lower floor. There in Room 36 they began to consider the structure of the new government they were going to form

"Vladimir Ilyich was extremely cheerful and gay," recorded party member A. A. Yoffe. He teased Kamenev about his earlier doubts that even if they could gain power, they could hold it for more than two weeks. Kamenev had now given his support to the party, but he was still uncertain about the future. The taking of one city, even the capital city, was not the whole of Russia.

"Never mind," Lenin told him with a grin, "when two years pass you'll still be saying: " 'We can only hold on for another two years.' "

Yoffe remarked how good it was that the revolution had been achieved virtually without bloodshed. Immediately, Lenin became serious. "Don't be too happy about it," he said. "There will still be plenty of blood spilled. Anyone with weak nerves had better resign from the Central Committee at once."

They began to discuss what the new government should be called. Lenin, according to Kamenev, suggested it should be named the Workers' and Peasants' Government. The title "Minister," reminiscent as it was of the old Tsarist regime, would clearly have to be discarded. "Why don't we call the new authority the Council of the People's Commissars?" proposed Kamenev.[3]

Later, before it was light, Lenin went upstairs to the MRC operations room for the latest reports on the rising. The pace had slowed down. The Winter Palace had not been taken. "May I please have an explanation!" he demanded of Podvoisky.

Poor Podvoisky, in command of the attack, did not know the reason. He was not getting adequate answers to his telephoned demands for information. In fact, the assault plan, involving eight regiments, large contingents of Red Guards and sailors from both Kronstadt and several warships, was just too large to deploy efficiently in the time allocated to the operation. Small storm groups, similar to those that had taken the other main parts of the city, would probably have captured the palace more easily.

By seven o'clock in the morning the assault units were only

just beginning to assemble in the streets surrounding Palace Square. The main contingents of sailors had not even arrived in the city. Podvoisky assured Lenin that the assault would be mounted by noon—but it was not. Nor by three o'clock in the afternoon, nor even by the evening.

It was fortunate for the Bolsheviks that they faced no serious opposition, for this aspect of the uprising was appallingly badly organized.

It was a cold bitter morning as the people of the city began to absorb the fact that the Bolsheviks controlled it. The yellow streetcars, crowded as always, were running as normal. The shops were open. On the walls were appeals to the people of Petersburg to reject the call to revolt.

In front of the State Bank, troops were standing on guard with bayonets fixed on their rifles. John Reed, in his capacity as a foreign correspondent, approached one of them. "What side do you belong to?" he asked. "The government?"

"No more government," the soldier answered with a grin. "*Slava bogu!* Glory be to God!"

At ten o'clock the MRC issued a proclamation written by Lenin, that was broadcast and also posted on walls throughout the city: "The Provisional Government is deposed. All state authority has passed into the hands of the Military Revolutionary Committee. . . . Long live the revolution of workers, soldiers and peasants!"

Three hours later soldiers and sailors surrounded the Mariinsky Palace where the Pre-Parliament was sitting, and the delegates were ordered to leave. A sailor mounted the rostrum and told the president, "No more council. Go along home now."

At two thirty-five the Petersburg Soviet went into session at Smolny, and a triumphant Trotsky announced, "In the name of the Military Revolutionary Committee I declare that the Provisional Government has ceased to exist. . . ."

As Trotsky was speaking, Lenin—looking strange to the

275]

delegates without his beard—entered the big hall. Applause—
thin at first, then growing in volume as he was recognized—
began to sweep through the Soviet.

"In our midst," declared Trotsky, "is Vladimir Ilyich Lenin,
who, by force of circumstances, has not been able to be with us
all this time. . . . Hail the return of Lenin!"

There was a roar—a "tumultuous ovation"—as Lenin
stepped forward on the platform. His eyes swept over the crowd
of faces before him; his chin thrust forward; his small eyes
brightened. "The oppressed masses will form a government,"
he announced. "The old state apparatus will be destroyed root
and branch and a new administrative apparatus will be created in
the form of Soviet organizations. Now begins a new era in the
history of Russia and this third Russian Revolution must finally
lead to the victory of socialism. . . ."

Meanwhile, as darkness enclosed the city, the ministers of
Kerensky's government were still in the Winter Palace, stoutly
insisting that they had not been deposed. For Lenin, the failure
to capture the palace had begun to be a severe embarrassment.
For the All-Russian Congress of Soviets that was due to open
that evening should be faced with a *fait accompli*.

By four o'clock in the afternoon the streets surrounding
Palace Square were crammed with troops, sailors and Red
Guards. There were now five naval vessels in the river. Yet four
hours later the palace had not been taken, indeed, had not even
been attacked although thousands were poised for the assault.
Guns from the ships on the river and even from the fortress were
trained on the mud-red palace. By contrast, the defense was
minimal—some Junkers, a few Cossacks who had opted to fight
for the government despite their colleagues' refusal and one of
the "Death Battalions" of women that had been mustered into
the army during the past few months. One of these female
battalions had even been sent to the front lines to serve as an
example to the men. But determined as they had been to fight for
Mother Russia, the women soldiers had not made much of an
impact. Certainly the morale of the soldiers now waiting to

defend the palace, eyeing the massed troops and workers at every entrance to the square, was not high.

So why, demanded Lenin in note after note from Smolny, had operations not commenced? Actually there were several reasons: a desire to avoid bloodshed, confusion, but, above all, the fact that the ministers had held a delegation that had entered the palace with a surrender demand as hostages. At last, however, with the help of the nervous troops within the palace, the delegation had escaped.

The assault could now proceed, but the commanders were still hoping they could avoid storming the palace. They had managed to insinuate agitators within it, some dressed as liveried servants, and the infiltrators were pressing the troops to surrender.

The opening of the Congress of Soviets was put back two hours to provide a little more leeway, but in Smolny Lenin's anger and impatience were growing. In a furious note he threatened Podvoisky with a court-martial and even a firing squad if he did not order an immediate attack on the palace. At last at nine o'clock the crash of guns reverberated over the Neva. They were only blanks fired from the *Aurora* and the fortress, but they were the signal for a long burst of firing. Machine guns opened up, firing across the square. The troops edged closer, shooting, but they did not charge. Two armored cars lumbered across the square and traversed the front of the palace, firing as they passed.

Men were still jammed in the streets adjoining the empty square, waiting for the order to assault the palace, as the Second All-Russian Congress of Soviets finally opened in the ballroom at Smolny at 10:40 P.M. The hall was packed with grim-faced men in the gray military greatcoats worn by many civilians as well as soldiers—though some of them, of course, *were* delegates from the army. Tobacco smoke obscured the 160-year-old chandeliers, shaped like enormous saucers, that hung from the high ceiling of the pillared hall.

And the chairman, appointed way back in June, was the

277]

Menshevik Theodor Dan, who years ago had worked with Lenin on *Iskra* but was now one of his bitterest foes. Dan rang his chairman's bell for silence. "Comrades," he said sadly. "The Congress of Soviets is meeting in such unusual circumstances . . . that you will understand why the Central Executive Committee considers it unnecessary to address you with a political speech. . . . At this very moment our party comrades are in the Winter Palace. . . ."

Lenin and Trotsky were at that moment in a nearby room which contained no furniture except for a couple of chairs. A blanket and pillows had been laid on the bare floor, and the two men were stretched out resting—"side by side; body and soul were relaxing like overtaut strings. . . . We could not sleep so we talked in low voices."

It is interesting that neither was attending the opening of the congress—the formal, if technical, handing over of power to the Soviets that had been at the heart of Bolshevik demands. Lenin did not go to the platform all evening, preferring to wait perhaps until the Winter Palace had fallen and the ministers of the old government were confined in the cells of the Peter and Paul.

Suddenly, one of Lenin's sisters ran into the room. "Martov is speaking," she said urgently to Trotsky. "They're asking for you."[4]

The new presidium had been appointed, and fourteen of the twenty-five members were Bolsheviks. Another seven were left-wing Socialist Revolutionaries. Kamenev was in the chair.

There were angry attacks from the floor and emotional counterattacks. The Bolsheviks were labeled "political hypocrites," "renegades," "impostor delegates." The uprising was "a military conspiracy with the aid of the Petersburg Soviet."

The critics were howled down by party members as "counterrevolutionists," "Kornilovists," "provocateurs." Army delegates accused other army delegates of lying about the attitude of the troops.

At one stage a large group of Mensheviks stalked out of the

hall "to perish with the government" in the Winter Palace, to expose their "breasts to the machine guns of the terrorists. . . ."

They left the Soviet to the accompaniment of catcalls and curses. . . .

Suddenly above the noise of the shouting, the boom of heavy guns was heard through the windows. The fortress artillery had opened up on the Winter Palace with live shells. So, too, had a field gun under the triumphal arch in Palace Square.

Julius Martov, the friend of Lenin's youth who had started *Iskra* with him, demanded the floor. Wracked with consumption, his shoulders were bent, his voice a hoarse croak: "Comrades, the civil war is beginning . . . our brothers are being shot down in the streets. . . . The question of power is being settled by means of a military plot organized by one of the revolutionary parties. . . ."

Through the noise of cheers and catcalls, he pleaded for the formation of a united democracy, for a coalition government of the socialist parties. "Comrades," he insisted hoarsely, "we must put a stop to bloodshed."

Trotsky moved forward on the platform to answer him. He had known Martov for fourteen years. Together, they had co-edited *Nashe Slovo* in Paris. They had quarreled, like so many of the exiles, but they had shared a belief in socialism. But this was the past. Martov's challenge had to be answered with an eye on the future.

"We have tempered and hardened the revolutionary energy of the Petersburg workers and soldiers. . ." declared Trotsky. "Our insurrection has conquered and now you propose to us: Renounce your victory; make a compromise. With whom? I ask: with whom ought we to make a compromise. . . ? your role is played out. Go where you belong from now on—into the rubbish can of history!"

Martov, wounded by the virulence of this attack croaked bitterly, "Then we *will* go," and began pushing his way through the crowd on the platform. As he walked out of the hall, he heard Trotsky's voice harshly demanding an indictment of the

279]

compromisers and their "criminal attempt to smash the All-Russian Congress."

By eleven o'clock the women's battalion in the Winter Palace had surrendered, and the lull that this caused in the fighting was over. The guns opened up again. John Reed joined the crowd of men waiting for the attack in Morskaya Street which led directly under the triumphal arch into Palace Square. "Voices began to give commands and in the thick gloom we made out a dark mass moving forward, silent but for the shuffle of feet and the clinking arms. We fell in with the first ranks. Like a black river, filling all the street, without song or cheer we poured through the Red Arch. . . ."

From all sides, Red Guards and troops surged into the enormous square. Halfway across, they checked, formed a rough line by the giant Alexander Column, then charged toward the palace. Its entrances were protected by barricades of firewood, and the attackers clambered over these, expecting to encounter bayonets. But the Junkers who had been posted there had gone. Their abandoned rifles lay in heaps

Through every door, troops and workers streamed into the palace and charged up the marble staircases. There was little fighting. In one room in the East Wing, according to John Reed, some packing cases had been broken open with gun butts. "Comrades," someone shouted. "Don't touch anything. This is the property of the people." Looting had been declared a crime by the MRC. At the palace entrances, Red Guards were searching every man who left.

In an inside windowless ivory-paneled room on the second floor the ministers of the Provisional Government waited. They had left their usual conference room with its big windows overlooking the river when the shelling had made it dangerous.

The door burst open to admit a crowd of soldiers, sailors and Red Guards. With them was Antonov-Ovseenko, one of Podvoisky's co-commanders. "I am arresting you in the name of the Military Revolutionary Committee," he told the ministers and, while the men who were with him jeered at them, proceeded to list their names.

Lenin drove with Bonch-Bruevich to his apartment to spend the night. He was so tired that he fell asleep in the car. The nap must have revived him, for when he got to the apartment, he could not sleep. According to Bonch, who gallantly elected to spend what remained of the night on the sitting-room sofa, the bedroom light remained on for hours. Lenin, he discovered later, was drafting the decree to confiscate private land.

When Lenin emerged from the bedroom in the morning to have a cup of tea with Bonch, he appeared in a jaunty mood. "Congratulations on the first day of the socialist revolution," he said. Shortly afterward, he drove back to Smolny.

That Thursday morning, as he entered the massive pillared building of Smolny, his new power was shaky indeed. Kerensky was at Pskov, massing a counterrevolutionary army to march on Petersburg. Before the end of the day several key unions—including the railwaymen, the telegraph operators and the postmen —would declare their opposition to the usurping of power by a single party.

Lenin displayed no concern. At a meeting of the party Central Committee Kamenev, and probably Zinoviev, pressed him hard to open the government to socialists of other parties, as Martov had pleaded. This, they argued, would broaden their base and help answer the accusations that they had acquired power by a coup d'état rather than with public support. "We can't hold on," argued Kamenev. "Too much is against us."

But Lenin was firm. "We won't give way an inch!" he insisted. He would permit no one and nothing to mar his socialist revolution, his world revolution. "The compromisers can come in," he said, "provided they accept our program." And he proceeded to consider who would be appointed as the first People's Commissars as he formed a government.

All day, the operations room of the MRC—still the technical and actual holder of the power—was a scene of hectic activity.

281]

Order after order was issued. Anyone giving any assistance to Kerensky would be punished as having committed a serious crime against the state. Government employees (Kamenev's "huge third camp" of the petty bourgeoisie) were ordered to continue with their work and threatened with severe penalties if they refused. Death would be the punishment for pillage, disorder or speculation. Priority was to be given to food transport. Capital sentences in the army were abolished.

And most critical of all, an appeal was made to the Cossacks on whom Kerensky's hopes of retaking the city were mainly built: "Cossack brothers! You are being led against Petersburg. They want to force you into battle with the revolutionary workers and soldiers of the capital. . . . Cossack brothers, execute no orders of the enemies of the people. Send your delegates to Petersburg to talk it over with us . . . the All-Russian Congress of Soviets extends to you a fraternal hand. . . ."

In Berlin that day, the mood was less taut. For Count Diego von Bergen, the official in charge of political subversion, and his new Foreign Minister, Richard von Kühlmann, the Bolshevik take-over of Petersburg was the crowning success for a policy that the Foreign Office had been conducting since the day Parvus had appeared in the Wilhelmstrasse in January, 1915. The Sealed Train and the millions of marks that had followed it had produced results almost beyond the Germans' fondest hopes. For Lenin, as he had promised, must now negotiate peace, and within four months more than 1,000,000 German and Austrian troops would be withdrawn from the Eastern line. In March, Germany would launch a devastating offensive against the Allied line in France with the help of forty-four divisions now facing Russian troops. And Russia itself would be defenseless and subject to whatever course the Kaiser might choose to take.

On the afternoon of November 8, however, the fragility of the thread by which Lenin held power was the main object of discussion among men in the Foreign Office. How could he be sustained? The situation was delicate, as a telegram just received from the embassy in Stockholm outlined clearly: "I urgently recommend that all public announcements of amicable agreement with Russia be avoided in the German and Austrian Press. Amicable agreement with imperial states cannot possibly be accepted as a watchword by the Bolsheviks. They can only justify peace with Germany by citing the will of the people and Russia's desperate situation. . . ."

Kühlmann agreed completely. "The view that the utmost moderation should be exercised is shared here," he wired back. "The press has been instructed accordingly." To bolster the new regime, 2,000,000 marks were immediately dispatched to Stockholm at the urgent request of the minister there—and a further 15,000,000 marks for "political propaganda in Russia" was requested from the Treasury.

In Petersburg that evening the delegates to the Congress of Soviets gathered again in Smolny's ballroom. Many of them now carried rifles with bayonets fixed, for the MRC was arming everyone who did not already possess a weapon in view of the expected attack by Kerensky and the forces from the front. This must have pleased Lenin, for it conformed with the concept he had visualized in his room in the Spiegelgasse of the armed proletariat, of rule from below by the people.

This time the delegates had assembled for a practical working session: to approve a new form of government, a council of People's Commissars under the presidency of Lenin, that would be responsible to the Congress of Soviets; to pass into law a decree confiscating without compensation all private land except that owned by peasants and Cossacks; and, most important of all, to stop the war.

Soon after eight thirty the members of the new Central Executive Committee, Lenin among them, entered the hall to a roar of welcome and took their places on the platform. As always, there was routine business to be processed before the congress could turn to the important issues, a report to be read by Kamenev, as chairman, some points of order, a few short speeches both of complaint and of greetings.

Then Lenin rose and went to the podium, "gripping the edge of the reading stand," as John Reed described the scene, "letting his little winking eyes travel over the crowd as he stood there waiting, apparently oblivious to the long-rolling ovation, which lasted several minutes."

When he could make himself heard, he declared, "We shall now proceed to construct the socialist order!" And there was another "overwhelming human roar."

"The first thing," Lenin went on, "is the adoption of practical measures to realize peace. . . ." In a long proclamation, addressed to the peoples and the governments of all the belligerent nations, he proposed a three-month armistice so that negotiations to end the war could take place.

"This proposal of peace," Lenin asserted, "will meet with resistance from the imperialist governments—we don't fool ourselves on that score. But we hope that revolution will soon break out in all the belligerent countries; that is why we address ourselves especially to the workers of France, England and Germany. . . ."

When Lenin had finished speaking, Kamenev stood up and asked all in favor of the proclamation to hold up their cards.

"Suddenly," recorded Reed, "by common impulse, we found ourselves on our feet, mumbling together into the smooth lifting unison of the 'Internationale.' A grizzled old soldier was sobbing like a child. Alexandra Kollontai rapidly winked the tears back. The immense sound rolled through the hall, burst windows and doors and soared into the quiet sky. . . ."

The incredible metamorphosis of Lenin's life had completed its first stage. The man who only thirty-four weeks before had been living in poverty in one room in Zurich's Old Town was now the ruler of Russia. The revolutionary who for years had plotted against the Tsar had now taken his place as head of state.

That night, as the hundreds of delegates to the Congress of Soviets watched in acute consciousness, Lenin executed an event that was unique in the annals of history, one that compared in significance with such occasions as the signing of Magna Carta at Runnymede or of the Declaration of Independence at Philadelphia—which events were, in truth, among its roots. The Bolshevik take-over was to change the way men thought, to create a global power of immense magnitude, to transform the lives of hundreds of millions of people.

It is fascinating to contemplate the delicacy of the timing on which this momentous event depended, to consider what would have happened in Russia if Lenin had not reached Petersburg when he did, if German interests had not for a few short months coincided with his own, if there had been no Sealed Train.

Chapter 17

"'IF THE LENINISTS succeed in bringing about the promised armistice," Count Czernin, the Austrian Foreign Minister, wrote to Berlin two days after Lenin's speech to the Congress of Soviets, "then it seems to me we shall have won almost a complete victory on the Russian sector for . . . the Russian Army in its present state will surely pour back into the hinterland in order to be on the spot when the estates are distributed. In the present circumstances, an armistice would make this army vanish. . . ."

The new situation was the result of brilliant military diplomacy. The plan to transport Lenin back to Russia in the Sealed Train and to finance him after his arrival there had given the Germans more than the separate peace they so badly needed. The negotiating team that met with the Soviet delegates to discuss peace terms at Brest-Litovsk demanded that the new government should relinquish the Russian claim to Finland, Poland, the Baltic states and the Ukraine. Turkey, Germany's ally, was to be given a large area in the Caucasus.

The Soviet commissars were appalled, for the demands were far greater than they seemed. The territory contained one-third of the nation's population, one-third of its cultivated land and half its industry. When at last the Germans tired of the discussion and ordered what was left of their army to advance, the Russians were forced to sign the humiliating treaty.

The final irony was that the Germans' investment in Lenin was returned to them—with enormous interest. Under a supplementary agreement to the Brest-Litovsk Treaty in August 1918, the new Soviet government paid the Germans 120,000,000 gold rubles—at contemporary rates of exchange more than 240,000,000 marks and far more than the Foreign Office supplied to the Bolsheviks.

As for Lenin himself, once the Germans had launched their spring offensive with the support of the divisions he had enabled them to transfer from the Eastern Front, he had, as they saw it, served his purpose to them. Like the right-wing Russians, they did not believe he would be able to retain power. "He will have the whole Cossack army against him," asserted the Kaiser, although already Kerensky's attempt to advance on Petersburg had failed and he had fled the country. But the German ruler reckoned without the fanatic determination and dedication of the Bolsheviks and the Red Army in the two-year civil war against the enormous forces arrayed them.

It was not Lenin but the Kaiser who would lose power. The offensive in the West, for which Wilhelm had used Lenin to provide so many troops, was almost successful—but not quite. It proved to be the Germans' last desperate effort in the long and debilitating struggle between the imperial powers. And once it failed, the German nation was left too exhausted to defend itself against the counteroffensive with which the Allies responded, now with the help of the newly arrived American troops.

Lenin's new society did not, however, emerge in the form he intended. Certainly, he destroyed the capitalist system. But Lenin's vision of a society constructed on the lines of the Paris Commune, as he outlined in his letters from Switzerland and in his April Theses speech in the Tauride Palace, did not materialize. He managed to create a socialist state with a keynote of equality, but his concept of rule from below by the people as opposed to rule from above by the establishment never even began to appear.

Indeed, the system of rule from above which he set up was far more rigid than that of the Tsar he replaced. And the secret police he established proved far more repressive than the Okhrana. Ultimately Lenin controlled his Russia by means of terror.

Nor did he ever truly give power to the Soviets. He gave it to

287]

the party. When elections to the Constituent Assembly were held at last and the Bolsheviks won only twenty-five percent of the seats, Lenin decided that the Assembly had no place in his new Russia. Although he insisted again and again during those early months in 1917 that he would give autonomy to the regions, he never did.

Lenin was proved wrong in two of his basic beliefs. First, he assumed that he was starting a world revolution, that the new system he established in Russia in 1917 would very quickly spread by means of proletarian revolts in other countries.

Secondly, he believed that the imperialist governments would be unable to end the war, that only by transforming the conflict into a civil class struggle could it be terminated.

In 1924 Lenin died of a stroke. Nadya lived on until 1939, when she died of a heart attack. Inessa had gone even before Lenin—struck down by typhus in the Caucasus in 1921. Her body was brought to the Kremlin for a state funeral. At her graveside Lenin displayed a degree of emotion that, for him, was astonishing. "He was plunged in despair, his cap down over his eyes," wrote Alexandra Kollontai. "At every moment we thought he would collapse."

Lenin's closest comrades did not fare well. Trotsky was forced into exile and then murdered. Kamenev and Zinoviev like so many others, were executed in the purges.

As for Parvus, the socialist tycoon, he found himself deserted after November, 1917. He had been of great value to the Germans, but his socialist ideas soon made him dangerous to them. To Lenin, he was political anathema. From Stockholm, he asked permission to come to Russia. When at last Lenin replied, the rejection was curt. "The cause of revolution," he wrote, "should not be touched by dirty hands."

Afterword

THE EVIDENCE of Lenin's links with the Germans is discussed at length in the relevant chapters, and the purpose of this afterword is to display the facts and the arguments that stem from those facts in isolated form so that the pattern can easily be seen.

Most modern Western historians—America's Adam Ulam of Harvard, Britain's Leonard Schapiro of the London School of Economics and Fritz Fischer of Hamburg are eminent examples—take the view, first advanced by Dr. George Katkov, that the case that Lenin received funds from the Germans is proved.

The Sealed Train starts from this base (evidence being detailed below) and also attempts to study and even reinterpret Lenin's actions and policy in the setting of this most important motivation. It explores the logical projections of the situation and by this means speculates possible answers to some of the questions that have puzzled students of Lenin during this short but critical period of his life that was to have such vast repercussions on the world.

The most important area of this speculation concerns the possibility that Lenin was in communication with Berlin. Certainly, this would have been logical. For if he was prepared to accept finance on a major scale to pursue the aims he had in common with the Germans, surely it was probable that he would also establish liaison with them in other ways if this was necessary to achieve the same objective. There is no proof that Lenin did communicate with Berlin, but there is no doubt that the channels for contact existed, and there is some evidence that these were used by members of the Bolshevik organization.

The evidence and arguments are as follows:

1. *The Germans supplied finance on a large scale to the Bolsheviks.* The key evidence is two telegrams in September and December, 1917, in which the German Secretary of State informed the Kaiser that his department had supplied the Bolsheviks with "a steady flow of funds" and that the party could not have attained "the scale or influence which it has today without our continual support." This is supported by an analysis, dated February 4, 1918, among the German documents of Foreign Office expenditure overseas for propaganda and special purposes. This gives an allocation to Russia of 40,580,997 marks, of which by January 31, 1918, a sum of 26,566,122 marks had been spent. From other documents, indicating expenditure after the Bolshevik seizure of power, it is clear that 11,500,000 marks were spent before November.

Although the analysis merely mentions "Russia," as opposed to "Lenin," the Secretary of State's wording in the telegrams indicates a high volume of expenditure, and it can be assumed, therefore, that Bolsheviks were the main recipients.

There is corroborating evidence, such as Eduard Bernstein's assertion of support amounting to 50,000,000 marks, the logic of the Germans' backing the Bolsheviks because of their peace policy, the lack of other major sources of funds for the party for a very major propaganda effort, the flow of money through the Fürstenberg commercial channel. However, the bastion of the case is the Secretary of State, who must be regarded as a prime source of the expenditure of his own department.

The big weakness of the case is the complete lack of evidence from Bolshevik sources, although this is not surprising. After Lenin's death in 1924, all documentation concerning Lenin was by law placed under government control—and censorship. Before that date, the whole issue of German assistance—which of course Lenin consistently denied—was far too traumatic for any Bolshevik to mention, though it is probable that very few knew of it.

Although the fact that Lenin received German funds is regarded as proved, by me and many others, the evidence regarding the channels employed to convey it to the party is inadequate. Almost certainly, the key to this puzzle is Jacob Fürstenberg, but it has never been completely substantiated. Probably the most important evidence is the confession of Eugenia Sumenson, but Colonel Nikitin was a highly suspect, unpleasant character who actually revels in print in his book over the fact that the troops who arrested her beat her up. Her confession has to be seen against the possibility that it was tortured out of her and the fact that she was never cross-examined in court.

2. *Lenin was possibly in communication with Berlin.* Without question, the information channels existed. There is evidence that Parvus was in contact with the Wilhelmstrasse and even with Zimmermann himself, that Parvus was very closely connected and in contact with Jacob Fürstenberg, who was in communication with Lenin.

An additional route between Fürstenberg and Berlin was Gustav Mayer, who has gone on record in his book *Erinnerungen* with the fact that he was the link between Fürstenberg and Karl Radek and the German authorities, that furthermore he reported direct to Diego von Bergen, the minister responsible for political subversion in Russia.

Much play was made by Kerensky and Nikitin that the German newspaper *Berliner Lokal-Anzeiger* published as early as July 16 a *Pravda* report on the trouble in the city—telegraphed to Jacob Fürstenberg from Petersburg. This was hardly important evidence of treason, but it reveals how fast communication could be.

Conclusions: (1) Lenin could have communicated with Berlin very easily if he had wished through established channels. (2) At times, notably in July and October, he had reason to. In short, he had incentive and opportunity, but there is no proof that he did.

3. *Lenin met Germans in Berlin during the Sealed Train journey, learned the scale of the finance available to him and*

291]

because of this changed his mind on revolutionary tactics. This is dramatic but logical speculation based on these facts: (1) Lenin did receive funds from the Germans on a large scale; (2) Lenin did change his mind between leaving Zurich and arriving in Petersburg (see Note 2, Chapter 7, for detail) and this change conformed with German interests; (3) the train was held up in Berlin for some twenty hours, even though this was not the intention of the Foreign Office earlier the same day; (4) during this wait, Lenin was in close proximity to the Foreign Office officials who were about to make a very major investment in him; (5) the station was under rigid military control, which would enable a meeting to take place under conditions of complete security; and (6) no one has adequately explained Lenin's change of mind. (Professor Schapiro has suggested that the sight of the crowds at the Finland Station was the reason, but I find it difficult to accept this because he made his first speech, reflecting the new policy, very shortly after his welcome, and I cannot believe that Lenin would make a major policy change so impulsively.)

Conclusions: Because a meeting with Lenin was easy, practical and desirable, German officials probably met him for financial discussion. This I believe, was the reason he changed his mind—primarily on timing—because the resources he now knew were available to him would enable him to mount a much larger propaganda campaign with greater impact than he had visualized in Zurich, but this is, of course, pure speculation.

4. *Lenin left Petersburg in its highly explosive state on July 12, not merely because he was ill but because he knew the date of the German counterattack and had planned his coup for the national humiliation that would follow defeat of the Russian Army—i.e., he had time to leave the city.* This is speculation rooted in the unproved assumption, already discussed, that he was in communication with Berlin and arises from the following facts: (1) It was out of character for Lenin to leave the city to take a rest at this sensitive moment, despite ill health; (2) the Bolshevik plan was to time the uprising to exploit the national humiliation caused by Russian defeat—as shown by the efforts of Lenin and

others to restrain the party militants in early July and confirmed by Stalin at the Sixth Party Congress in August; (3) the uprising would not therefore be staged for at least a week and probably two weeks after this defeat—which gave Lenin ample time for a rest; (4) contact with Berlin over so important an issue as a Bolshevik strike for power, which in this case was linked to some extent with the actions of the German Army, was logical—given that the communication channels existed; and (5) all the evidence indicates that the Bolshevik leaders tried to stop the uprising that had been inspired by militants, who were not in the top ranks of the party.

5. *Lenin decided not to stand trial after the July debacle because of the facts that might emerge if he did.* Sukhanov mocked the idea that during those months in 1917 Lenin would have been in danger of execution, which is the reason he himself gave for flight, and pointed to the experience of Kamenev and Trotsky, who *were* arrested. Certainly, the case against him was clearly weak.

According to Nadya and others, he planned at first to give himself up—then changed his mind under pressure from the Central Committee. According to Sulimova, by contrast, within twenty-four hours of going into hiding, he stated his belief to her that he would be executed if he were found.

It was natural during that traumatic period for there to be vacillation while the best course of action was decided. However, Soviet sources (Nadya and Sulimova) can never be completely trusted. Sukhanov's account was, in effect, independent. Sukhanov could not understand his flight, but now that the fact of German finance has been substantiated—*i.e.,* that the government's charges were soundly based, even though its case was weak—it is reasonable to speculate that this was the reason he did not wish to submit to detailed questioning. Also, while there was no trial, the government could be accused of smear tactics.

6. *One reason for Lenin's frantic urging of the party to rise against its will in October was information from Berlin that the Austrians were going to offer Kerensky a separate peace deal*

which would destroy any Bolshevik chance of gaining power.
This is speculation—and dramatic speculation—that there was
an additional motive for speed beyond Lenin's published
reasons, *i.e.*, that there was enormous danger of another right-
wing coup that, unlike Kornilov's, could well be successful; that
the timing for the seizure of power was now cdeal; that the army
would support the party. These are not challenged as being
among Lenin's reasons, but the danger of a separate peace—
which is not so widely appreciated—was possibly even greater
than the danger of failing to grasp the revolutionary opportunity.

There is, of course, no proof that Lenin had any information
from Berlin, but the following is the setting of the famous
meeting of November 23: (1) There *was* an imminent Austrian
peace initiative (see Kerensky's memoirs); (2) Austria's
disenchantment with the war was no secret; the news of the
peace initiative was no doubt picked up in advance by
Germany's efficient intelligence service and was therefore
known in Berlin; (3) although the previous communication
channels between Lenin and Fürstenberg were broken after
July, they were in touch by the old courier system before Lenin
left Finland—as is shown by a published letter from Lenin to
Fürstenberg; Fürstenberg's channels to Berlin from Sweden had
been unaffected by the July debacle in Russia; (4) both Lenin (as
he wrote from Finland) and Kerensky (as stated in his memoirs)
believed that if Kerensky could offer the Russian masses peace,
it would destroy the Bolshevik chance of seizing power; and (5)
although Lenin does not mention Austria in his letters from
Finland, he does express extreme anxiety of a separate peace,
anticipating that the greatest danger of this lies in a deal between
Germany and Britain.

Glossary

OF POLITICAL PARTIES AND INSTITUTIONS IN ST. PETERSBURG IN 1917

THE GOVERNMENT

DUMA: The nearest institution to a parliamentary-type elected house that existed under an autocratic Tsar. Only property owners and taxpayers were represented through a system of electoral colleges. The Tsar could dissolve the Assembly at will.

DISTRICT DUMAS: These were local municipal councils, elected by limited franchise.

SOVIETS: Literally meaning "Councils," the Soviets were assemblies of delegates from factories or other places of employment. Each city and large district had its Soviet which, in makeup, was similar to a local trade union congress, though it was not limited to unions.

PETERSBURG SOVIET: Because St. Petersburg was the center of the March Revolution, the St. Petersburg Soviet carried out the role for a few months of a national Soviet but relinquished this in June to an All-Russian Congress of Soviets. After this, in theory at least, it became solely a local city Soviet. Its voice and directorate was the Executive Committee which the delegates elected.

ALL-RUSSIAN CONGRESS OF SOVIETS: A congress of delegates from Soviets all over Russia who in June, 1917, appointed a Central Executive Committee that sat permanently in St. Petersburg. Some of the leaders of this were also leaders of the Executive Committee of the St. Petersburg Soviet, having attended the congress as delegates. The same characters, therefore, remained at the center of events, even though there was a technical change in the principal body they represented.

295]

PROVISIONAL GOVERNMENT: The system which emerged from the March Revolution and the deposing of the Tsar was one of "dual power." The ministers ruled the country under the supervision of the Soviet, which had the support of the people.

The first ministry consisted primarily of men from the liberal Kadet Party that, after the March Revolution when it was no longer wise to be a monarchist or even a conservative politician, absorbed many members of the right-wing parties. But two members of the Petersburg Soviet were also in the first Cabinet.

In the early days the Soviet was very left-wing. As time went on, more Soviet leaders were brought into the government in a "coalition" ministry. Gradually—and especially after the arrival of Lenin with his radical new policies—the political attitudes within the Soviet moved right, a process that Lenin saw as a betrayal to "compromise."

CONSTITUENT ASSEMBLY: A Parliament that was planned in the full electoral sense of the word. No elections were held within the time span with which this book is concerned, although there was talk and even preparation— though the obvious vested interests of the parties caused delays in settlement of the electoral system. Elections were held after Lenin's assumption of power, but the Assembly was closed when the fact that the Bolsheviks were a minority presented Lenin with too many problems.

PRE-PARLIAMENT: A preliminary assembly, sometimes known as the Council of the Republic, set up as a kind of temporary constitutional assembly on Kerensky's initiative in October, 1917. Because it was rigged in Lenin's view, the Bolsheviks walked out of it on the first day. It was closed down in the uprising as part of the seizure of power.

THE PARTIES

RUSSIAN SOCIAL DEMOCRATIC LABOR PARTY (RSDLP): The party believed in socialist development on the lines predicted by Karl Marx. In 1903 it split into two sections, which sometimes cooperated and sometimes feuded but divided irrevocably in 1917. These were:

The Bolsheviks: The smaller faction headed by Lenin, who

[296

believed that the party should consist of full-time professional revolutionaries.

The Mensheviks: The far larger faction was much more democratic in the Western sense and was prepared to tolerate supporters as well as militants. Plekhanov, Axelrod and Vera Zasulich were its leaders among the older generation of revolutionaries, but Martov became its main force. Later, after the Revolution, such men as Chkheidze, Skobelev, Tseretelli became the key figures.

SOCIALIST REVOLUTIONARY PARTY (SR's): The largest political party in Russia, primarily because it represented the peasants, the biggest section of the population. Its policies included some Marxist tenets, but it believed broadly in socialist development based on the peasant communes that already existed. Kerensky and Chernov were the principal SR's.

KADETS: The name was formed by the initials of the Constitutional Democratic Party, which represented the bourgeois and petty bourgeois—civil servants, army officers, shopkeepers, etc. It was headed by Milyukov, who sought a Constitutional Republic or monarchy on British lines. Nearly all the ministers in the Provisional Government were Kadets.

ANARCHIST-COMMUNIST: An utterly militant party whose members held many similar views to the Bolsheviks on individual issues, such as ownership of land, but, unlike them, did not believe in any state structure.

THE BOLSHEVIK PARTY COMMITTEES

The party was built in cellular fashion within a pyramid of organizations each of which had its elected committee. Thus each city had its party committee, as indeed did each district within each city. At the head was the party Central Committee that was elected by vote at the party conferences by representatives of the main party committees from all over Russia.

CENTRAL COMMITTEE: Until the March Revolution, there were in effect two Central Committees—one within Russia, where the party was illegal, and the other in exile: the Foreign Bureau of the Central Committee. After Lenin returned to Russia, there was no longer a need for a foreign section.

PETERSBURG COMMITTEE: This was responsible for running the party within the city through the hierarchy of the local district committees. During 1917, when the existence of the party depended mainly on events within the city, the functions of the St. Petersburg Committee overlapped those of the Central Committee.

MILITARY ORGANIZATION: This controlled the party cells within the army and the navy and also ran the Red Guards, the units of armed civilians. It operated very closely, but not always harmoniously, with the Petersburg Committee. The two principal MO leaders were Nevsky and Podvoisky.

THE BUILDINGS IN PETERSBURG

TAURIDE PALACE: Home of the Imperial Duma and of the Petersburg Soviet. For a very short time was also used by ministers of the Provisional Government.

MARIINSKY PALACE: The offices of the Provisional Government until it moved in August into the Winter Palace. Later home of the Pre-Parliament.

WINTER PALACE: Once the Tsar's formal home, from August the seat of the Provisional Government.

KSHESINSKAYA MANSION: Bolshevik Party headquarters until July.

SMOLNY INSTITUTE: Seat of the Petersburg Soviet and of the All-Russian Congress of Soviets after September.

NAVAL ACADEMY, VASILEVSKY ISLAND: Meeting place of the All-Russian Congress of Soviets in June.

Notes*

CHAPTER 1

1. Main sources: *Collected Works of Lenin*, 4th Edition, Vols. 35,36,37,43; G. Zinoviev, *Pravda*, April 16, 1924 (R); N. K. Krupskaya, *Memories of Lenin*, and *Pravda*, April 16, 1924 (R): for Fritz Platten's account, L. D. Davidov, *Leninskaya Gvardia Planet†* (R); Valentinov, *Encounters with Lenin*; A. Lunacharsky, *Revolutionary Silhouettes*; Bertram Wolfe, *Three Who Made a Revolution*; W. Gauchi, *Lenin in Switzerland* (G); Edmund Wilson, *To the Finland Station.*

2. Non-Soviet historians tend to mock the contention of Soviet historians that the execution of Lenin's brother turned him into a revolutionary—which raises the question: How does one define a revolutionary? The facts at this period of his life are hazy. Possibly, he did not become truly active until after he had qualified as a lawyer some four years after Sasha's death, but the impact on his studying and his reading must have been enormous

CHAPTER 2

1. Main sources: N. K. Krupskaya, *Memories of Lenin*; Richard Pipes, *Social Democracy and the St. Petersburg Labor Movement*; J. Freville, *Inessa Armand—a Great Character of the Russian Revolution* (F); Bertram Wolfe, *Three Who Made a Revolution* and "Lenin and Inessa Armand," in *Slavic Review*, 1963; R. H. McNeal, *Bride of the Revolution*; Leon Trotsky, *Lenin and My Life*; Valentinov, *Encounters with Lenin*; Lilina (Zina Zinovieva), *Leningradskaya Pravda*, 1924, No. 22 (R); Z. A. B. Zeman and W. B. Scharlau, *Merchant of Revolution*; D. W. Treadgold, *Lenin and His Rivals.*

2. I refer to Joseph Djugashvili as "Stalin" to avoid confusion, though, in fact, he did not assume this cover name until 1912, some five years later.

3. According to Marcel Body, an aide in Alexandra Kollontai's embassy

---

*The letters (R), (G) and (F) after sources indicate that it is in Russian, German or French respectively. All other sources are in English.

†This title is not translatable into English.

when she was a Soviet ambassador, in "Alexandra Kollontai," *Preuves* (April, 1952).

CHAPTER 3

1. Main sources: As for Chapter 1. Also, David Souliashvili, *Meetings with V.I. Lenin in Exile* (R); *Collected Works of Lenin*, Vols. 23, 35, 36, 37, 43; V.I. Lenin, *The Revolution of 1917* ; N. Sukhanov, *The Russian Revolution 1917* ; Leon Trotsky, *The History of the Russian Revolution*; Alexander Kerensky, *The Kerensky Memoirs* and *The Catastrophe*; M. Futrell, *The Northern Underground*; G. Safarov, "About Comrade Lenin," *Leningradskaya Pravda*, 1925, No. 17 (R); A. Senn, *The Russian Revolution in Switzerland, 1914–1917*.

2. Kerensky was head of the Trudoviks, a small party that was one of several that operated under the SR banner.

3. Technically, the two police forces of the Tsars had been disbanded by the Provisional Government—though possibly Lenin did not yet know this. However, many of the members of two forces were now in the militia that was carrying out policing duties. This should not be confused with Lenin's idea for a popular "militia."

CHAPTER 4

1. Main sources: For full list of sources of the journey to Russia, see Section 1 of the bibliography. Accounts of the journey were written by ten of the travelers, either in book form or in articles—namely, Fritz Platten, Nadya (Krupskaya), Radek, Safarov, Zinoviev, Lilina (Zina Zinovieva), Olga Ravich, Sokolnikov, Tskhakaya and Souliashvili. Lenin himself published a brief undetailed account for the Soviet.

The other main sources are the German Foreign Office papers that, of course, include correspondence to and from the legation in Berne; two reports by Swiss Customs; and, for British response to the journey, the Foreign Office files in London and *Theatre of Life* by Lord Esme Howard, British ambassador in Stockholm.

Two writers have combed the German sources—W. Hahlweg (in German) and Dr. Z. A. B. Zeman (in English)—and produced most useful books (see bibliography for full description. Nikolai Fritz Platten, the archivist son of Fritz Platten, has also written a lengthy paper—which he kindly made available to the author—some of which has been published without references in the journal *Grani*. The biography of Fritz Platten, written by the Soviet historian A. Ivanov, has also been used. Two other Soviet writers, Moskovsky and Semenov in *Lenin in Sweden*, are also an interesting source of detail.

Description of the sealed carriage itself and of the route taken is based on the travelers' own accounts, supported by most useful details of contemporary rolling stock, German rail systems and wartime conditions supplied by the Bundesbahn Verkehrsmuseum in Nuremberg.

Other sources for the journey and for the events that took place before the journey in this chapter were: Z. A. B. Zeman and W. B. Scharlau, *Merchant of Revolution*; Arthur Siefeldt, *Bakinsky Rabochii 1924*, No. 24 (on Lenin's meeting with Parvus) (R); General Erich Ludendorff, *My War Memories* and *The General Staff and Its Problems*; S. T. Possony, *Lenin, the Compulsive Revolutionary*; Barbara Tuchman, *The Zimmermann Telegram*; Paul Levi, *Poslyedriiya*, quoted in David Shub's *Lenin;* Gerard Walter, *Lenine* (F); Henri Guilbeaux, *Vladimir Ilyich Lenin*.

2. The company that Fürstenberg directed was, in fact, owned 50 percent by Parvus and 50 percent by George Sklarz, an associate of Parvus who was also a German agent.

3. The proof that this went to Parvus is not conclusive, but according to Zeman and Scharlau, no one else received sums of this size for political purposes in Russia.

CHAPTER 5

1. Main sources: See sources for Chapter 4.

2. There is a degree of mystery about the exact numbers. On arrival in Russia, Lenin stated that the party consisted of thirty-two. This would conform with the statement signed by the travelers at lunch in the Zahringerhof in Zurich on which were twenty-nine signatures, excluding Fritz Platten and the two children who, according to Zina Zinovieva, were in the party (four-year-old Robert and her own Stepan). But two travelers—Platten and Radek—were not still with the party when it arrived in Russia. This means either that Lenin referred to the arrival in Russia somewhat loosely, perhaps using the Zahringerhof statement as his basis for assessing the numbers, or others traveled with the party whose identity we do not know.

3. Platten in his book played down the behavior of Swiss Customs, but David Souliashvili's account of his anger is supported by reports of the examination by Swiss Customs at Schaffhausen and Thayngen.

4. A. Ivanov, a Soviet historian, does not give his source for this fact and indeed gives no citations for other material in his biography of Platten that exists nowhere else to the author's knowledge. Some of his other facts are wrong, though this criticism could be applied to many of the personal accounts. It would seem that he has used a personal account by one of the two officers—probably Lieutenant von Buhring—though attempts to confirm this in Moscow have failed. As a source, Ivanov must be suspect, but he is a member of the Institute of Marxism and Leninism, and his book was published by the Soviet State Publishers of Political Literature. There appear to be no political elements that would involve distortion or creation of facts.

5. Nadya wrote that Robert spoke only French. Karl Radek in *Pravda* insisted he spoke a Minsk dialect of Russian, the actual quote being

transliterated as *vusk dues*. Dr. Harold Shukman of St. Antony's College, Oxford, has suggested that Radek was in error, the phrase being unrecognizable in Russian but being vaguely similar to the Yiddish for "What's happening?"

6. Quoted by Moskovsky and Semenov in *Lenin in Sweden*.

7. Radek quotes Ben Baverk in *Pravda*, but information about this theoretician has eluded the author and everyone he has consulted.

CHAPTER 6

1. Main sources: See sources for Chapter 4. Also, Lilina (Zina Zinovieva), *Leningradskaya Pravda*, 1924, No. 22 (R); B. V. Nikitin, *The Fatal Years*.

2. It is assumed that Zina was in the remaining second-class compartment. It is known that Lenin had one second-class compartment—presumably an end one since it was to enable him to work—that Radek and company had the neighboring compartment, that the German officers had the third-class compartment at the far end of the coach. Platten recorded that women were given priority to second class, and it is assumed that Zina and Helen Kon availed themselves of this. Possibly, too, so did Robert's mother, but she may have preferred to stay with the other Jewish Bundists.

Of the other compartments it is probable that Platten occupied the third-class compartment adjoining the escort officers for easy communication.

3. My source is Zina Zinovieva, writing in *Leningradskaya Pravda* in 1924, and it is interesting that she does not mention if Inessa, who was at Longjumeau with them, joined them on the bicycle trips. This could have been tact or even jealousy, for, apart from her closeness to Lenin, Inessa was giving lectures which Zina would never have been asked to do. Perhaps Inessa just did not like bicycling, though it is strange that she should have been left out of this weekend activity.

CHAPTER 7

1. Main sources: See sources for Chapter 4. Also, A. Lunacharsky, *Revolutionary Silhouettes*; Leonard Schapiro, *The Communist Autocracy*, and *The Communist Party of the Soviet Union*; R. H. McNeal, *Bride of the Revolution*; John P. Nettl, *Rosa Luxemburg* (on Radek and Fürstenberg); Viktor Mushtukov, and Vadim Kruchina Bogdanov, *Lenin and the Revolution*.

2. The fact that Lenin changed his mind on the journey from Switzerland to Russia can be seen by comparing his writings in Switzerland *after* he knew of the revolution (notably two letters to Alexandra Kollontai, his five famous *Letters from Afar* and, in particular, since this ties it down to a date, his *Farewell Letter to Swiss Workers* which he read at lunch at the Zahringerhof on the date of his departure from Zurich) and the notes and descriptions of his speeches on the night of his arrival in Petersburg and the following day in the Tauride Palace when he presented his April Theses. See V. I. Lenin, *The*

Revolution of 1917, Vol. 1; N. N. Sukhanov, *The Russian Revolution 1917*; F. Raskolnikov, *The Proletarian Revolution*, 1923, No. 1 (R); Leon Trotsky, *History of the Russian Revolution*.

There is little doubt that his decision for the *immediate* leap into the second stage of revolution was made *after* leaving Switzerland and *before* arriving in Russia. All sources are agreed on the astonishment this caused, and the change is clear from his writings.

The fact that he altered his view about the role of the Soviet is more open to challenge because he *did* write about preparing for the Soviets to take power *before* leaving Switzerland, and the question is exactly what he meant by this.

Nadya Krupskaya in her *Memories of Lenin* wrote that he did not in Switzerland "write of the seizure of power by the Soviets of workers' deputies as a perspective, but urged that concrete measures be taken *for* the seizure of power, for the arming of the masses, for the fight for bread, peace and freedom." From this it would seem that he was thinking in terms of the Soviets as a method of organizing the workers rather than as an actual organ of government.

Professor Leonard Schapiro of the London School of Politics and Economics (London University) in *The Origin of the Communist Autocracy* wrote: "He did not while in Switzerland propound the doctrine that the Middle Class phase of the revolution should be cut short at birth. . . . There is nothing in his writings during the weeks of waiting in Switzerland to suggest that the soviet as opposed to the armed proletariat should assume power." In a letter to the author he has added subsequently his view that "whenever he [Lenin] talks about soviets seizing power in Switzerland, he seems to identify them in his own mind with some form of armed or insurrectionary mob. The change when he gets to Russia is quite clear—he then begins to talk about the actual Petrograd Soviet. . . ."

Professor Robert H. McNeal, chairman of the Department of History at the University of Massachusetts, writes in his biography of Krupskaya, *Bride of the Revolution*: Lenin's "April Theses probably came as a shock to her because Lenin's expressed opinions shortly before they left Switzerland . . . did not include the slogan 'All Power to the Soviets!' If Lenin came round to this stance during his trip to Russia, he told nobody. . . ."

Finally, it is a fact that by the time Lenin reached Russia the party had had more than two weeks to digest his two letters on policy to Alexandra Kollontai and his first two *Letters from Afar*. Yet there is no doubt whatever that they were astonished when he outlined his new policy on arrival. So clearly, they at any rate understood a different meaning to his new call for power to be given to the Soviets from that which he had written from Switzerland.

3. Jacob Fürstenberg was known by three identities: (1) Hanecki, his real Polish name; (2) Ganetsky, which is the Russian for Hanecki transliterated back into English; (3) Fürstenberg, which was cover name.

4. Joel Carmichael, "German Money and Bolshevik Honour," *Encounter* (March, 1974).

5. Although Souliashvili must be regarded as a prime source since he was there on the journey from Zurich to Petersburg, the way he writes is very suspect—both politically and emotionally. It seems astonishing that Lenin, who barely knew him, should ask him to share his compartment for a 600-mile journey when he had other far closer friends on the train—such as Kharitonov. It is interesting that Inessa, whom we know from several sources was in a separate compartment on the Sealed Train, should be with Lenin and Nadya now.

Certainly parts of Souliashvili's account—such as a vivid account later of how Stalin met the travelers, as the sole representative of the party, at Beloostrov—is quite clearly fabricated with many imaginative trimmings.

However, for lack of any other source about this particular train, I have written these paragraphs on the assumption that here, at least, Souliashvili was not lying.

6. Lenin did propose this change of name in a speech on his first day in Petersburg—as Souliashvili, writing years later, well knew. It rings a little false as written but is clearly a probability.

CHAPTER 8

1. Main sources: See sources for Chapter 4.

2. The Soviet line on this story in the carriage varies from my own. Safarov, Zinoviev and Zina all suggest in their accounts that the soldiers were "defensists"—supporting the war until victory. Podvoisky, however, quotes Lenin in his first speech in Petersburg on his arrival night as saying that the soldiers on the train had been unanimously in favor of stopping the war now and made a dramatic gesture to indicate the sticking of their bayonets into the ground. Sukhanov, who left the most elaborate record of Lenin's speech, made no reference to this point, though this does not mean it was not made. However, Podvoisky's book was published in 1958 after years of Stalin's rule, when Zinoviev had been almost written out of the history books, and I have relied on three people who were in the carriage at the time.

3. There is disagreement about who was in the welcoming party. Raskolnikov says that Alexandra Kollontai was there, while Shlyapnikov says she was waiting at the Finland Station with a large bouquet of flowers. Two accounts, one hopelessly subservient by David Souliashvili and the other by Zinoviev in *Pravda* in 1924 after Lenin's death, said that Stalin was there. No other accounts, not even Krupskaya's, record his presence. Almost certainly Zinoviev was being tactful.

CHAPTER 9

1. Main sources: N. N. Sukhanov, *The Russian Revolution* 1917; Leon Trotsky, *The History of the Russian Revolution;* V. D. Bonch-Bruevich, *Battle*

Positions in the February and October Revolutions (R); V. I. Lenin, *The Revolution of 1917*; Alexander Shlyapnikov, *The Year 1917* (R); N. I. Podvoisky, *The Year 1917* (R); Sir George Buchanan, *My Mission to Russia*; Alexander Kerensky, *The Catastrophe* and *The Kerensky Memoirs*; P. B. Browder and A. Kerensky, *The Russian Provisional Government 1917*; Elena Stasova, *Pages of Life and Fighting* (R); Frank Golder, *Documents of Russian History, 1914–1917*; N. K. Krupskaya, *Memories of Lenin*; V. Mushtukov and V. Kruchina-Bogdanov, *Lenin and the Revolution*; A. Ilyn-Genevsky, *From the February Revolution to the October Revolution*; British Foreign Office files; newspapers (See list at end of General Works in Bibliography).

CHAPTER 10

1. Main sources: As for Chapter 9. Also, F. F. Raskolnikov, *In Kronstadt and "Peter" 1917* (R); A. E. Ross, *The Russian Bolshevik Revolution*; A. Rabinowitch, *Prelude to Revolution*.

CHAPTER 11

1. Main sources: As for Chapters 9 and 10. Also, Isaac Deutscher, *The Prophet Armed*; N.V. Sorokin, *Leaves from My Russian Diary*; Leon Trotsky, *Lenin* and *My Life*; K. T. Sverdlova, *Jakob Mihailovich Sverdlov* (R); Albert Rhys Williams, *Through the Russian Revolution*; B. V. Nikitin, *The Fatal Years*.

2. According to Trotsky in *Lenin*.

3. In other words, the ten ministers in the Cabinet who were not socialists.

CHAPTER 12

1. Main sources: As for Chapters 9 and 11. Also, Erich Ludendorff, *My War Memories*.

2. M. Futrell, *The Northern Underground*, 222.

3. Kerensky states in his memoirs that he left because the Germans broke the Russian line on July 16. Ludendorff in his memoirs asserts the attack was not made until July 19. Something menacing at the front, however, clearly made Kerensky's presence as War Minister necessary.

4. Some historians, including Sukhanov, have stated that what was cut out of *Pravda* was a call to a peaceful demonstration—*i.e.*, a stepping down from the leadership in fear of what they had started. It is clear, however, from party sources that what was cut out was an order *not* to demonstrate. See Rabinowitch's *Prelude to Revolution*.

CHAPTER 13

1. Main sources: As for Chapters 9 onward, but in particular the highly detailed Rabinowitch's *Prelude to Revolution*. Also, G. Zinoviev, *Lenin in the July Days* and *Nicolai Lenin—His Life and Work*; N. Emelyanov, "Ilyich at Razliv," *The Banner*, No. 2 (1957).

2. Several eminent historians—notably Harvards's Professor Adam B. Ulam and St. Anthony's Dr. Harold Shukman at Oxford—have taken the view that Lenin organized the July uprising. In my view, the whole pattern of the party protocol and personal accounts—and Lenin's declared policy over several weeks—reveals a clear picture of a party out of control, of a mutiny against Lenin's orders.

CHAPTER 14

1. Main sources: G. Zinoviev, *Lenin in the July Days;* N. Emelyanov, "Ilyich at Razliv"; V. I. Lenin, *Toward the Seizure of Power;* A. Shotman, *Lenin in Hiding, July–October;* K. Rovio, "How Lenin Was Hiding in the House of the Helsingfors Chief of Police"; E. Rahja, "Memoirs of Vladimir Ilyich"; V. Nevsky, *October 1917;* David Shub, *Lenin;* H. Yalava, "Two Meetings with Ilyich on a Train."

2. I have leaned heavily on Zinoviev's detailed account of his time with Lenin at Razliv. It is interesting that the official Soviet line on this period is that Lenin was alone, yet Zinoviev's article was published in *The Proletarian Revolution* in 1927, the year Stalin established his control, when Zinoviev's star, like Trotsky's, was in descent. The journal's editor printed a preliminary note criticizing the article on the ground that Zinoviev was claiming too much personal kudos—which might well be justified—but he did not deny its accuracy.

3. In fact, although the death sentence had been reintroduced, no man had actually been shot.

4. In theory, Lenin was not opposed to the Constituent Assembly, and he had accused the Provisional Government of deliberately delaying the organization of elections. But he opposed the Pre-Parliament because, he said, it was rigged to give Kerensky control of it.

5. There is considerable argument about the date that Lenin returned to Petersburg though there is no question that he was back in the city by the twenty-third. However, I am following official Soviet sources.

CHAPTER 15

1. Main sources: Leon Trotsky, *History of the Russian Revolution, Lenin,* and *My Life;* N. N. Sukhanov, *The Russian Revolution 1917;* N. I. Podvoisky, *The Year 1917* (R); John Reed, *Ten Days That Shook the World;* Louise Bryant, *Six Months in Red Russia;* V. A. Antonov-Ovseenko, *In 1917* (R); V. I. Lenin, *Toward the Seizure of Power;* M. Fofanova, *Memories of 1917* (R); V. Nevsky, *October 1917;* A. Kerensky, *The Catastrophe* and *The Kerensky Memoirs;* V. Mushtakov and Kruchina-Bogdanov, *Lenin and the Revolution;* E. A. Ross, *The Russian Bolshevik Revolution;* O. H. Gankin, and H. H. Fisher, *The Bolsheviks and the World War.*

2. The sources of this important meeting are the minutes of the meeting; Trotsky's descriptions in *The History of the Russian Revolution* and in *Lenin;*

Sukhanov; the letter written by Kamenev and Zinoviev to the party (see Gankin and Fisher); V. Mushtakov etc., *Lenin and the Revolution;* Gankin and Fisher, *The Bolsheviks and the World War.* Although Sukhanov states in his *Russian Revolution* that he was unaware of this meeting in his apartment until he learned of it later and plays up the fact considerably, Alexander Solzhenitsyn in *The Gulag Archipelago* asserts he was fully aware of it.

3. When Lenin was on his way to Russia in 1905, he wrote from Stockholm that the Soviet could be "the germ of a provisional revolutionary government," but he changed his mind when he arrived in Petersburg and saw it in operation. He regarded it then more as "a fighting organization for specific purposes." Later this transient concept hardened in his mind and he suggested that the Soviet "may actually become superfluous."

4. Assuming that Kamenev said at the meeting what he wrote of the issue the following day.

CHAPTER 16

1. Main sources: As for Chapter 15. Also, A. Belyshev, *The Shot from the Aurora;* V. D. Bonch-Bruevich, *Battle Positions in the February and October Revolutions* (R), and *Lenin in Petersburg and Moscow* (R); P. Dashkevich, *The October Days;* A. Ilin-Genevsky, *From the February Revolution to the October Revolution;* K. Mekhonoshin, *Battle Headquarters of the October Revolution;* S. Pestkovsky, *About the October Days in "Peter"* (R); N. I. Podvoisky, *The Military Revolutionary Committee* (R); C. Piontkovsky, *Military Revolutionary Committee* (R), "Recollections About the October Uprising. . ." *Proletarian Revolution,* 1922, No. 10 (R); Kamenev quoted in E. A. Ross, *The Russian Bolshevik Revolution.*

2. This little story has been questioned by historians as Soviet propaganda—as well it may be. But it seems fairly likely that it happened as Rahja reports.

3. Kamenev claimed credit for the title. Trotsky, in his own account, also claimed credit.

4. Trotsky records the speaker as Dan, but it is clear from other sources that it was Martov.

Bibliography

The bibliography is in three sections: (1) sources of the Sealed Train and the journey from Switzerland to Russia (which are discussed in Note 1, Chapter 4); (2) personal accounts by participants of the events in the book, except for the Sealed Train and the journey to Russia; (3) general works, at the end of which is a section for newspapers consulted.

The titles of books and journals are given in English, a letter (R, F or G) indicating if the language of the source material is other than English. An exception to this rule is made with the list of newspapers since some of them—such as *Pravda*—are familiar in the Russian.

For the ease of the reader, if a source covers periods in more than one section—such as Krupskaya's *Memories of Lenin*—it is listed in each section.

1. *SOURCES OF THE SEALED TRAIN AND THE JOURNEY FROM SWITZERLAND TO RUSSIA, including departure and arrival dates.*

BONCH-BRUEVICH, V. D., *Battle Positions in the February and October Revolutions.* 1930 (R).

BRITISH FOREIGN OFFICE FILES: Correspondence between the Foreign Office and the ambassadors in Petersburg, Stockholm and Berne, the Admiralty and internal documents. Public Record Office, London.

DRABKINA, F., "The Arrival of Comrade Lenin," *The Proletarian Revolution 1927.* No. 4 (R).

ELMSTED, COMRADE, "In the Same Train as Ilyich"; "Memories of the Driver of the Train (in Finland)" *Leningradskaya Pravda,* April 16, 1924, No. 87 (R).

HAHLWEG, W., *Lenin's Journey to Russia 1917.* 1957 (G).

HANECKI (JACOB FÜRSTENBERG). "The Arrival of Comrade Lenin from Switzerland," *The Proletarian Revolution,* 1924, No. 87 (R).

HOWARD, LORD ESME, *Theatre of Life*. 1935.
IVANOV, A. I., *Fritz Platten*. 1963 (R).
KRUPSKAYA, N. K. (NADYA), *Memories of Lenin*. 2 v. 1959.
———, "From Exile to 'Peter,'" *Pravda*. No. 87, April 16, 1924 (R).
LENIN, V. I., *The Revolution of 1917*. 2 v. 1929.
———, *Collected Works*. 4th Edition. Vols. 23, 35, 36, 43, 19.
LENIN MISCELLANY, Vol. 37 (p. 56 for his baggage) (R).
LILINA(ZINA ZINOVIEVA), "Comrade Lenin Departs for Russia," *Leningradskaya Pravda*. April 16, 1924, No. 87 (R).
———, "On Life with Lenin in Exile," *Leningradskaya Pravda*. 1924, No. 22 (R).
MOSKOVSKY, P. V. and SEMENOV, V. G., *Lenin in Sweden*. 1972 (R).
PLATTEN, Fritz, Lenin's Journey through Germany in the Sealed Car. 1924 (G).
———, "Lenin's Return," included in *They Knew Lenin*. (1968).
PLATTEN, N. F., From the Spiegelgasse to the Kremlin: Grani, Nos. 77 and 79 (fuller-length paper kindly made available in German to the author). 1972 (R).
PODVOISKY, NIKOLAI, "The Return," *Goudok*. 1925, No. 17 (R).
RADEK, Karl, "In the Sealed Carriage," *Pravda*. April 20, 1924, No. 91 (R).
RASKOLNIKOV, F. F., *The Proletarian Revolution*. 1923, No. 13 (R).
RAVICH, OLGA, "The Journey Across Germany," *Pravda*. April 18, 1927, No. 88 (R).
———, "The February Days in Switzerland," *Katorga i Ssilka*. 1927 Vol. 1 (R).
SAFAROV, George, "Comrade Lenin," *Leningradskaya Pravda*. 1924, April 16, 1924, No. 87 (R)
———, "About Comrade Lenin," *Leningradskaya Pravda*. 1925, No. 17 (R).
SHLYAPNIKOV, ALEXANDER, *The Year 1917*. 1924 (R).
SOKOLNIKOV, G., "The Return of Lenin from Exile," *Leningradskaya Pravda*. April 18, 1928, No. 90 (R).
SOULIASHVILI, DAVID, "From Switzerland to Petersburg with Lenin," *Zaria Vostoka* (Tiflis). 1925, No. 781 (R).
———, *Meetings with V. I. Lenin in Exile*. 1957 (R).
STASOVA, ELENA, *Pages of Life and Fighting*. 1957 (R).
SUKHANOV, N. N., *The Russian Revolution 1917*. 1955.
SWISS CUSTOMS, Letters from Police Department of Direction Generale des Douanes at Schaffhausen and Thayngen Stations to the Minister of Foreign Affairs about Lenin's passage, Swiss National Archives, Berne. 1920 (G).
TSKHAKAYA, MIKHA, "Meetings with Lenin," included in *Reminiscences of V. I. Lenin*. 1960 (R).
ULYANOVA, MARIA, "Lenin's Arrival in Russia," included in *Reminiscences of V. I. Lenin*. 1960 (R).

ZEMAN, Z. A. B., *Germany and the Revolution in Russia*. 1958.
ZINOVIEV, GREGORY, "On the Journey," *Pravda*. April 16, 1924. No. 87 (R).
ZINOVIEVA, ZINA. *See* LILINA

2. PERSONAL ACCOUNTS RELATING TO THE PERIOD COVERED BY THIS BOOK EXCEPT FOR THE JOURNEY TO RUSSIA (in Section 1)

ANTONOV-OVSEENKO, V. A., *In 1917*. 1935 (R).
——, *In the Revolution*. 1957 (R).
BONCH-BRUEVICH, V. D., *Battle Positions in the February and October Revolutions*. 1930 (R).
——, *Lenin in Petersburg and Moscow*. 1956 (R).
BELYSHEV, A. "The Shot from the *Aurora*," included in *Petrograd October 1917*. 1957.
BRYANT, LOUISE, *Six Months in Red Russia*. (1919).
BUCHANAN, SIR GEORGE, *My Mission to Russia*. 2 v., 1923.
CHERNOV, V. M., *Great Russian Revolution*. 1936.
CHERNOVA, A., *New Horizons*. 1936.
DASHKEVICH, P., "The October Days," included in *Petrograd October 1917*. 1957.
DZERZHINSKAYA, SOPHIA, *In the Years of the Great Struggles*. 1964 (R).
EMILIANOV, N., "Ilyich in Razliv," *The Banner*. 1957, No. 2 (R).
FOFANOVA, M. "Memories of 1917," *Leningradskaya Pravda*. 1928, No. 19 (R).
GORKY, MAXIM, *Days with Lenin*. 1944. *Lenin*. 1967.
GUILBEAUX, HENRI, *Vladimir Ilyich Lenin*. 1923 (F).
ILIN-GENEVSKY, A., *From the February Revolution to the October Revolution*. 1917.
KAMENEV, L. B., See personal account "October Days" in E. A. Ross, *General Works*.
KERENSKY, ALEXANDER, *The Catastrophe*. 1927
——, *The Kerensky Memoirs*. 1966.
KOLLONTAI, ALEXANDRA, *A Great Life*. 1927.
KRUPSKAYA, N. K., *Memories of Lenin*. 2 v., 1959.
LENIN, V. I., *Collected Works*. 4th Edition, 1960–
——, *The Revolution of 1917*. 2 v., 1929.
——, *Toward the Seizure of Power*. 2 v., 1933.
LUDENDORFF, GENERAL ERICH, *My War Memories*. 1919.
——, *The General Staff and Its Problems*. 1920.

*Although published under these titles in four volumes, these constitute Volumes 20 and 21 of the 2d Edition of the *Collected Works*.

[310

LUNACHARSKY, A., *Revolutionary Silhouettes.* 1967.
MEKHONOSHIN, K., "Battle Headquarters of the October Revolution," included in *Petrograd October 1917.* 1957.
NEVSKY, VLADIMIR, "October 1917," included in *Petrograd October 1917.* 1957.
NIKITIN, B. V., *The Fatal Years.* 1938.
PESTOVSKY, S., "About the October Days in 'Peter.'" *The Proletarian Revolution.* 1922. No. 10 (R).
PIONTKOVSKY, C., "Military Revolutionary Committee in the October Days," *The Proletarian Revolution.* 1927. No. 10 (R).
PODVOISKY, N. I., *The Year 1917.* 1958 (R).
———. "Military Organization of the Central Committee of the Bolshevik Party in 1917," *Krasnaya Letopis.* 1923. No. 8, (R).
———. "The Military Revolutioary Committee and the Red Guards in the October Revolution," included in *Petrograd October 1917.* 1957.
RAHJA, E., "Memories of Vladimir Ilyich," included in *Reminiscences of V. I. Lenin.* 1956–60 (R).
RASKOLNIKOV, F. F., *In Kronstadt and "Peter." 1917.* 1925 (R).
RECOLLECTIONS About the October Uprising: Meeting of Participants in the October Revolution That Took Place in Petersburg, November 7, 1920," *The Proletarian Revolution.* 1922. No. 10 (R).
REED, JOHN, *Ten Days That Shook the World.* 1960.
ROVIO, KUSTAA, "How Lenin Was Hiding in the House of the Helsingfors Chief of Police," included in *They Knew Lenin.*
SHLYAPNIKOV, ALEXANDER, *The Year 1917.* 1924 (R).
———. "Towards October," *The Proletarian Revolution.* 1924. No. 10 (R).
SHOTMAN, ALEXANDER, "Lenin in Hiding, July-October," included in *Reminiscences of V. I. Lenin.* 1956 (R).
SIEFELDT, ARTHUR, *Bakinsky Rabochii* (Baku). 1924. No. 24 (R).
SKARIATINA, IRINA, *A World Can End.* 1931.
SOROKIN, N. V., *Leaves from My Russian Diary.* 1925.
STASOVA, ELENA, *Pages of Life and Fighting.* 1957 (R).
———. *Such Was Lenin.* 1961 (R).
SVERDLOVA, K. T., *Jakob Mikhailovich Sverdlov.* 1939 (R).
SUKHANOV, N. N., *The Russian Revolution 1917.* 1955.
TROTSKY, LEON, *The History of the Russian Revolution.* 3 v., 1932.
———. *Lenin.* 1925.
———. *My Life.* 1930.
VALENTINOV (N. V. VOLSKY), *Encounters with Lenin.* 1968.
WILLIAMS, ALBERT RHYS, *Through the Russian Revolution.* 1921.
YALAVA, HUGO, "Two Meetings with Ilyich on a Train," *Leningradskaya Pravda.* 1924. No. 87 (R).
ZALEZHSKY, V. I., "First Legal Meeting of the Petersburg Committee," *The*

Proletarian Revolution. 1923. No. 13 (R).
ZINOVIEV, GREGORY. "Lenin in the July Days." *The Proletarian Revolution.*
1927. Nos. 8–9 (R).
————. *Nikolai Lenin: His Life and Work.* 1920.
————. *V. I. Lenin.* 1924.

3. GENERAL WORKS

ABRAMOVICH, RAPHAEL R.. *The Soviet Revolution.* 1962.
AGAFANOV, V. K.. *The Okhrana Abroad.* 1918 (R).
BROWDER, P. B.. and KERENSKY, A.. *The Russian Provisional Government*
1917. 3 v., 1961.
CARR, E. H.. *The Bolshevik Revolution.* 3 v., 1950.
CHAMBERLIN, W. H.. *The Russian Revolution.* 2 v., 1935.
DAVIDOV, L. D.. *Leninskaya Gvardia Planet* (article on Fritz Platten on March
15, 1917). 1967 (R).
DEUTSCHER, ISAAC. *The Prophet Armed—Trotsky 1879–1921.* 1954.
FISCHER, FRITZ. *Germany's Aims in the First World War.* 1967.
FISCHER, LOUIS. *The Life of Lenin.* 1965.
FREVILLE, J.. *A Great Character of the Revolution—Inessa Armand.* 1957 (F).
FUTRELL, MICHAEL. *The Northern Underground.* 1963.
GAUCHI, WILLI. *Lenin in Switzerland.* 1973 (G).
GANKIN, O. H.. and FISHER, H. H.. *The Bolsheviks and the World War.* 1940.
"GERMAN Foreign Office Documents on Financial Support to the Bolsheviks."
International Affairs. April, 1956.
GOLDER, FRANK A.. *Documents of Russian History, 1914–1917.* 1927.
KATKOV, GEORGE. *Russia 1917.* 1967.
KUSKY, G. S.. *Train No. 293.* 1965 (R).
MASKULIA, A. B.. *Mikha Tskhakaya.* 1968 (R).
MCNEAL, ROBERT H.. *Bride of the Revolution.* 1972.
MOOREHEAD, ALAN. *The Russian Revolution.* 1958.
MUSHTUKOV, V.. and KRUCHINA-BOGDANOV, V.. *Lenin and the Revolution.*
Undated.
NETTL, J. P.. *Rosa Luxembourg.* 2 v., 1966.
PAYNE, ROBERT. *The Life and Death of Lenin.* 1964.
POSSONY, STEFAN T.. *Lenin—The Compulsive Revolutionary.* 1964
RABINOWITCH, A.. *Prelude to Revolution.* 1968.
Reminiscences of V. I. Lenin. 3 v., 1956–60.
ROSS, E.A.. *The Russian Bolshevik Revolution.* 1921.
SCHAPIRO, LEONARD. *The Origin of the Communist Autocracy.* 1955
————. *The Communist Party of the Soviet Union.* 1960.
SENN, ALFRED ERICH. *The Russian Revolution in Switzerland 1914–1917.*
1971.
SHUB, DAVID. *Lenin.* 1951.

SHUKMAN, HAROLD. *Lenin and the Russian Revolution.* 1967.
SMITH, E. E., *The Okhrana.* 1967.
TREADGOLD, D. W., *Lenin and His Rivals.* 1955.
TUCHMAN, BARBARA, *The Zimmermann Telegram.* 1958.
ULAM, ADAM B., *Lenin and the Bolsheviks.* 1966.
WALTER, GERARD, *Lenin.* 1950 (F).
WARTH, ROBERT, *The Allies and the Russian Revolution.* 1954.
WILSON, EDMUND. *To the Finland Station.* 1960.
WOLFE, BERTRAM. *Three Who Made a Revolution.* 1956.
―――. "Lenin and Inessa Armand." *Slavic Review.* 1963.
ZEMAN, Z.A.B., *Germany and the Revolution in Russia.* 1958.
―――. *A Diplomatic History of the First World War* (1971)
―――with SCHARLAU, W. B., *Merchant of Revolution (Parvus).* 1965.

NEWSPAPERS CONSULTED

Bakinsky Rabochii
Birzhevye Vedomosti ("The Stock Exchange News")
Den ("Day")
Izvestia ("News")
Novoye Vremya ("New Times")
Pravda ("Truth")
Rech ("Speech")
Russkaya Volya ("Russian Liberty")
Times, London
Zhivoe Slovo ("Living Word")

Index

Alexandrovna, Maria, 17; death (1916), 44
Alexeyev, Michael, 119
Alexinsky, Gregory, 216
Alliluyev, Sergei, 221
American involvement in war, 66
Annexation of territory, 142
Antonov-Ovseenko, Vladimir, 250
April Theses, 141, 287
Armand, Inessa, 22, 24
  arrest, 40
  background and character, 37–38
  conflict with Lenin, 46
  death in 1921, 288
  decision to go to Moscow, 89
  increasing coolness toward Lenin, 88–89
  involved in Lenin's train journey plans,
    52–53
  joins Troika, 37
  passenger on Sealed Train, 76
  relations with Nadya, 39
  relationship with Lenin, 38
  subdued behavior on train, 87–88
  translator for Lenin, 38, 45
Army
  Bolsheviks gain partial control, 204
  female regiments, 276
  propagandized, 168–69
Arras, 72
Aurora, 262, 264
  anchors in midstream, 272
  proceeds upriver, 269
Axelrod, Paul, 28, 36; writings on need for
    Soviet, 33

Balfour, Arthur, 71
Bank raids, 35, 87
Baverk, Ben, 85
Bedny, Demyan, 195
Belenih. See Shlyapnikov, Alexander
Beloostrov, 123
Bergen, Diego von, 63
Berlin
  impressions made on travelers, 107
  train delayed, 103
Bernstein, Eduard, 115
Bethmann-Hollweg, Theobald von, 70, 108

Birzhevye Vedomosti, 148
Black Hundreds, 34, 35, 154
"Bloody Sunday" (1905), 32
Blum, Oscar, 79; suspected of spying, 79
Bogdanov, B. O., 143–44
Boitsov, Nicholas, 43
Bolshevik Central Committee. See Central
  Committee
Bolshevik Military Organization, 168
Bolsheviks, 20, 31
  complete take-over, 284–85
  consider coalition with Mensheviks, 238
  control of mobs, 159–60
  control Petersburg, 275
  deny German funding, 114
  essentially professional revolutionaries, 31
  financed by bank raids, 35
  German financial links implied, 174
  hostility from other revolutionaries, 147–48
  importance of propaganda, 165
  money received from Keskula, 63
  need for Russian support, 107
  new Central Committee elected, 163
  newspaper distribution, 168
  organization of growth, 170
  organization of Lenin's welcome, 127
  party achieved acceptance in Germany, 63
  party committees, 297–98
  party membership, 153
  plan to arrest leaders, 262
  possibility of German funding, 112–13
  propaganda to the man in the street, 167
  public support drops, 224
  repercussions for uprising, 227
  underrated by Russians, 106
  uprising begins, 272
  virtually ruined, 227
  welcome Lenin at Beloostrov, 123
Bombs, 33
Bonch-Bruevich, Vladimir, 127, 140, 281
  host to Lenin, 195
  warned of plot against Lenin, 215
Bretten, 97
Brockdorff-Rantzau, Count Ulrich von, 64,
  112
Bronski, Mieczyslav, 18–19

Buchanan, Sir George, 71, 72, 144, 261
  communication with London, 84
  requests release of Trotsky, 84
Bukharin, Nicholas, 46

Central Committee, 177, 238, 239
  considers Lenin's journey plans, 72
  decides timing of coup, 265
  Kamenev attacks policy proposals, 151
  meeting with Lenin, 242–49
  ordered to overhaul Moscow leadership, 234
  overseas bureau planned, 110
  vote for armed uprising, 247
Chernov, Victor, 211–12
Chkheidze, Nicholas, 25, 55, 128
  acts to prevent newspaper story leak, 216
  appeals for ban on demonstration, 185
  chairman of Tauride Palace meeting, 142
  receives Lenin, 129–30
Chugurin, Ivan, 129
"Communists" used as title for first time, 117
Congress of Soviets, 177
  against demonstrations, 185
  at Smolny, 250
  blamed for cancellation of demonstration, 187
  definition, 295
  members armed, 283
  second, 277
Constantinople, 142
Constituent Assembly, 149
Cossacks
  appeal from Bolsheviks, 282
  beaten by First Reserve Regiment, 214
  refuse to charge, 50
  reserves to counter demonstration, 208
  search for Lenin, 228
Crime increase following Revolution, 139

Dan, Theodor, 278
Dardanelles, 142
"Day of the Soviet," 261
Decembrists, 26
Demonstration
  dangers of cancellation, 185–86
  peaceful, 183–84
  strategic plan, 207–8
Dreyfus case, 223
Duma, 20
  Bolshevik delegates, 40
  definition, 295
  election permitted by tsar (1911), 40
  political constitution, 22
  provisional government, 50
Dzerzhinshy, Felix, 243

Elections permitted by tsar, 33, 40
Elizarov, Anna, 44
Elizarov, Mark, 43, 136–37
Emelyanov leases land to Lenin for refuge, 228

Ermolenko, Lieutenant, 174, 216

Financial backing. See Funding
Finland, 218
Flakserman, Yuri, 243
Fofanova, Marguerite, 221, 240; reports to Lenin on state of Petersburg, 267
Food shortages, 175
Fotieva, Lydia, 39
Frankfurt, 100
Freedom of speech granted by tsar (1905), 33
Funding, 112, 144, 150
  convincing proof of German funds, 193
  evidence of German provision, 289–94
  explanations proposed, 152
  influence on Lenin's decision to stand trial, 223
  of Foreign Bureau, 237
  of propaganda, 169
  passed through German Legation in Stockholm, 174
  through Bolshevik Foreign Bureau, 224
Fürstenberg, Jacob, 49, 216, 291
  accused by press of spying, 219
  agrees to work with Parvus, 61
  association with Lenin, 101–2
  at Trelleborg, 101
  offer of transit across Germany, 57
  request made for Swedish identity papers, 52
  use of Russian diplomatic bag, 112
  welcomes passengers from ferry, 109

Gapon, Father, 32
Germany, 22–23. See also relevant entries under Funding
  appearance of wartime countryside, 94
  army engaged by Russian troops, 190
  breakthrough near Tarnopol, 221
  evidence of Lenin's collaboration, 289–94
  interest in sparking off Revolution, 60
  moves troops westward, 176
  receives return on investment in Bolsheviks, 286–87
  success of Bolshevik strategy, 282
Goldenberg, I. P., 144
Gorky, Maxim, 43; 219; owner of Letopis, 132
Gottmadingen, 74, 81; train departs, 82–83
Grimm, Robert, 65
Guchkov, Alexander, 161
Guilbeaux, Henri, 74

Haparanda, 117, 118
Helphand, Alexander. See Parvus
Horb, 94
Howard, Lord Esme, 98; report to London on Lenin's progress, 119

Ilyin-Genevsky, A. F., 168
Iskra, 26
  editors move to London, 29

315]

printed on illegal press, 28
started in Moscow, 28
Ivanov, A., 81, 107
Izmailovsky Regiment, 34, 155–56; protects Soviet, 217–18
Izvestia, 144; publishes explanation of Sealed Train journey, 146

Janson, Wilhelm, 96, joins Sealed Train, 79
July Days, 196–97
  arms used, 210
  sparked by mutiny, 200
Junkers occupy railway station, 266

Kadet Party, 51, 141, 145, 235, 297
  clash with workers' march, 161
  processions through Petersburg, 190
  support of Provisional Government, 160

Kaiser, 65
Kalinin, Michael, 205
Kamenev, Leo, 36, 124, 246, 251
  arrested, 40
  becomes part of Troika, 37
  executed, 288
  public appeal in press against armed insurrection, 253
  reply to Lenin's Bolshevik policy speech, 135
  supports war, 121
  takes control of Bolsheviks, 72
  writings in *Pravda*, 124–25
Kamenev, Olga, 36
Kamo, 35
Karl, Emperor of Austria, 70
Karlsruhe, 97
Kerensky, Alexander, 67, 126, 264
  appointed War Minister, 162
  becomes Premier, 226–27
  conflict with Lenin for control of army, 163
  counterrevolutionary danger, 246
  "Declaration of Soldiers' Rights," 176
  disillusioned by Soviet, 149
  dismisses garrison commander, 220
  flees Petersburg, 273
  opposed to Lenin, 54
  organizes anti-Bolsheviks, 238, 281
  public conflict with Lenin, 179
  speaking tour of armed forces, 173
  takes control of government forces, 273
  threat to life in July Days uprising, 200
Kesküla, Alexander, 63; money paid to Bolsheviks, 63
Kharitonov, 21, 43, 76
Kienthal Manifesto, 70
Kollontai, Alexandra, 39, 49, 52, 54, 127, 284
  plot of *A Great Love*, 89
  welcomes Lenin at Petersburg, 128
Kon, Helen, 91
Konstantinovna, Nadezhda, 18
Kornilov, Lavr, 99, 146

advances on capital, 235
arrested, 235
commander in chief Russian forces, 235
relinquishes command, 161–62
Kozlovsky, Mecheslav, 150, 216
  accused by press of spying, 219
  warns Bonch-Bruevich of plot against Lenin, 215
Kronstadt, 166; votes to form independent republic, 170–71
Krzhizhanovsky, Gleb, 18
Krupskay, Nadya. *See* Nadya
Kühlmann, Richard von, 113, 237, 282

Laurent, Pierre, 193
Lenin, Vladimir Ulyanov
  accused by press of spying, 219
  addresses Artillery Regiment, 157
  addresses Bolsheviks in Tauride Palace, 140
  addresses Congress of Soviets after seizing power, 284
  addresses sailors during demonstration, 206–7
  attack on Parvus in *Die Glocke*, 61–62
  attitude to patriotism, 47, 48
  bank raids, 35
  becomes part of Troika, 37
  Central Committee forbids return to Petersburg, 240
  changes tactical plans during train journey, 104
  conceived *Iskra*, 26
  contacts in Sweden, 49
  daily routine in Zurich, 41
  death in 1924, 288
  death of mother, 44
  decides to cross Germany under own aegis, 68
  decides to stand trial, 221–22
  decision to reach Petersburg, 52
  departure in train to hostile farewell, 78
  desire for privacy, 27–28
  Development of Capitalism in Russia, The, 30
  disregarded by Kaiser, 64
  edits *Proletarii*, 36
  edits *Sotsial Demokrat*, 45
  escape plan, 232
  escapes disguised as train stoker, 233
  exile ended (1900), 26
  exiled shared by Nadya, 29
  family background, 19
  fits of rage, 46–47
  given bodyguard, 148
  goes with Rahja to Smolny, 270–71
  hides in Finnish woodlands, 225–26
  hunted in Petersburg, 225
  in Zurich, 17
  increasing coolness with Inessa Armand, 88–89
  insists on "sealed train," 68

lecture attempts in Zurich, 44
lives in Elizarovs' flat, 136–37
loses stature over demonstration cancellation, 187
love of bicycling, 92–93
meeting with Parvus in Berne, 61
meets opposition from party leaders, 145
moves to Finland (1906), 35
moves to Vyborg (Finland), 239
physical appearance, 18
plan to prosecute by government, 215–16
poverty in Zurich, 42
progress to Kshesinskaya Mansion, 131
propaganda techniques, 165–67
public conflict with Kerensky, 179
public support diminishes, 224
quarrels with contacts in Europe and America, 46
questions Trotsky on planning of uprising, 271
recalled from holiday by uprising, 196
refusal to meet Parvus in Stockholm, 111
refused permission to go to Smolny, 268
relationship with Radek, 86–87
relationship with Inessa Armand, 38
rents rooms in London, 29
returns to Petersburg during riots, 204
searched at Tornio, 118
seeks support of international socialists, 74
speaking tour of factories, 169
split with Trotsky, 31–32
splits party, 30
standard of life in Zurich, 41
stays in Helsinki, 233
study of military tactics, 33
tries to expel Kamenev and Zinoviev, 254
two-hour speech on Bolshevik policy, 133
ultimate control by terror, 287
unwell and takes holiday, 194
welcome at the Finland Station, 128–29
wife. See Nadya
working methods in Zurich, 41–42
Letopis, 43, 132
Levi, Paul, 67
Lilina. See Zinovieva, Zina
Lomov, George, 243
Ludendorff, General Erich, 81, 234
Lunachavsky, Anatol, 43, 172
Luxemburg, Rosa, 46
Lvov, Prince, 162

Malmo, 110
Mannheim, 97
Martov, Julius, 26
    addresses Congress of Soviets, 278
    character, 27
    indicts Lenin (1911), 36
    invited to join Bolsheviks, 172–73
    involved in Sealed Train journey arrangements, 53
    living with Vera Zasulich, 29

split with Lenin, 30–31
Marx, Karl, 27; Lenin's visit to grave, 108–09
Marxism, 152; discarded by Lenin, 143
Mayer, Gustav, 198
Mekhonoshin, K., 218
Mensheviks, 31, 35, 92, 137
    attack Bolsheviks at Congress of Soviets, 178
    attract Marxist intellectuals, 31
    dominant in Soviet, 51
    join counterrevolution, 229
Mesopotamia, 142
Mikhailovsky Regiment, 156
Military Organization, 154
Military Revolutionary Committee, 250; control of state, 275
Militia used as means of law and order, 55
Milyukov, Paul, 51, 67, 229
    determines to destroy Soviet, 145
    forced resignation, 161
    maligns Lenin as pro-German, 146
    note to Allied ambassadors, 158
Molotov, Vyacheslav, 72; sets up press bureau, 167
Moor, Karl, 237
Moscow suggested as new capital, 250

Nadya, 17
    death in 1939, 288
    difficutlics of role in Petersburg, 152–53
    family background, 29
    lack of contact with Lenin in Petersburg, 195
    member of Vyborg Duma, 181
    relations with Inessa Armand, 39
    rents rooms in London, 29
    secretary of Iskra, 28
    threatens to leave Lenin, 39
Narodniks, 27, 51
Nashe Slovo, 279
National strike, 33
Nevsky, Vladimir, 132, 154, 156
Nikitin, B. V., 98–99, 213
    leades opposition to demonstration, 208
    raids Elizarovs' flat, 220
    searches for contact between Lenin and Parvus, 180
    surveillance of Eugenia Sumenson, 193
Nobs, Ernst, 45
Novaya Zhizn, 223
Nuratov, 126

Okhrana infiltration, 35

Paris Commune, 143
Parliament granted by tsar (1905), 33
Parliamentary republic denounced by Lenin, 134
Parvus, 28, 291
    agreement with Germans to create revolution, 60

317]

change to bourgeois outlook, 57–58
contact with German ambassador, 59
contact with Lenin via Beloostrov, 180
disagreement with Lenin, 59
German Treasury pays him 5,000,000
   marks, 64
in Stockholm, 111
involved in Sealed Train journey arrangements, 57
meeting with Lenin in Berne, 61
partnership with Trotsky, 58
sources of income, 58, 288
takes German nationality, 60
wishes to meet travelers at Malmo, 83
writings stressing need for Soviet, 33
Patriotism
   emerges as threat to Lenin, 191
   Lenin's attitude, 47, 48
People's Will Party, 27
Pero. *See* Trotsky
Peter and Paul Fortress, 263
Petersburg, 21, 138
   awaits either uprising or right-wing coup,
   255
   City Committee, 151
   confusion during coup, 266–67
   consideration of Lenin's imminent arrival,
   126
   dismissal of garrison commander, 220
   increase in Bolshevik seats in Soviet, 181
   Lenin recalled by uprising, 196
   under Bolshevik control, 275
Petersburg Soviet, 295
Petrograd. *See* Petersburg
Platten, Fritz, 24, 68, 79
   at Frankfurt, 100
   involved in fight before Sealed Train's
   departure, 78
   leadership accepted, 77
   meeting with Wilhelm Janson, 96
   refused entry to Russia, 119
Plekhanov, George, 28, 36, 48, 92
   joins board of *Iskra*, 28
   opposes Trotsky's appointment to *Iskra*
   board, 30
Podvoisky, Nicholas, 120, 130, 154, 274
   chief of staff of MRC, 250
   organizes demonstration, 155
   reports on military plans for uprising, 257
   trains sailors in techniques of agitation, 166
Political prisoners, 34
Potresov, Alexander, 28
Pravda, 40
   circulation soars, 169
   raided by government troops, 219
Pravda Bulletin, 223
Press bureau, 167
Proletarii, 36
Pskov, 281
Putilov workers, 212–13

Queen Victoria ferry, 107, 108, 109

Rabochy Put, 243, 254; closed down by
   Junkers, 263
Radek, Karl, 46
   at Frankfurt, 100
   causes trouble on train journey, 85–86
   danger from Janson, 96–97
   meeting with Parvus in Stockholm, 111
   relationship with Lenin, 86–87
Rahja, Eino, 240
Raskolnikov, Theodor, 123, 135, 170–71;
   arrives in Petersburg with Kronstadt sailors,
   206
Ravich, Olga, 46, 82, 85
   accounts of Lenin's problems with Radek,
   86
   irritates Lenin, 87
   last-minute passenger on train journey, 76
Razliv, 228
Rebellion in armed forces, 139
Rech, 160
Red Guards, 154
   attack snipers, 210
   instructed as fighting units, 251
   Lenin questions ability, 257
   man Smolny, 262
   training program in factories, 169
Reed, John, 265, 280, 284
Revolution, 49
   announcement, 19
   first newspaper accounts, 20
   immediate social effects, 140
   street fighting (1905), 34
Rolland, Romain, 74
Romberg, Gisbert von, 63
   asked to guarantee safe transit, 69–70
   attempts to arrange transport of SR mem-
   bers, 75
   instructed to expedite train journey, 66–67
Roshal, Simon, 132, 212
Rottweil, 93
Rovio, Kustora, 233
Rumbold, Sir Horace, 71
Russian Social Democratic Party, 20, 29;
   Lenin returns to Central Committee
   (1906), 35. *See also* Bolsheviks
Ryazanov, D. B., 78, 172

SR's, *See* Socialist Revolutionaries
Safarov, George, 76, 85; arrested, 40
Safarov, Valentina, 85
Saint Petersburg. *See* Petersburg
Sailors
   arrest Chernov, 211
   join riots, 205
   returned in disgrace to Kronstadt, 227
   training in political agitation, 166
Sassnitz, 84, 102; transfer to ferry, 107
Schaffhausen, 80

Sealed Train. *See* Train
Semashko, A., 200
Semenov, V. G., 108
Semenovsky Guards, 34
Sestroretsk, 231
Shlyapnikov, Alexander, 42, 73, 77
Shotman, Alexander, 169, 231, 240
Shushenskoye, 26; Nadya shares Lenin's exile, 29
Siefeldt, Arthur, 58
Simbirsk, 162
Singen
   overnight stop, 85
   train departs for Stuttgart, 90
Skariatina, Irina, 167
Skobelov, M.J., 128, 158
Smilga, Ivan, 239
Smolny Institute, 249; fortified, 262
Social Democratic Party, 137
Socialist Revolutionaries, 297
   dominant in Soviet, 51
   Kerensky's membership, 54
Sokolnikov, G., 76, 243; experiences following 1905, 95
Soldat closed down by Junkers, 263
Soldatskya Pravda, 168; article on erosion of Lenin's authority, 192
Sotsial Demokrat
   edited by Lenin, 45
   Zinoviev's editorial assistance, 48
Souliashvili, David, 76, 79, 108, 116
Soviet
   appeal by Kamenev to stop uprising, 201
   arrested by Izmailovsky Regiment, 34
   attempt to avoid national collapse, 175
   Bolshevik minority tactics, 141
   control of street violence, 161
   discussion on organization, 33
   initial development, 50–51
   proposal for government, 106
   revolutionary aspects, 51
   supervisory role, 51
Soviet Republic, 143
Soviets
   Congress, 177
   definition, 295
   do not receive autonomy, 288
   for whole nation, 56
Lenin's proposal for role, 134
Spring-Rice, Sir Cecil, 72
Stalik, Ludmilla, 124
Stalin, Joseph V., 164, 182, 216, 243, 265
   arrest, 40
   takes control of Bolsheviks, 72
Stasova, Elena, 152–53, 171
State and Revolution, 230, 234
Steklov, 144
Stetskevich, Maria, 73, 98
Stockholm, 110, 116
Strategy, 104–5

Strikes
   by workers in Vyborg area, 183
   financed by German Treasury, 60
   national, 33
   scale unimpressive, 62
Stuttgart, 94
Sukhanov, Galina, 242
Sukhanov, N. N., 131, 242; account of train's arrival, 126–27
Sumenson, Eugenia, 193, 216, 224, 237
Sverdlov, Jacob, 171–72
   acting as information liaison, 259
   opposition to Lenin standing trial, 223
Sweden, 49

Tauride Palace, 50
Terijoki, 233
Thomas, Albert, 149–50
Tiflis, 87
Tornio, 117
Train
   anti-Leninist result, 147
   explanation of "sealing," 146
   leaves Singen for Stuttgart, 90
   passes through several state railway systems, 90
   searched by customs at Schaffhausen, 80
   separation of Russians from Germans, 82
Trelleborg, 101, 107, 108, 109
Troika, 37
Trotsky, Lev, 202
   achieves power base, 258
   addresses mass meeting, 259–60
   addresses men at Peter and Paul Fortress, 263
   arrives in London, 30
   arrives in Petersburg, 172
   attacked by Lenin, 46
   complementary to Lenin, 249
   directory of Military Revolutionary Committee, 250
   forced into exile, 288
   formally joins Bolshevik Party, 230
   meeting with Lenin during demonstration, 209
   partnership with Parvus, 58
   plans uprising, 245
   president of Petersburg Soviet, 236
   reaction to Lenin's Bolshevik policy speech, 133
   release requested by Buchanan, 84
   removal from SS *Christiana Fiord*, 71
   split with Lenin, 31–32
   tries to free Chernov, 211–12
   writings on need for a Soviet, 33
Tsar
   arrests Petersburg Soviet Executive, 34
   rule ended, 22
Tseretelli, Irakli, 158, 178, 213
Tskhakaya, Mikha, 24, 75–76, 81, 108

319]

Tuttlingen, 94, 95

U-boats, 66
Ulyanov, Vladimir Ilyich. *See* Lenin
Ulyanov family move to Cracow, 40
Uprising. *See* July Days
Uritsky, Moses, 172, 243
Ussievich, Gregory, 76
Ussievich, Grisha, 43

Vailingen, 95
Volksrecht, 45
Vyborg, 129, 181
   army officers killed in river, 236
   rabid Bolsheviks, 153
   strike by workers, 183

Wilson, Woodrow, 66
Winter Palace
   attack, 276-77
   massacre by Palace Guards (1905), 32
   taken by Bolsheviks, 280

Yakovleva, Varvara, 243
Yalava, Hugo, 233; assists in Lenin's return to
   Petersburg, 240
Yoffe, A. A., 274

Zalezhsky, V. I., 144
Zalkind, Rosalya, 43-44
Zasulich, Vera, 28; living with Martov, 29
Zhivoe Slovo, 219; libel on Lenin, 231
Zimmermann, Arthur, 60, 83
   background, 62
   interviews Parvus after fall of tsar, 62
   kept informed of Sealed Train's progress,
      97-98
   plan to sink shipping, 66
   supervises transport of revolutionaries, 65
Zinoviev, Gregory, 24, 124, 151, 213, 251, 265
   arrives in Geneva (1908), 36
   assistance with *Sotsial Demokrat*, 48
   becomes part of Troika, 37
   executed, 288
   hunted in Petersburg, 225
   on Sealed Train with his family, 76
   proposes postponement of uprising, 252
   public appeal in press to avoid armed
      insurrection, 253
   role as speech-maker. 209
Zinoviev family move to Cracow, 40
Zinovieva, Zina, 40
   co-editor of *Soldatskaya Pravda*, 168
   meets Lenin, 91-92
Zurich library, 17, 42

JUL   1975   STACKS

947.084   Pearson, M.
Pea   The sealed train